TAPPING THE RICHES OF SCIENCE

Roger L. Geiger and Creso M. Sá

# Tapping the Riches of Science

Universities and the Promise of
Economic Growth

**HARVARD UNIVERSITY PRESS**

Cambridge, Massachusetts, and London, England   2008

*Library of Congress Cataloging-in-Publication Data*

Geiger, Roger L., 1943–
    Tapping the riches of science : universities and the promise of economic
growth / Roger L. Geiger, Creso M. Sá.
        p.   cm.
    Includes bibliographical references and index.
    ISBN 978-0-674-03128-9
    1. Universities and colleges—Economic aspects—United States.   2. Technology
transfer—United States.   3. Business and education—United States.   4. Economic
development—Effect of education on.   I. Sá, Creso M., 1976–   II. Title.
    LC67.62.G45 2008
    378.1'03—dc22                                                           2008030548

# Contents

# Preface

For the past decade, discussions of economic growth, competitiveness, or the relative strength of the U.S. economy have centered on the notion of innovation. Embraced by corporations, writers on management, as well as federal, state, and local governments, innovation has been touted as the nation's comparative advantage, the best hope for achieving economic growth in the context of relentless globalization. This "innovation narrative" accords a strategic role to research universities. Their leadership in cutting-edge scientific and technological research is seen as a crucial source of innovation. Specifically, universities are expected not only to create discoveries and inventions, but also to convey them to the productive economy through patenting and licensing, launching and nurturing spin-off firms, and collaborating with corporate research. Thus, the riches of university science are joined with the promise of economic growth.

Social narratives of this kind possess a great deal of validity. After all, journalists, scholars, and decision makers in industry, government, and higher education find them compelling. Typically, they marshal extensive evidence, anecdotal and scholarly, to buttress their case. However, the broad and plausible outline they depict is seldom a complete picture. Often ignored are questions of how far the indicated policies should be pursued and what ancillary or unanticipated consequences they might bring. Of course, detractors often reject the premises of social narratives entirely or give higher priority to different values and outcomes.

This book seeks to be neither booster nor detractor, but rather to examine, critically and empirically, the actual role of universities in this innovation scenario. It thus provides a more complete picture of this key component of the innovation narrative. It examines in some depth how university research connects with innovation in industry, what policies state governments have adopted to harness university research for economic development, the challenge of creating and licensing university intellectual property, and finally how these activities are changing universities themselves. The book does not attempt to quantify the contribution of university research to economic growth. While past research has often found that contribution to be substantial, it has also shown it to be contingent on other crucial factors. What this book does show is that contemporary universities have been doing far more to enhance their economic contribution; and, unequivocally, that the promise of aiding economic growth has brought them vitally needed resources for advancing strategic frontiers of science and technology.

Much of the research and writing for this study was accomplished in 2006 and 2007 at Pennsylvania State University and the University of Toronto, but considerable effort preceded the actual writing. Two grants from the National Science Foundation supported related research. The first allowed us to investigate a microcosm of state policy formation and university-industry linkages for nanotechnology in Pennsylvania. The second supported Creso Sá's study of interdisciplinary strategies at research universities. A Connaught Award from the University of Toronto provided Sá with valuable support. The Penn State College of Education provided Geiger with a sabbatical leave and research support. The Penn State Office of the Vice President for Research has assisted this project in several ways, especially with the investigation of corporate-university research relationships. The Penn State Office of Outreach and the Ben Franklin Technology Partners of Central and Northern Pennsylvania also contributed to this effort. We are grateful for all this support. We would also like to thank Paul Hallacher for continuing assistance and intellectual input. Dr. Radhika Prabhu was a valued colleague for portions of this research, and Irwin Feller was a frequent source of wisdom on this subject. The editorial suggestions of David R. Jones greatly improved this manuscript. Finally, we would like to thank the innumerable individuals at the many universities and corporations we visited who gave us their time and shared their knowledge. These unstructured and unrecorded interviews are seldom referred to in the notes, but many parts of this book reflect the experiences and the lives of the interviewees. The involvement of universities in economic activities has not ceased with the completion of this book, and for that reason we continue to make our contributions to comprehending these developments available at our Web site: www.tappingtherichesofscience.info.

# TAPPING THE RICHES OF SCIENCE

# Introduction: Innovation and Economic Relevance

      Universities in the United States are currently perceived—and expected—to be founts of innovation for a growing economy. In addition to their traditional roles of teaching, research, and outreach, most institutions now recognize an obligation to promote economic development—or, viewed more widely, to optimize their economic relevance. Modern universities have always had a large economic footprint, frequently being their regions' largest employers. But economic relevance implies a different kind of impact. It refers above all to the conviction that research universities must not only generate inventions, but also take steps to ensure that the inventions will be transferred to and developed into innovations in the private sector. Thus, "economic relevance" is a general term for the university activities that are directly or indirectly linked with the private sector, like patenting and licensing, launching and nurturing new firms, conducting research for industry, and cultivating academic fields that contribute to technological advance.

The expectation that universities should optimize their economic relevance is endorsed by a broad coalition of legislators, entrepreneurs, economic growth pundits, and academic leaders. Although American universities have long engaged in some of these activities, and have greatly enlarged this role since about 1980, the twenty-first century has witnessed an intensification of external inducements and internal willingness to emphasize these tasks. This book explains what this recent intensification of economic relevance means for American universities.

The movement to consecrate the university as a source of innovation for industry is driven by several powerful rationales. First, changes in the global economy have made advanced industrial countries like the United States increasingly dependent on the generation and utilization of sophisticated knowledge. At the same time, global competition has created a "flat world"

1

in which traditional manufacturing and some service industries are being exported to more efficient producers. A consensus has consequently formed that the vitality of U.S. industry is increasingly based on the capacity to generate innovations. The comparative advantage of the United States lies in its huge base of advanced science and technology, especially in its universities. Competing or even surviving in a globalized setting, according to this scenario, demands that universities fulfill a crucial role in the innovation process.

Second, this view of the economy has been assimilated into public policy. The principal federal science agencies require industrial partners for many major grants. Even more targeted policies have been adopted by the states. Nearly every sta e has launched initiatives to stimulate technology-based economic development. These programs typically encourage universities to found new companies and to assist small enterprises in conducting research. More ambitious states have committed substantial resources to provide research infrastructure in critical technologies likely to spawn innovation and economic activity. Universities have responded to these initiatives with alacrity, eager to be seen as loyal contributors to economic growth and grateful for contributions to needed scientific infrastructure.

Third, developments within science itself have greatly expanded the possibilities for high-tech innovations. Molecular biology, or biotechnology, was this era's most prominent pathbreaking "science-based technology"—a field in which the most basic scientific research yielded discoveries with unmistakable commercial potential. This scientific revolution in the foundations of biology thus turned basic scientists into inventors and entrepreneurs. A pattern was set, and to varying degrees it has been replicated in nanotechnology, photonics, informatics, and other emerging fields of science. Major universities are inherently committed to these areas as rapidly advancing frontiers of scientific discovery; but these fields are also rich with potential for commercially valuable innovations.

Despite the powerful momentum behind economic relevance, many of its features raise doubts as well. Although government policies deserve some credit for the vigor of science-based technologies, state policies are often poorly designed, and the economic theories ("assumptions" might be a better term) that lie behind them can be questionable. Unlike the federal government, states face a dual problem of both stimulating economic activity and capturing it within their own borders. Optimistic assumptions about innovation systems or economic clusters are echoed but seldom critically examined. The long-term benefits of these investments involve multiple contingencies that are virtually impossible to evaluate in the short run.

University efforts to develop and commercialize innovations have undergone a progressive rationalization. While some university inventions find a niche in the marketplace, far more have found commercial success elusive. The reality is that substantial market risk exists in starting a new company or finding a licensee for a patent. Universities realized through experience that careful planning and timely assistance would materially improve the chances for success. Thus, the technology transfer process itself has demanded increasing resources to expand the scope of activities to include, for example, the nurturing of new firms and the marketing of licenses.

The lures of economic relevance have affected the core academic mission of universities in both obvious and subtle ways. Most conspicuous have been efforts to accommodate the "innovative" sciences. Support for science-based technologies has been welcomed by faculty members and university leaders alike. Deliberate steps to restructure academic programs on an interdisciplinary basis are now ubiquitous, as is the proliferation of special institutes for science-based technologies. Incorporating these new fields—or new combinations of older fields—into the departmental and curricular structure of universities has been a challenge. A limiting factor in virtually all cases has been the need for expensive new facilities. Even when new facilities have been financed and built, the new fields present an organizational conundrum of avoiding isolated "silos" and integrating teams of specialists into academic units. Universities have experimented with various models to blend new ways of organizing scientists with the traditional structure of colleges and departments, leading some to believe that the future lies in a heavier emphasis on entrepreneurial research centers and institutes.

How or whether to teach these research specializations has been less clear. For example, degree programs in nanotechnology are rare, although perhaps not for long. University concerns about making serious commitments to novel educational offerings dissipate as rival institutions chart new terrain, often where a continuous flow of research funding creates new scientific niches. The necessity of maintaining critical mass in emerging hybrid fields has affected the recruitment and composition of students. The rapidity with which U.S. universities have embraced and developed these demanding subjects has been a remarkable accomplishment, but there is no slowing down on this fast track, and continuing progress poses ever-larger challenges.

Universities have created senior administrative positions devoted to economic development and have encouraged a more entrepreneurial culture among the faculty. New upper-administrative offices dedicated to fostering entrepreneurship bring a distinctive outlook on university roles and responsibilities to institutional decision making, adding to the already ingrained structures for technology transfer, community outreach, industrial liaison, and business assistance.

All these adaptations feed the momentum behind economic relevance. Substantial doubts nevertheless remain about elevating it to the status of an explicit university mission. Within universities, economic relevance is far from enjoying consensus support. The largest task of universities is the education of young people, and in the popular mind this function overshadows all others. Next largest is the advancement of knowledge, whether through scientific research or critical interpretation. Both these roles presuppose objective scholar-teachers and disinterested institutions. Universities are expected to be honest brokers in the pursuit and dissemination of knowledge—and rightly so. Universities are above all concentrations of experts in myriad fields whose reputations and careers are based upon rigorously evaluated contributions to knowledge and understanding. All these activities are generally distanced from the shadow of commercial interest and assumed to contribute to the public good. The American university today harbors a latent antagonism between its intrinsic commitment to learning and its purported embrace of economic relevance, an ideological tension combined with practical coexistence.

Whether or not new conditions in the global economy demand that U.S. universities change their mode of operations to bring forth the innovations desired by American industry is a question as daunting as it is perplexing. What should be clear is that the forces bringing change to science, technology, industry, and the economy will also affect universities. But myriad questions remain about the implications for universities.

The next chapter places the role of economic relevance in context. American universities have been creating technology and conveying it to external users since the nineteenth century. The technology transfer activities they have embraced since 1980 are new in many respects, but scarcely alien. They have nevertheless been assailed by critics who consider entanglements with industry to be incompatible with the norms of disinterested scholarship. Critics have eagerly publicized occasions when these norms seemed jeopardized, but the general forebodings that involvement with technology transfer would fundamentally alter the nature of universities have not come to pass. Instead, since 2000 a consensus on the enhancement of university interactions with industry has encompassed federal science agencies, state governments, donors, corporations, and virtually every university. University involvement with economic relevance is the reality of the twenty-first century, yet it remains widely resisted or misunderstood. The remainder of this book endeavors to clarify the complexity and ambiguity of this relationship by examining four key features.

Chapter 2 addresses how universities contribute to innovation—the desired fruition of economically relevant research. Although innovation is usually considered an undifferentiated phenomenon, this chapter describes two distinct tracks of innovation and how universities relate differently to each. One entails university patenting and licensing, and the small technology companies or spin-offs that attempt to commercialize most university intellectual property. These companies are particularly prized for purposes of economic development, and universities have steadily enlarged their efforts to assure their success in the face of unfavorable odds. However, the far larger track of innovation runs through the laboratories of established corporations, and their relationships with university research have been more contentious. Research is conducted quite differently across industries, and universities have generally not been flexible in adapting their policies accordingly. Most corporate labs have in fact deemphasized fundamental research and now look increasingly to external performers to complement internal R&D. Capitalizing on this opportunity, at least some universities have become more accommodative to research relationships with industry, and some corporations have established long-term partnerships with university units.

Chapter 3 examines how state policies to promote technology-based economic development have affected universities. Since 2000, virtually every state has established or expanded these initiatives. Most important has been the trend toward "upstream" policies that focus on stimulating university research in economically relevant fields. Such initiatives are analyzed for California, New York, Georgia, and Arizona. In the first two, the largest state economies, large expenditures have managed to produce fairly large actual or potential impacts. More carefully targeted programs in Georgia and Arizona have seeded units oriented toward economic relevance in their respective universities. In general, upstream state policies have provided a powerful incentive for universities to embrace economic relevance. Initiatives in these states have yielded positive results for increasing federally funded research and recruiting firms, and they have strengthened individual universities as well.

Chapter 4 analyzes university patenting and licensing and the operations of the offices charged with these responsibilities. Controversy has surrounded technology transfer offices as they seek to mediate between the world of academic inventors and that of commerce. Critics have charged that university patenting of research tools and overreach in intellectual property claims can inhibit technology transfer, diminishing the public good. But tech transfer professionals argue that the public good is only served when inventions are licensed and developed into commercial products. Evidence presented here qualifies both these claims. This chapter identifies current practices that seek to bridge the gap more effectively between embryonic academic discoveries and marketable products. Universities have continually enlarged the scope of technology transfer operations in an attempt to generate more innovation and licensing revenue, but relative productivity has apparently declined. Tech transfer offices primarily are oriented toward the small-company track of innovation, but diminishing returns suggest that more emphasis should be directed toward the corporate track.

Chapter 5 explores how the pursuit of economic relevance has challenged departments and schools at the academic core of universities. The science-based technologies that inform relevant fields are inherently interdisciplinary and hence not easily assimilated into traditional academic departments. Universities have consequently had to devise new organizational structures, formulate new strategies for hiring faculty, and create large research institutes for fields with substantial external support. Contrary to popular misconceptions, economic relevance has not produced a tilt toward applied research. Universities have been willing to make these adjustments to the academic core because the science-based technologies represent cutting-edge science. Hence, the race for economic relevance has been a competition for academic eminence.

The final chapter argues that economic relevance has had a substantial though not transformative impact on American universities. It has developed and expanded a complementary role for these multipurpose institutions, but a role with inherent limitations. Despite metanarratives about globalization and the knowledge society, university contributions to innovation and the social resources available for this purpose are both finite. Effort and luck may be required just to sustain current levels. Some possibilities for growth may be found from cultivating deeper ties with corporate research, but industry ultimately determines this relationship. Many of the upstream initiatives of state governments were designed to provide singular boosts to economically relevant research and may not have sequels. Nevertheless, the mandate to spawn innovations for the U.S. economy has brought universities the resources to augment their expertise and research capacity in crucially important fields of science. And discoveries in those fields have contributed, and promise to contribute more, to the technological edge of U.S. industry. Economic relevance will remain attractive for American universities as long as this vital relationship holds.

# CHAPTER 1

# Technology Transfer as University Mission

The contribution of university scientists to innovation in the private economy has been a contentious issue virtually from the time that it became a realistic possibility. The first academic scientists to master useful scientific knowledge studied the fields of chemistry, mineralogy, and geology early in the nineteenth century. Benjamin Silliman of Yale, his son and namesake, and other pioneers not only taught this subject in colleges, but also hired out their talents to states and private ventures to survey the mineral wealth of the young republic. After 1840, the discovery of how plants derive nourishment from soil raised a demand for experts in applied, or agricultural, chemistry. These developments fed popular calls for the colleges to offer separate courses in the "practical arts," which they were ill suited to do. In the most robust antebellum effort, Yale created a separate school to teach advanced and practical subjects—to anyone except Yale college students. Geologist William Barton Rogers advocated a more ambitious plan for an organization that would teach and advance all branches of applied science, a project not realized until the Massachusetts Institute of Technology (MIT) opened in 1865.[1]

By that date, the 1862 Morrill Land-Grant Act had ostensibly answered the call for the teaching of practical subjects. By inducing the creation of institutions that would teach agriculture and the mechanic arts, in conjunction with liberal arts subjects, the Land-Grant Act raised great expectations of academic assistance to the nation's paramount industry. However, the colleges receiving land-grant funds had almost no capacity to aid agriculture, or even to educate savvy farmers. The result was a generation-long controversy in which these institutions were continually attacked by well-organized agricultural groups, forcing the removal of land-grant funds from some flagship universities in favor of new agricultural colleges. A resolution only emerged when agricultural interests succeeded in passing the Hatch Act in 1887, establishing agricultural experiment stations. Hatch Act funds allowed land-grant colleges to form these distinct units, thus creating a separate and largely separated mission.[2] Subsequent legislation strengthened this system, especially when Agricultural Extension was created for technology transfer—to convey the findings of agricultural science to practitioners. Land-grant universities thus developed a permanent mission of technology transfer—fostering agricultural innovations and conveying them to farmers.

As the effectiveness of this system became apparent, the notion of extending it to engineering and manufacturing gained adherents. Particularly after World War I, advocates proposed creation of federally supported engineering experiment stations. No legislation was enacted, although some individual states did establish such units, albeit poorly funded. However, universities and America's young science-based industries found other ways to interact. Engineering schools, most notably at MIT and the University of Michigan, performed applied research for industry during the 1920s, but this practice withered in the following decade as industry expanded internal laboratories. A different pattern then emerged as pharmaceutical companies relied on university chemists to manipulate refractory compounds. In both these cases, direct funding for university research largely complemented efforts within firms rather than being an independent source of innovation.[3]

Innovative research was more likely to result from philanthropy than from fee-for-service arrangements. The Daniel Guggenheim Fund, for example, provided support to universities for research to advance the development of aviation. More generally, basic university research in this era began to produce patentable inventions. Although it was controversial, leading universities gradually reached a consensus: patenting was necessary for the development and dissemination of such innovations (although there were reservations about medicine); and patents ought to be managed by intermediaries like the Research Corporation (founded in 1912) or the Wisconsin Alumni Research Foundation (1925).[4] Overall, the interwar years saw the development of several kinds of working arrangements between universities and industry. Prevailing theory took a black box approach: support for basic research in universities from foundations, industry, and possibly government would yield, somehow, someday, discoveries of eventual value to industry, the economy, and the public.

The mobilization of university scientists during World War II permanently altered the perception and the reality of academic research. Having developed major innovations in radar, proximity fuses, rocketry, and most spectacularly atomic energy, the government and the armed services had no intention of abandoning these fields. The innovation system that had functioned so effectively in wartime was given a permanent peacetime configuration. In a complex division of scientific and technical labor, R&D was conducted in military labs, in corporations, in university-administered federal laboratories, in special university-based facilities, and within academic departments. Some of this funding proved a boon to basic research and fundamental science; another part accelerated the development of mixed-use technologies, including electronics, computers, aviation, materials science, and atomic energy; and yet another portion supported technology transfer from universities to the defense establishment. Special units dedicated almost exclusively to defense-related research grew large at Michigan, Penn State, Stanford, UC Berkeley, Johns Hopkins, Caltech, and most prominently MIT.[5]

Critics of these arrangements pointed to the inappropriateness of academic research depending on military patronage, but the mission of creating and transferring military technology was long unquestioned. This role, for one thing, was never presented as a separate mission, nor did it develop its own administrative structure beyond the special labs. It brought resources to universities, rather than making claims on general funds, and virtually sustained certain academic departments. However, these conditions changed rather abruptly in the mid-1960s when student protests against an unpopular war focused on defense research as a proximate target. In fairly short order, most campus units sponsored by the Department of Defense shed their university affiliations.

The Defense Department continued to support university research, but far more selectively. After 1970, technology transfer from universities to the military diminished to insignificance, at least for a time. Its demise suggests an inherent weakness. Many of the related research units grew closer to their patrons as they evolved, and more distant intellectually and administratively from their academic settings. Units like the Draper Laboratories at MIT and the Stanford Research Institute welcomed independence for the freedom it gave them to pursue their real missions. For their part, universities were initially reluctant but soon reconciled to separation from these nearly autonomous appendages. Clearly, developments over a quarter century had attenuated the connections with university scientists that had been the original reason for this union. The defense establishment had numerous ways to seek innovation, and universities, purged of these impure relationships, happily embraced the comforting self-image of the ivory tower.[6]

A different pattern emerged in medicine. Here too federal commitments to underwriting discovery in university laboratories were established during wartime and institutionalized afterward in the National Institutes of Health (NIH). Consistently favorable treatment by Congress brought steadily increasing appropriations to NIH, which chiefly supported basic biomedical research in academic settings.[7] As early as the 1960s, the research role in major medical schools had grown to rival the education of physicians. At the same time, however, medical schools expanded their ties with health care delivery. Patient care, and the revenues it brought, soon overshadowed both teaching and research in emerging academic health centers.[8]

These new entities represented a distinctive organizational form with their own hybrid mission. They aspired to educate both physicians and biomedical scientists, to advance medical practice through both applied and basic research, and to provide both advanced and routine patient care. It mattered little whether they were part of a traditional university or were constituted as freestanding institutions; academic health centers were all shaped by the same forces: the system of health care reimbursements, research funding from NIH, and rapidly advancing medical technology. Academic medicine played a crucial role in the innovation system that propelled advances in health care, but the health centers were tied to the politics and economics of the national health care system. Health centers consequently embody a separate university mission that evolved to be not an integral commitment of universities, but rather affiliated, semiacademic organizations.

Agriculture, defense, and medicine demonstrate the capacity of the American university to embrace and assimilate external technology transfer missions. Three conditions are present in these cases. All were predicated on the advancement of knowledge through research; all had some academic foothold in university instruction; and all were not only self-supporting but accretive in bringing knowledge resources to the university. Colleges of agriculture and medicine were institutionalized as part of the academic structure, while defense labs had a more tenuous relationship. In all cases, though, the evolution of the university's technology transfer mission was largely determined by the circumstances of the external partner. Agriculture has been relatively stable, reflecting its dependence on regular government subsidies. Academic health centers have been buffeted by NIH, commercial interests, and the economics of health care. And the Defense Department has been flexible in utilizing or substituting for academic research. All these factors are relevant to the enlargement of the technology transfer mission in the twenty-first century.

In the years around 1980 a rising chorus of voices demanded that universities contribute to overcoming the prevailing economic stagnation. Universities were urged to help revitalize U.S. technological competitiveness by taking steps to transfer technology to industry. The influences on this development have been fully explained elsewhere.[9] Essentially, universities were encouraged to abandon the ivory tower aloofness that characterized the 1970s and to seize opportunities to collaborate with firms. For universities, these injunctions proved convincing for reasons well beyond the economic competitiveness rationale. These years witnessed the first wave of commercialization of biotechnology, providing a powerful paradigm for the economic potential of basic university research.[10] With real federal support for academic research stagnant, and cutbacks anticipated, universities noted the success of those maverick institutions that had cultivated productive ties with industry. Finally, the Bayh-Dole Act of 1980 gave universities an unrestricted right to patent discoveries made through federally supported research. Powerful trends impelled the reorientation of universities toward civilian technology transfer during the 1980s.

Developments moved on parallel tracks inside and outside universities. Bayh-Dole was only one of a series of steps that strengthened intellectual property rights and thus encouraged university patenting. Before 1980 most universities had entrusted their occasional patents to external patent management organizations, but after 1980 every major research university brought this task in-house by creating offices for patenting and licensing. Another innovation of this era was the proliferation of publicly subsidized university-industry centers for collaborative research. Several states enacted policies to support such centers, and in mid-decade the National Science Foundation (NSF) launched a program to create Engineering Research Centers. By 1990, most industrial states were supporting university-industry centers, while the NSF supported 21 large Engineering Research Centers and numerous smaller projects for collaborative research. With universities as eager partners, and public subsidies to boot, industry tripled real spending for academic research during the decade. Building university research parks to promote interaction with industry was another manifestation of this trend. In 1979, 24 such parks were operating, but another 100 were opened during the 1980s.[11]

By 1990 or shortly thereafter, virtually every research university not only had accepted the desirability of technology transfer to industry, but had created internal units to work toward that end. However, this imperative was by no means embraced with equal fervor at all institutions. The pre-1980 leaders, like Stanford and MIT, continued with business as usual. A few ambitious institutions perceived the industrial connection as a means of enhancing their research profile. Other universities to varying degrees viewed technology transfer as something that occurred in engineering centers or in the medical school. In fact, the climate of the early 1990s fed skepticism toward these developments.

Academic research lay under a cloud for much of the 1990s. Federal support stagnated for several years, and research universities were besmirched by sensational allegations of gouging on indirect costs. Inside universities, undergraduate teaching was accorded rhetorical top billing, and undergraduate tuition was paying an ever-larger share of the bills.[12] In this atmosphere, no new commitments for university-industry centers were made by NSF or the states; industry support for academic research temporarily leveled off; and new research parks generally failed to live up to their optimistic expectations. Scholarly studies tended to emphasize disappointment with the ambitious goals of the 1980s.[13] However, beneath this gloomy surface university-industry relations were undergoing consolidation rather than backsliding. Arrangements valuable for both sides prospered, and in the process solidified the university's commitment to this role. The number of patents awarded to universities steadily rose, doubling from 1991 to 1997, while licensing revenues tripled. Although this income was highly skewed toward a handful of big earners, the results were plain for all to see: technology transfer could be very lucrative indeed.

The final years of the twentieth century may forever be known for "irrational exuberance" and the "dot-com bubble." Despite these pejorative rubrics, these years saw the largest creation of wealth in the nation's history. Private research universities were among the principal beneficiaries—in their endowments, gifts, and ability to raise prices. They soon abandoned the trepidation of the early 1990s and began to make major investments in faculty quality and research capacity. Public research universities, despite a relative financial disadvantage, sought strategies to do the same. All universities in fact confronted similar challenges: how to adapt university structures to better incorporate the emerging science-based technologies; how to derive greater return from actual and potential intellectual property; and how to contribute to community and economic development.

The twenty-first century opened with a hangover from the fin-de-siècle prosperity and a new sense of economic crisis. The challenges now were intense global competition, the massive exodus of U.S. manufacturing, and even the outsourcing of service industries. Once again, universities were envisioned as part of the solution. Research-based innovation was seen as the comparative advantage of the United States in a brutally competitive global economy. America may have lost its edge in the old industries, but its base of advanced research had the potential to maintain an advantage in the new high-growth, high-tech fields, like software, biotechnology, broadband, and the Internet. Thus, the national investment in research was framed as an antidote to the looming economic crisis, and universities, with their scientific leadership, were expected to play a crucial role. This logic, moreover, was repeated at the state and local levels: relative economic gains for regional economies would require the stimulation of activity in areas of advanced technology and high potential growth. Universities had not received a more welcome mandate since the post-Sputnik science race with the Soviets. It came with only one proviso: university research must be linked with economic development.

This, then, was the context for the emergence of a distinct university commitment to economic relevance in the twenty-first century. In a sense, universities seemed to be recapitulating the injunctions of the 1980s; however, important differences are evident. Rather than devising new organizations, universities were building on and intensifying twenty-some years of efforts. Industry had changed as well, in ways that will be explored below. Where the policies of the 1980s stressed collaborative research with technology-based corporations, the signature feature of contemporary efforts has been the formation of spin-off firms. That development signaled the preeminent position that intellectual property has assumed. State policies for science and technology are focused more intently than ever on economic development, but they are now shaped by more sophisticated conceptions of the levers of economic growth. Above all, universities have become more proactive in all aspects of promoting their economic relevance.

Economic relevance, as an enlarged form of the technology transfer mission, shares the three features of university technology transfer in agriculture, medicine, and defense. It is rooted in specific areas of university research. It adds new knowledge resources in those same areas. Linkages with instruction, however, are diffuse. And the institutionalization of this "mission" consists chiefly of administrative offices charged with coordination and liaison with external actors. Thus, economic relevance has a tenuous academic home. This mission naturally depends on the behavior of private industry, but a key feature of current practice is the effort to counteract this external dependence through university-based initiatives. One thing that has not changed, however, is the presence of controversy. Critics of the active involvement of universities in the economy have consistently denied the necessity and the desirability of this course of action.

## Commercialization and Economic Relevance

The participation of industry in university research has always generated controversy, but probably never more so than in the current era. Among the voluminous writings on this topic, two general perspectives have been most influential. One school of critics has stressed the incompatibility of the norms of academic science with the self-interested motives of profit-seeking firms. A second camp, interested in the economics of innovation and wealth creation, finds the relationship to be not without problems, but historically and currently constructive for both sides.[14]

The academic community has long harbored numerous skeptics toward university collaboration with industry and commercial entanglements generally. Their concerns are founded partly on ideological predisposition and partly on a traditional view of the autonomy of universities and the sanctity of academic values. During the 1970s, hostility toward university involvement with the "military-industrial complex" prevailed on most university campuses, and the traditional image of the university went largely unquestioned. Thus, when Harvard in 1980 proposed taking partial ownership in a faculty member's biotech firm, the gambit not only divided the campus but raised the ire of alumni as well. Throughout the 1980s, however, support for commercialization gained momentum and more acceptable kinds of linkages evolved. In 1988, for example, Harvard overcame its previous reluctance and established an arm's-length arrangement for making equity investments in faculty firms.[15] But even as support for university ties with industry grew, detractors remained implacable.

The era of economic relevance has seen no lessening of these critiques. Among the most prominent is Derek Bok, who presided over Harvard's growing involvement with industry and patenting in the 1970s and 1980s but has since condemned commercialism in college athletics, research, and distance education. Sheldon Krimsky, who writes on science ethics and public policy, asks, "has the lure of profits corrupted biomedical research?" Higher education scholars Sheila Slaughter and Gary Rhoades considered the cultivation of university-industry ties to be part of a more pervasive phenomenon that they call "academic capitalism." Journalist Jennifer Washburn offered a comprehensive critique of "the corporate corruption of higher education."[16] All these authors offer sensible arguments, raise legitimate concerns, and present anecdotes to support their cases. On the other hand, their negative perspectives, foreshadowed in the titles and subtitles of their works, limit their analyses.[17]

A touchstone for all these critics (save Bok) is sociologist Robert K. Merton's classic formulation of the "normative structure of science." Merton held that science as a social system rested on four fundamental norms: universalism, communalism, disinterestedness, and organized skepticism.[18] Clearly, the intrusion of profit seeking and intellectual property challenges these norms. Disinterestedness is directly contradicted when a scientist or university has a financial interest in the outcomes of research. Communalism—the sharing of results through publication—can also be compromised when scientists withhold results in order to gain advantage in the marketplace. More generally, the Mertonian norms describe ideal-typical behavior for science, but not the application of science as technology. The generation of intellectual property raises the concern with conflict of interest and secrecy in science.

Universities have been mindful of these problems and have instituted policies to prevent them: to preclude conflicts of interest by separating commercial and academic activities; to limit the amount of time a corporation can delay the publication of research findings; and to protect students from being unwittingly diverted to work on commercial projects. How well such policies are enforced is difficult to judge, since they operate in the murk of university research bureaucracies, only becoming visible when alleged malfeasance is reported. Critics have seized upon some notorious transgressions to argue that commercial interests have undermined Mertonian norms. Bok, Krimsky, and Washburn, for example, all cite the experience of Betty Dong, a pharmaceutical researcher at UC San Francisco. Dong's 1990 research findings on the bioequivalence of a popular drug were legally blocked from publication for two years by the research sponsor, until the case was finally exposed in the press.[19] Still, the fact that these authors all had recourse to the same dated instance of injustice, that the sponsor committed and was punished for obvious wrongdoing, and that the incident occurred under the high-stakes conditions of drug testing (discussed below) might raise doubts about the generality of this problem for academic science.

Another concern of critics has been expressed metaphorically as the shrinking scientific commons: the fear that the growing prevalence of ownership claims over fundamental scientific tools or processes has reduced the open area of scientific knowledge available for all to use.[20] Critics seek changes that would restore or strengthen what they deem to be the public character of academic science and universities in general. Thus, Slaughter and Rhoades depict academic capitalism as superseding knowledge for the public good. Both they and Krimsky advocate the creation of public-interest science—the creation of knowledge to ameliorate "social, technological, and environmental problems"—to counteract the increasing weight of private interests.[21] The difficulty with these and similar injunctions is knowing just what "public" means and to whom. These authors would have universities become proactive in public spheres that are chiefly the responsibility of governments and that are just as distant from academic learning as start-up companies and venture capital. Conversely, as will be seen, proponents of economic development see these latter activities as public services—and sometimes support them with public funds.

The distinction between public and private is perhaps clearer in matters of intellectual property. The villain here is not so much industry but the patent system, where universities are often more aggressive than corporations in filing broad and inclusive claims. The cause is not simply the Bayh-Dole Act, but subsequent legal decisions that expanded *what* could be patented.[22] Universities operating in commercial markets are accused of behaving increasingly like profit-seeking firms.[23] This situation raises the question of whether universities can be profit maximizers in their intellectual property portfolios and still remain guarantors of academic values in education and research. Critics are not alone in asking if there is a tipping point at which universities would forfeit their most valuable asset—public confidence in the integrity of academic knowledge. Derek Bok, for one, judges that such a point has not yet been reached: "Commercialization of research is still relatively new, and universities are not yet bound irrevocably to indefensible policies." Still, he finds it "unhealthy for universities to have their integrity questioned repeatedly by reports of excessive secrecy, conflicts of interest, and corporate efforts to manipulate and suppress research."[24]

Daniel Greenberg, a longtime critic of federal science, has concluded that universities are moving away from, not toward, that tipping point. In an extensive inquiry into "campus capitalism," he perceived a heightened sensitivity on the part of universities to upholding academic norms. He found greater "public and academic scrutiny and the specter of embarrassment or disgrace for ethical shortcomings. Together they produce a strong, perhaps irresistible, academic insistence on shared governance over use of industrial money; quick, if not immediate, publication of results; and adherence to academe's concept of the rules of the game."[25] In other words, for any given transaction with industry, universities stand to reap limited benefits from the terms of the agreement, but risk substantial losses in reputation and managerial burden if accused of an ethical breach. Accusation is tantamount to conviction in such situations. Critics of university-industry ties generally fail to appreciate how heavily the balance scales are weighted in favor of academic values.

However, Greenberg finds one persistent ethical concern—the testing and evaluation of actual or potential commercial products by scientists with ongoing and often undisclosed relationships with sponsor companies. This problem is particularly acute with the pharmaceutical industry, where vast sums of money ride on the interpretation of the results of drug tests or clinical trials. Greenberg's study recounts the often-ineffectual efforts of universities, NIH, and medical journals to remedy this situation. And these are the cases, like Betty Dong's, that critics invariably cite. Here the argument is a strong one: university scientists should be wary in general of evaluating the merits of commercial products, and they should avoid completely doing so for products of companies that support their research.

But hard-and-fast rules are difficult to apply over the vast terrain of science. For example, scientists in nutrition or food science frequently have research relationships with companies whose products they evaluate. Yet when a research project supported by the Walnut Growers Association reports nutritional benefits from eating walnuts, the marketplace for nuts is unperturbed. However, when scientists with undisclosed ties to a drug company publish a scientific paper showing the efficacy of a new application for one of the firm's products, hundreds of millions of dollars may be at stake.[26] Money is obviously a factor in such situations, but it does not require a bioethicist to know that the second situation is wrong.

Clinical drug trials are an area where potential for conflicts of interest abounds. Derek Bok dismissed this whole area as "potentially lucrative but usually of little scientific interest."[27] But these trials can be exceedingly complex. Doing them properly requires painstaking design; and interpreting results requires analytical rigor. The Duke Medical Center established the Duke Clinical Research Institute, which calls itself the "world's largest academic clinical research organization," for this purpose. Most other academic health centers also engage in these activities. Although this may be shaky ground for university science, the alternative could be worse for the integrity of drug testing. Private contract research organizations now compete for much of this business.[28] A product of the current era, these commercial organizations have a number of advantages for drug firms over academic settings, and these advantages have become more attractive as universities tighten standards. Where human subjects are concerned, they deal with more pliable institutional review boards; sponsoring firms can exercise much closer control over testing, the better to avoid inconvenient findings like those of Betty Dong; commercial research organizations readily conform with material transfer agreements and pose no threat to intellectual property; and they will happily ghostwrite articles reporting desired conclusions. These companies are therefore the smoking gun of privatized science—the exemplar of commodified research.

However, these areas of university-industry relations are not the subject of this book. For one thing, the world of academic health centers and drug testing is actually removed from the conditions surrounding economic relevance in the nonmedical portions of the university. There, our subject resides in the relationship between academic research and the generation of ideas, inventions, and expertise of use to industry. In one respect, however, the imbroglios over drug testing and medical subjects have influenced all university-industry relations. Efforts to control actual or potential conflict of interest in this area have largely driven the adoption of the rigorous standards that Greenberg found to be governing university-industry research relationships generally.

Quite a different view of university-industry relations emerges from economists who approach this topic from the side of industry. Richard R. Nelson and Nathan Rosenberg have studied why firms engage in basic research, partly to illuminate the role of innovation in the economy, but also to deepen understanding of the specific contribution of university research.[29] These authors find basic research to be an intermediate good that serves chiefly to stimulate and enhance the value of research performed in industry. They have also described it as a ticket of admission to the networks of scientific fields. Being plugged into scientific networks is a necessity for corporate R&D labs that engage extensively in research, as opposed to development. Such connections normally mean interacting with academic scientists and engineers. However, this model describes a traditional relationship that existed throughout much of the twentieth century between large firms that perform R&D and university research. The model is predicated on such firms seeking to develop discovery and intellectual property within the organization.

This traditional relationship has been described as the "enhancement function." Firms enhance the effectiveness of their internal R&D by seeking academic partners who have cutting-edge expertise in their own areas of specialization or, alternatively, have expertise in related fields they cannot cover adequately in-house. Tapping expert university personnel, as hires or as consultants, also contributes to enhancement, as does sharing instrumentation.[30] This relationship includes much wider interactions than industry funding of university research. The bottom line for these studies, as an assessment of the economics of science concluded, is that "academic science and industrial science are complementary activities when viewed from the societal perspective."[31] Indeed, in the traditional model they are. However, for these authors universities represent "open science," by definition. But precisely that openness is now at issue.

These same scholars have all recognized that the emergence of biotechnology and the growing role of university patenting complicated this model.

Instead of academic research representing intermediate goods, to be developed into valuable products within corporate R&D labs, key discoveries in biotech were quickly converted to intellectual property. They still were largely intermediate in terms of an eventual product, but now ownership became entangled among scientific entrepreneurs, universities, small spin-off firms, and multinational corporations. Moreover, the amounts of money at stake were enormous—for biomedical research and for potential profits. The inherent commercialization of this entire field raised the very issues that troubled the Mertonians.[32]

These authors regard the current regime of academic patenting as an arena in which universities lack a comparative advantage.[33] According to this view, patenting should be a means for universities to foster innovation, not an end in itself. The pattern of revenue-producing biotech patents has come to dominate university tech transfer offices at the expense of this larger mission. The historical record shows that these units serve their clients poorly when they strive simply to maximize income. These authors are also concerned that ownership claims are diminishing the scientific commons and threatening the privileged position of academic science. Ultimately they, like others, find fault with the current liberality of the patent laws and the broad claims allowed for intellectual property.[34] Thus, from this perspective too, discontent with commercialization largely focuses on the difficulties arising from intellectual property.

## Universities and Innovation in the Knowledge-Based Economy

From the perspective of the global economy, the notion that U.S. universities should refrain from commercializing the discoveries of academic science appears ludicrous. According to journalist Thomas Friedman, globalization has created a "flat world" in which the United States will have to accelerate its innovative capacity if it hopes to maintain a competitive edge. Its assets in this challenge "start with America's research universities, which spin off a steady stream of competitive experiments, innovations, and scientific breakthroughs—from mathematics to biology to physics to chemistry." Friedman backs his point by quoting Microsoft chairman Bill Gates, who testifies: "our university system is the best," because the large number of research universities allow talented individuals to try out different approaches, to innovate, and to turn innovation into products; "it is a chaotic system, but it is a great engine of innovation in the world."[35] Friedman pungently expressed a view that has now become conventional wisdom in many quarters, but that nevertheless rests upon sophisticated interpretations of economic change: the key role of innovation in economic growth; a trend in U.S. industry from internal to external sources of innovation; and the effectiveness of universities in supplying potentially valuable innovations to industry.

If explaining the sources of economic growth has been a holy grail for economists, innovation has long been seen as playing a key role. Both Adam Smith and Karl Marx pointed to the importance of advances in productive technologies in the capitalist economy. Joseph Schumpeter, the Austrian-born Harvard economist, coined the phrase "creative destruction" in his work on business cycles: entrepreneurs bring about waves of disruptive innovation that transform the basis of economic competition, creating new market opportunities. These spurts of innovation are followed by imitation and enhanced competition, which diminish profit margins and generate incentives for entrepreneurs to seek new opportunities to innovate.[36] For Schumpeter, innovation is the central element driving productivity gains that yield long-term economic growth. He placed special emphasis on the competition brought about by innovation—"competition which commands a decisive cost or quality advantage and which strikes not at the margins of the profits and the outputs of existing firms, but at their very foundations and their very lives."[37] Innovation understood in this broad sense is echoed in recent management literature supporting the incorporation of learning and invention into core firm strategies.[38]

Schumpeter's contemporary and fellow Nobel Prize winner Simon Kuznets proposed that technological innovation often creates new industries with novel classes of products, and that their high rate of growth can offset the declining profitability of mature industries, contributing to overall economic growth.[39] This notion still carries much currency in policy circles, forming the underlying "theory" of state efforts to promote technology-based economic development (TBED). But the impact of technological innovation reaches much farther than the introduction of new products, particularly in its influence on more traditional industries. David Mowery and Nathan Rosenberg have argued that during the twentieth century, a fundamental feature of the U.S. economy was the intersectoral flow of new technologies—the adoption of innovations by mature industries. They point to the institutionalization of innovation as a key condition shaping the choice of American industry for knowledge-based strategies of competition. Universities were crucial to this institutionalization, supplying the trained scientists to staff industrial labs, accommodating and legitimizing practical engineering disciplines, and producing and disseminating useful scientific knowledge.[40] Thus, innovation has been a critical force driving productivity gains, whether in new or mature industries, especially in the long run.

The special relation of innovation to economic growth has only been magnified with the coming of age of the knowledge-based economy. The hallmark of one key part of the entrepreneurial sector is firms that produce new technologies with high consumer demand. However, in the older industrialized sector, access to innovation has been altered in the current environment. The role of the corporate research lab, which first used organized science for commercial purposes in the early twentieth century, has changed. Since the "competitiveness crisis" of the 1980s, a variety of factors have led to the decentralization of large in-house R&D units that once spearheaded the pursuit of innovation in high-technology sectors.

This development has been driven by the same conditions producing global privatization, inside and outside the corporate world. Internally, competitive conditions in the 1980s and 1990s undermined the viability of the vertically integrated corporation. The reduction of Cold War defense research further weakened corporate R&D by shrinking a lucrative portion of its financial base. Important changes in the external environment included the strengthening of intellectual property, the removal of antitrust obstacles to cooperative research, the emergence of foreign labs as attractive venues for corporate research, the enormously enhanced efficiency of communication technologies, and finally the willingness of universities to work for and with corporate investigators. The prominent role of new science-based technologies further complicated the mission of corporate labs. The emergence of these fields widened the scope of technological opportunities for firms, but also made it more difficult for them to cover the range of specializations with internal expertise. At the same time, many of these new technologies were commercialized by small or start-up companies, providing additional external sources of new technology. Technology-based corporations consequently adapted in part by looking to these research-focused companies to develop innovations while orienting the efforts of their internal labs toward monitoring and integration.[41]

This latter development helps to account for the fact that industry spending on R&D did not slow with the decline of the big corporate labs, but rather experienced a robust expansion throughout the 1980s and 1990s. In this complicated universe, research-intensive firms, including university start-ups, became indispensable intermediaries in the innovation process. They frequently made significant discoveries, but often lacked the complementary assets to commercialize them. This vibrant core of the innovation system might best be viewed as a matrix of firms of all sizes and orientations—and in constant evolution as well.

One testimony to the heightened expectations now attached to innovation in promoting economic growth has been its apotheosis in the management literature. Formulas have been offered for "open innovation" or achieving a "sustainable edge" that urge firms to strive for mastery of niche specializations and rely on other firms for complementary knowledge or resources. One author has even declared that the central corporate R&D lab is dead.[42] This overstatement is based on interpretation of just one portion of the innovation system. In fact, the pressure to innovate has led firms to devise numerous strategies and patterns for R&D. Outsourcing can occur by licensing technology from universities, forming alliances with fledgling technology companies, hiring third-party organizations to perform development work (for example, drug testing), or, especially recently, utilizing offshore laboratories. However, these and other approaches all require firms to maintain an internal capacity for understanding and interpreting basic science and related research.

If the innovative matrix is indeed a wellspring for economic growth, then universities are obviously important contributors. With the greater reliance on building innovative capabilities across firms and sectors, universities now play an increasing role in the system of innovation through substantial interactions with industry. Universities contribute in at least three ways. Directly, they are one source of innovation through the creation and disposition of intellectual property. Less directly, they collaborate and cooperate with other intermediaries in the innovation system, through continued relationships with start-ups, business incubators, research parks, and collaborative research centers. Indirectly—but crucially important—the public knowledge generated by universities and disseminated through publications, presentations, and graduates is a vital input into all levels of the innovation system. Universities now simultaneously fulfill roles of creator, proprietor, partner, and disseminator in the commercialization of knowledge.

## Research Universities in the Twenty-First Century

The dawn of the twenty-first century witnessed an escalation of hopes for the efficacy of technology-based economic development. These expectations extended beyond journalists and academics, affecting the behavior of corporations, governments, and universities. Such pervasive shifts in thinking can seldom be attributed to the power of ideas alone. Rather, ideas persuade when they convey plausible interpretations of underlying realities. These interpretations, broadened and elaborated through multiple iterations and permutations, become narratives that convey contemporary understanding of unfathomably complex processes like TBED, innovation, and globalization.

Since 2000, a distinctive view of TBED has superseded the attitude that prevailed in the 1990s. For much of that decade an undercurrent of skepticism toward the value of basic research had held sway. However, actual research was only slightly affected. The benefits of basic research are long-term, and its conduct is deeply embedded in permanent institutions. Thus, research is far more stable than the public discourse surrounding it.

During the last years of the decade these associations began to change. After 1995 the economy began a long, steady expansion—the so-called "Goldilocks economy" that was neither too hot nor too cold. But a few areas sizzled, most notably biotechnology and, driven partly by the vast expansion of the Internet, information and communication technology. These industries drew directly from the nation's scientific and technological resources, including university research. Public opinion began to link basic research with economic growth, and attitudes shifted decisively in government, industry, and universities. In 1998 Congress committed to doubling the budget of the National Institutes of Health, which subsequently rose from $11 billion in 1998 to $22 billion in 2003. The doubling of the largest federal science budget by Republican Congresses would not likely have occurred without the tacit support of the business community.[43] The giant biomedical industry clearly saw public science as a contributor to the development of future products. Similarly, in 2006, President George W. Bush consulted with business leaders before announcing the American Competitiveness

Initiative, which promised to double federal spending for the physical sciences, including the NSF. Between these two events, in 2000, the federal government announced the National Nanotechnology Initiative, which focused $1 billion of annual federal research spending on the scientific foundations of what many believe to be a nascent industry.[44] These steps may well prove to be wise investments in the nation's future; they also reflect a level of faith in the efficacy and utility of basic science that had not been in evidence since the early 1960s.

This faith carried its own lexicon of terms that evoke underlying narratives. The "knowledge economy," which social scientists had variously described for decades, was now invoked by public figures as diverse as Newt Gingrich and President Bill Clinton. An umbrella term, it signified the growing importance of knowledge industries, knowledge-based (high-tech) industries, knowledge applied to rationalizing operations in industry, and/or the growth of knowledge services. Reference to the knowledge economy, whichever version, privileged the roles of science, technology, and education.[45] "Innovation" was championed as the key to economic growth. Also an umbrella term that usefully encompasses the creation of all manner of new and better things, its importance for the economy has inspired a recent outpouring of scholarly and hortatory literature.[46] Most treatises with "innovation" in their titles present it as an imperative for U.S. industries—at once an objective of a knowledge economy and a necessity for firms in a competitive global economy. Thus, "globalization" too is a concept that validates the continual push to innovate in our knowledge economy. Given intense competition from other countries, and the resulting decline of mature, manufacturing industries, the chief competitive advantages of the United States are its knowledge resources and its capacity to mobilize technology for innovation.[47]

The forces behind these narratives had clearly been building for some time. However, after the dust had settled from Y2K, the apocalypse that wasn't, and the bursting of the dot-com bubble, an evanescent catastrophe, a consensus reigned over the linkage between scientific research, technology, and economic development. This was not mere happenstance; the world was changing in profound ways that directly touched people's lives. According to Thomas Friedman, the principal drivers of change "needed time to converge and start to work together in a complementary, mutually enhancing fashion. That tipping point arrived sometime around the year 2000."[48] In subsequent years, this consensus has only strengthened, and with it the impact on industry, universities, and public policy. The notion that economic relevance ought to be a mission of the university rests heavily on the assumption that these unprecedented developments have given universities a new role and a responsibility in generating innovations for industry. How best to harness this potential is still very much at issue, as is the question of whether universities ought to be "harnessed" at all. The place of the American university in these far-reaching developments is the subject of the following chapters.

# CHAPTER 2

# Universities and the Two Paths
# to Innovation

The rhetoric of universities and economic development invokes fundamental features of universities, contemporary industry, and how they interact. The notion that economic relevance ought to be a mission of the university rests heavily on the assumption that universities have a role and a responsibility in generating innovations for industry. From the opposite perspective, it also encompasses the activities of industry that draw upon universities. These two spheres of activity represent two different tracks for the creation of innovation—one drawing from university inventions and the other centered on industrial R&D labs.

## The Case for Innovation

The underlying premise for the economic importance of university research and expertise rests upon their contributions to innovation. Although such contributions may be relatively small, the phenomenon of innovation has huge repercussions for economic development. Economist William Baumol provocatively suggests, "it can be argued that virtually all of the economic growth that has occurred since the eighteenth century is ultimately attributable to innovation." "Ultimately" is a key word in this argument: investments in education and productive capacity have been indispensable, but "only the productive surpluses that innovation began to make possible . . . made feasible the enormous increases in inanimate and in human capital that are widely judged to have contributed greatly to economic growth."[1] Thus, viewed from this standpoint, the university's contribution to innovation becomes the bottom line for evaluating its role in economic development.

The study of innovation emerged as a minor academic field in the 1970s, but has mushroomed since the late 1990s. For the most part the term has been employed broadly, as it has in this book: "invention is the first occurrence of an idea for a new product or process, while innovation is the first attempt to carry it out in practice."[2] Linked as it is to basic human inventiveness, the scope for innovation is almost limitless. The distance between invention and innovation can be long or short. The agency that connects the two—the entrepreneur in Joseph Schumpeter's seminal analysis—can similarly play a crucial or marginal role. Besides products and processes, Schumpeter also identified innovations in inputs, business organization, and marketing. In addition, an important distinction exists between incremental innovations to established products ("new and improved" laundry detergents) and radical new technologies (Internet search engines). This distinction also has a bearing on how and where innovations occur.

Many breakthrough innovations emanate from individual inventors or small firms. On the other hand, by far the greatest amount of private sector R&D is conducted by large corporations.[3] This apparent paradox should not suggest that single inventors are cleverer than their corporate counterparts, but rather signals that different processes are at work. Innovation in the U.S. economy occurs on two different tracks—one oriented to invention and traveled by technology start-ups and small firms, and another taken by large corporate laboratories. The relationships of universities to these two sectors vary accordingly.

Baumol's encomiums to innovation preface an analysis of the factors underlying its institutionalization in modern economies. The first factor is oligopolistic competition. Mature high-tech industries largely consist of a limited number of dominant large corporations that compete only obliquely with one another (oligopolies). By constantly developing new and improved products, they differentiate their goods and services from those of rivals. Distinctive products ensure market domination and comfortable profit margins, which in turn provide the resources for continued investment in innovation. The most successful American corporations of the twentieth century, beginning with DuPont and General Electric (GE) and continuing through such firms as Microsoft and Amgen, have principally used internal R&D to generate the innovations that continually reinvent their product lines. Thus, the second key factor: the innovative activities of corporate laboratories have been institutionalized as a permanent part of their corporations' operations. Product enhancement in these settings is predominantly incremental, and the bulk of activity is applied research and development; the result is the continual perfection of products and the occasional major advance. A third factor that enables this system to function is the selling and trading of technology, made possible by the legal protection of intellectual property. Corporate labs need not do all the work of discovery alone, but rather can purchase or trade for useful technologies. They also sell technologies that they have developed when circumstances warrant. This market for intellectual property makes corporate innovation an open rather than a closed system.[4]

Baumol depicts corporate R&D as anything but entrepreneurial: "many of these undertakings," he writes, "are subjected to complex bureaucratic controls that discourage free-swinging and heterodox approaches."[5] Routine corporate innovation brings enormous benefits to the economy, but only of a certain type. With established product lines and a large base of customers, corporations strive above all to improve their offerings and better serve their clientele. To spend additional resources on exploratory research would risk producing "spillovers" (benefits) that could not be captured by the firm.

This general picture sketches the modal behavior of corporate research but not the variety of contexts that have permitted more ambitious strategies, especially during the golden age of central labs. The legendary research portfolio of Bell Labs was justified because, as a regulated, vertically integrated monopoly, parent AT&T would assuredly be the principal beneficiary of any radical innovations. IBM similarly counted on first mover advantage to assimilate novel findings from fundamental research into its extensive operations. Pharmaceutical companies relentlessly search for breakthrough drugs, confident that any discoveries will be protected by patents. In contrast, the invention of the graphical user interface now standard on personal computers by the Xerox Palo Alto Research Center is regarded as a classic example of brilliant corporate research that exceeded the company's capacity to make use of it.[6]

The institutionalization of innovation in large corporate research labs has undergone a significant evolution since its golden age. Throughout the 1980s the suspicion grew that the purely scientific accomplishments of central corporate labs were contributing little to the financial performance of their respective companies. In the cases of GE and Xerox, competitive pressures mounted, particularly from Japanese corporations. Bell Labs had to adapt to the legal termination of AT&T's monopoly status. IBM reoriented its corporate strategy toward business services.[7] In general, to use Baumol's terms, their oligopolist advantages had eroded. Instead of employing innovation to remain comfortably separated from competitors, they now had to innovate to keep up with the competition. In the late 1980s and early 1990s, all of these companies reorganized corporate R&D to bring it into closer relations with their product lines. What this meant specifically was less "blue-sky" basic research and more mundane development.

In most cases these changes brought dispersion of R&D away from the prestigious central laboratories where, for Bell Labs and IBM, Nobel Prizes had been earned. But the most crucial aspect of decentralization was financial. Instead of being supported with direct budget allocations, the laboratories were now expected to earn their keep. The labs were compelled to negotiate research contracts with other corporate business units, or external customers, so that R&D would be directly linked with product needs. After the revolution at GE, 30 percent of core funding for the R&D center was provided centrally and the rest had to be derived from contracts. Xerox and IBM were somewhat more generous with core support, but the principle was the same: corporate R&D would henceforth be integrated more tightly with product development to enhance the competitiveness of the firm.[8]

These wrenching changes were accompanied by dire predictions of the death of corporate science.[9] However, such forebodings should be tempered with an appreciation for the enormous variety of corporate research, the constant emergence of new technology-based industries, and indeed, the inherent contribution of fundamental research. Robert Buderi, who has chronicled this revolution, believes that corporate research rests on a sounder foundation in the twenty-first century for being more closely aligned with product innovation. Nor has this orientation obliterated the need to conduct basic research. Fundamental investigation creates a "climate of discovery that attracts people to the lab"; it is needed "to gain a deep understanding of the processes involved"; and, "in order to partner . . . dynamically with the rest of the world," companies need a core "that can understand, relate, and adapt discoveries from outside . . . and apply them." Buderi estimates that perhaps 10 percent of corporate research at these leading firms is basic in character, and perhaps 10 percent of that is purely exploratory. Since the R&D budgets of these firms often exceed $1 billion, even one-tenth of one-tenth represents an appreciable amount of blue-sky research.

The implications for universities of this new configuration of corporate research are still evolving. The downsizing of central laboratories might well imply that industry scientists would have more frequent need to "partner dynamically" with academic peers, and especially to gain access to advances in basic science. Given the increased salience of science-based technologies, corporate labs should experience pressure to cover broader and more challenging scientific frontiers in fields like nanotechnology. On the other hand, if their focus has moved to a narrower concern for applied research and development, perhaps they have less need to monitor advances occurring elsewhere. These crosscurrents will be considered below, after first exploring the revolution in university relations with industry and the expanded role of universities in the second innovation track.

## University Inventions and Academic Patenting

Before the current era, industry rarely looked to universities for actual inventions. Commercially valuable discoveries were occasionally made in universities, but generally as a by-product of academic research, not as its objective. Patenting such serendipitous events was long a controversial matter, especially where medicine or human health was concerned. Most universities consigned inventions to patent management organizations, predominantly to the Research Corporation, a nonprofit foundation that had the professional staff for patenting and licensing and a formula for sharing any profits with universities. Prior to 1970, MIT and the universities of Wisconsin and California were among the few institutions to administer their own patents, but soon more universities established these offices, including Stanford (1970) and Harvard (1977).[10] However, if any single event precipitated a new regime in university relations with industry, scientifically and commercially, it was the patents on recombinant DNA filed in 1978 by the University of California and Stanford on behalf of Herbert Boyer and Stanley Cohen.

The three Cohen-Boyer patents covered the discovery of techniques for transporting genetic material from one organism to another. Two decades earlier, James Watson and Frances Crick had discovered the molecular basis for life itself in the double helix structure and replication of genes. Cohen-Boyer described the technique for the manipulation of genetic material (recombinant DNA), and thus permitted life forms themselves to be engineered. This was literally the birth of biotechnology at the molecular level, a scientific revolution that transformed the knowledge base and the nature of research throughout the life sciences. The biotech revolution also transformed the way the results of university research were conveyed to industry.

Cohen and Boyer made their breakthrough in 1973, and by the time the patents were granted in 1978 recombinant DNA was already widely used in research. The Cohen-Boyer patents were thus one of the first cases of patenting a scientific research tool—still a controversial practice. The Stanford Office of Technology Licensing devised a nonexclusive license, which it offered for $10,000 per year, plus a "reach-through" royalty (0.5 to 3 percent of sales) on products developed using the license. The patents ultimately drew several hundred licensees and became one of the most lucrative academic patents, earning around $200 million for the two universities.[11] The commercial potential was exploited further by Boyer, who in 1976 became a founder of Genentech, the first true biotechnology company. By the end of the 1970s, a new paradigm for university commercialization of intellectual property had emerged and, oddly for such an esoteric endeavor, burst into public awareness.

Four features characterized the new paradigm. Foremost, the Cohen-Boyer patents emerged directly from basic research in molecular biology. Second, they broke new ground by patenting a research tool or technique.[12] Third, biology patents are quite strong since they cannot be "invented around." Hence, such patents can have great commercial value. And finally, the Cohen-Boyer discovery tapped this commercial value in three ways—licensing fees, reach-through royalties, and launching a new company. Each of these elements has had far wider implications in the subsequent decades.

Biotechnology was the first, and the most spectacular, of what came to be called science-based technologies. These are, quite simply, areas of basic research where certain discoveries are highly likely—at some point—to produce practical innovations. Situations like this had arisen in the past, but the biotechnology paradigm forced the research system to adapt to their existence; and there were soon many more. National Academy of Sciences president Frank Press defined this phenomenon in 1992, identifying as examples high-temperature superconductivity, optoelectronics, sensor technology, and artificial intelligence. Soon nanotechnology would prominently enter that list.[13] Although each of these fields has unique characteristics, investments in basic research in all these areas could be justified not only to advance knowledge, but for their potential to yield patentable discoveries.

Changes in the patenting system soon made this last outcome more likely. Discussion of this issue has been dominated by the Bayh-Dole Act of 1980, which removed restrictions on the patenting of discoveries made through federally sponsored research. This legislation purported to unlock the economic potential of federal research dollars, allowing the resulting technologies to be brought to the marketplace. The act was a green light on the highway that a few universities, like Stanford and MIT, had already started down.[14] However, other significant developments broadened the scope of what could be patented, including research tools, organisms, and sometimes basic scientific discoveries. The rights of owners of intellectual property were bolstered as well. The U.S. patent system became more accommodating for the kinds of discoveries made in universities, especially biotechnology.

The 1980s witnessed a transformation in the ways universities interacted with industry. The vast majority of research universities established their own intellectual property offices, research parks, and other modes of technology transfer during that decade. However, the increase in patenting has been the distinguishing feature of the current era. Prior to 1970 American universities produced on average fewer than 100 patents per year. That figure rose to 350 by 1980. Twenty years later, it had increased tenfold. Biomedical fields were in the forefront, accounting for half of all academic patents and up to 87 percent of licensing income.

Universities converted to the cause of technology transfer at different times and with different degrees of commitment, but they all felt the pull of powerful external inducements. Besides the new patenting regime, a host of government policies sought to boost the competitiveness of U.S. industry (Chapter 3). An even more fundamental motivation was provided by the changing academic knowledge base, particularly science-based technologies. Universities were producing discoveries of considerable value in their laboratories. The creation of potentially valuable intellectual property (IP) within university laboratories produced real problems of secrecy and conflict of interest, which critics quickly seized upon; but in the absence of public disclosure and ownership, established through patents, these problems could have been worse: "patent trolls" who steal IP, now considered a nuisance, might have become a scourge of university laboratories. Universities in the current era had to develop new relationships with private industry and the economy; they found themselves on a long learning curve, yet to be completed.

The patenting of academic discoveries brought challenges from the outset. Patenting is something of an art as well as a demanding professional skill. The challenges universities face in operating intellectual property offices will be examined in Chapter 4. Here, some implications of academic patenting are relevant, since they stem from the nature of science-based technologies and the liberal patent regime.

Perhaps the most salient feature of academic patents is their "embryonic" nature. Most represent proofs of concept or lab-scale prototypes at best, which means that extensive development is required before an operational product is achieved. For the relatively few academic discoveries that can be used right away, like the University of Florida's Gatorade, the process is not problematic. A clean handoff to industry is possible for such devices without any confusion of roles. For most university patents, however, the developmental period represents an awkward combination of proprietary and university connections. Three basic challenges need to be surmounted.

First, the knowledge of the inventor is usually a critical factor for the development of early-stage inventions. A patent may show how a concept or prototype should work, but the inventor has a deeper, tacit knowledge that is crucial for making it operational. Second, the risk of failure is clearly substantial in this type of venture, and all the more so the more embryonic the discovery. Lengthy periods of development and lack of involvement by the faculty inventor also increase the risk of failure.[15] Third, the inherent risk in early-stage discoveries shapes the market for university patents. Few of these patents attract more than one bidder for a license, and usually the interest comes from small companies, which are generally willing to assume greater risk. Exclusive licenses are demanded by licensees who need protection during the lengthy period it takes to bring an innovation to market. Universities have long been criticized for granting exclusive licenses, but under such circumstances alternative approaches scarcely seem feasible.

University-spawned innovations thus need to be viewed as evolving through stages. A span of 15 years from a discovery arising from basic research to a commercial product has been suggested as typical, but in an arena characterized above all by variety such estimates are of little use. Rather, understanding what occurs at each stage is more important for tracing how or if university discoveries reach the economy. In this process, basic science, which in the language of economists yields public goods (available to everyone without diminishing their value to anyone), is transformed into technology, which has properties of both public and private goods. Moreover, the balance shifts toward the private as an invention moves closer to the realization of a product. The outcome of this process depends on two kinds of uncertainty—technical risk (will it work?) and market risk (will the returns justify the investment?).[16]

In theory, the process begins with basic research, particularly in science-based technologies.[17] When a potential future application dimly emerges, further investigation can be characterized as "generic research." In fact, many departments of the university engage largely in generic research. These fields include pharmacy, bioengineering, computer science, most of agriculture, and the whole realm of what Herbert Simon famously called the "sciences of the artificial." While the long-range applications orientation of these fields is clear, they get there by different routes. In engineering and other fields that work with processes and systems, collaborative research with industry is commonly pursued in consortia and special institutes. Participating firms anticipate taking the results of such research into their own corporate laboratories, where products will ultimately be developed. Patents may play a role here, but corporations depend heavily on their own internal know-how, embodied in first-mover advantages and trade secrets.

In strong-patent fields, principally biotechnology and medicine, generic research leads to patentable results as soon as a use or application can be foreseen. However, these inventions are usually just proofs of concept, and much developmental work inevitably follows under patent protection. Under both scenarios, further generic research is needed before the more focused stage of applied research is reached. The difference is where this stage takes place. In corporate laboratories, university involvement would be minimal, or indirect at best, and the firm assumes the risk. Where universities own and license IP, they have a vested interest, together with inventors and licensees, in the eventual realization of value. Since few university technologies can be "handed off," universities have had to find ways to advance technology beyond the proof of concept stage, while also dealing with the fact of ownership. The general principle is that proprietary research should be separated from academic research, but this has proved to be something of a dilemma for universities that wish to promote commercialization without violating this standard.[18] How universities can best ensure success in this initial stage of commercializing technologies is a burning contemporary issue that will be examined further. Once an innovation progresses to the next stage, applied research and development usually take place outside the university, and private investors can be relied upon to gauge technical risk and market risk.

The relationship between universities and the economy that has emerged in the current era is characterized, above all, by the prominent role assumed by patenting. It was the strong-patent field of biotechnology that largely inspired and led the development of these practices. The rhetoric that accompanied the Bayh-Dole Act stressed the likely benefits that would ensue from moving technology out of university laboratories and into the private economy, but little attention was given to the complications inherent in this time-consuming process.[19] In fact, the patenting paradigm for university commercialization failed to appreciate (or neglected to heed previous debates on) the tangle of public and private interests that characterize this middle stage of the technology transfer process in strong-patent fields. This issue is also inherently bound up with how universities convey innovations to industry.

Despite the considerable range of research that corporate labs undertake, there is still a class of potential innovations that they generally do not pursue. They eschew early-stage inventions where lengthy development will be required and the eventual product is initially ill defined. They are also wary of discoveries that will depend heavily on the inventor's tacit knowledge to bear fruit. They have little interest in pursuing radical technologies that might undermine existing product lines or production processes. Corporations also tend to pass over general-purpose technologies that apply to more than their own product lines. For these potentially significant types of innovations, small and spin-off firms are more promising vehicles.

When the phenomenon of research-inspired innovation is viewed across the entire economy, it clearly operates on two different tracks, and these tracks, in turn, relate to university research in different ways. The R&D labs of oligopolist corporations are black boxes in some ways.[20] They operate through unspoken combinations of patents, licenses, trade secrets, first-mover advantage, and simple know-how; and they largely generate incremental innovations around their own product lines. Universities make important contributions to this mix, greater in some industries than in others; but corporations draw upon universities in numerous ways chiefly to enhance the effectiveness of their own innovative capacities. Small and especially spin-off firms are more apt to create radical innovations that can spur or alter new industries. Of course, to be successful, they must grow large themselves, or find a large partner with complementary assets. The university contribution here is numerically quite small, but nevertheless strategic. University spin-offs, in particular, represent a distinct type of new firm based on scientific or technological inventions. They aspire to transform new science-based technologies into marketable products. Such contributions are qualitatively different from the vast bulk of innovations produced by corporate labs, independent entrepreneurs, or corporate spin-offs. Their significance, then, is precisely that without university engagement such innovations would be unlikely to see the light of day. In this respect, they represent a net addition to the stock of innovation, principally in technologies having future growth potential.[21]

## The Innovation Track for Small Companies and Spin-offs

Outside of high-tech fields, small firms generally have little capacity for innovation. They lack the resources to support internal R&D or even to keep abreast of technological advances. For most of the postwar era it was assumed that innovation was the province of large corporations.[22] In fact, the Bayh-Dole Act was intended specifically to redress this situation. Small firms were supposed to be given priority in licensing university inventions, but this restriction never proved workable. The Small Business Innovation and Development Act that followed in 1982 established the popular Small Business Innovation Research Program, which still provides research grants for firms to develop commercial products (discussed in Chapter 3).

Since then, small and newly founded firms have been increasingly recognized as important sources of innovation. Indeed, new firms, arising from small beginnings in emerging industries like software, broadband, and biotechnology, have played a large role in the resurgence of technological leadership by the United States. "Small business" is a nebulous category, usually defined as firms having fewer than 500 employees. Undoubtedly the majority of that group would, as indicated, qualify as technologically challenged. However, the small firms that do perform R&D make a distinctive contribution to innovation. Such firms account for 18 percent of industry R&D and employ 25 percent of industry scientists and engineers.[23] More importantly, they are the chief conduit for knowledge spillovers from universities. Spillovers represent underutilized knowledge that provides opportunities for entrepreneurs. In fact, small businesses take out the majority of licenses of university patents (70 percent in 2004), most often negotiating exclusive rights to develop the technology.[24]

Three basic types of new firms contribute to innovation—independent inventor-entrepreneurs, corporate spin-offs, and university spin-offs. Each creates value from underutilized knowledge in different ways.

The first group includes unique individuals about whom it is difficult to generalize. Bill Gates and Michael Dell, for example, left college to follow their respective entrepreneurial visions; more recent entrepreneurs of this stripe are responsible for Facebook and YouTube. Although such entrepreneurs may flourish in high-tech industries, their distinctive innovations seldom contribute new technologies per se, but more likely are based on exploiting market opportunities. They apply their unique marketing insights to some piece of an existing, or more typically emerging, technology platform.

Industrial spin-offs are probably the largest source of innovative firms. Entrepreneurs of this breed are steeped in the practices of their respective industries. However, they tend to embody precisely those free-swinging and heterodox initiatives that oligopolistic corporations have difficulty accommodating. In one historically significant example, discontented employees defected from Fairchild Semiconductor in the late 1960s to lead at least 10 different electronics firms in what soon became known as Silicon Valley. They realized that Fairchild's expertise in semiconductor manufacture could be extended to numerous other products; they chafed under unimaginative corporate leadership; and they felt they were not adequately rewarded for their contributions.[25] These extraordinary companies—including Intel and Advanced Micro Devices—were characteristic of many industrial spin-offs: they were embedded in industrial processes and manufacturing, and they envisioned products with relatively short developmental horizons. Industrial spin-offs thus tend to be rather remote from university research, at least at their launching.

University spin-offs, for all their variety, are most likely to be based on scientific or technological inventions.[26] Other inherent features follow from this and differ from corporate research. Radical or breakthrough innovations are frequently entrusted to spin-offs because of the large degree of risk. And spin-offs by faculty inventors are particularly effective as a means of commercialization because the tacit knowledge and continual involvement of the inventor are assured. Indeed, the majority of university spin-offs are led by faculty inventors, and consequently remain closely linked with university laboratories.[27] At MIT and other hotbeds of innovation, entrepreneurs and venture capitalists often prospect for promising technologies for launching new firms. These outside entrepreneurs particularly seek out inventions that are relatively close to being market-ready.

The weaknesses of university spin-offs correspond to these same inherent features. First, technologically inspired inventions must find markets that have use for them. This sequence is largely the reverse of that followed by most new firms. The most successful independent entrepreneurs tend to perceive and exploit market opportunities. The more radical the departure from existing technology, the more formidable the obstacles to gaining market acceptance are likely to be. Second, embryonic inventions face the challenge of securing funding during the lengthy developmental period that precedes any sales or revenues, known as the "valley of death" among entrepreneurs and their backers. Clearly, many ventures do not survive the crossing. And third, inventors are notoriously weak on managerial skills and vision and are sometimes distracted by competing academic obligations.

University spin-offs tend to occur in younger fields of technology. Such areas are typically populated by large numbers of relatively small firms that can locate market niches in which to operate. University spin-offs have been accused of being second-best alternatives, since in some cases they are formed when other licensees are lacking. A more accurate depiction, however, would relate them to situations where the continued application of the inventor's tacit knowledge is essential. Moreover, they appear in many cases to be transitory organizations, intended to develop a specific product to a point where it can be acquired by a larger firm with the complementary assets needed for commercialization. At the University of California (UC) this type of firm is nicknamed "krill companies"—suitable to be gobbled up by the whales. Indeed, in one sample of UC spin-offs almost all the firms that developed salable products were acquired, usually before significant sales were achieved.[28]

Biotechnology, the leading area for university spin-offs, exemplifies many of these features. Although it is more than three decades old, unceasing advances keep this field a youthful technology. It is characterized by numerous small firms that by their very constitution occupy market niches. Most characteristic, biotechnology consists of relatively discrete inventions guarded with patent protection.[29] It has long been an open question whether other science-based technologies will follow the same path to commercialization blazed by biotechnology. However, biotech is unique in several ways.

A successful innovation must surmount three generic hurdles: Can the invention be developed into an actual product? Can the product be manufactured? Is there demand in the marketplace at an acceptable price?[30] Biotech has been particularly fecund in generating inventions directly from basic research. However, the consequence of such early-stage inventions is a long lag time in developing workable products. In the universe of the Food and Drug Administration, additional years are required to prove safety and efficacy for human health products. Patent protection and product uniqueness permit lengthy development horizons that would prove fatal in other industries. The second hurdle, manufacturing, can be formidable for biotech and is sometimes a limiting factor. But the third hurdle is almost nonexistent. That is, health products of proven efficacy can be assured of a market with little price resistance. Thus, biotech innovations that survive this gauntlet can be enormously lucrative, and this prospect, in turn, justifies the large investments needed to fund the grueling development process.

Other science-based technologies, by comparison, have less financial potential, and this fact dampens the entire process of developing innovations. They too produce mostly early-stage inventions, but financing the development of prototypes is likely to be more difficult. Patent protection, another requirement for surviving this protracted process, varies with different technologies but is generally less airtight than for biotech. Marketability, finally, is an ever-present concern for innovations that will compete for consumer favor against established products. Nevertheless, the decentralized character of these new industries, combined with embryonic patents, tacit inventor knowledge, niche products, and potentially radical breakthroughs, all point toward spin-offs playing a large role in commercializing science-based technologies.

Probably most important for economic development, however, is the connection between highly productive scientists, major research universities, and firm formation. Evidence confirms that star scientists tend to congregate and that their presence has a positive effect on the creation of new firms.[31] University research may contribute through corporate intermediaries to national or international economies, but the commercialization of university innovations through spin-offs directly stimulates local economic activity.

This last insight has been magnified by the current vogue of economic clusters. This notion is at once conceptually confusing, given the multiple dimensions of clusters, and superficially compelling, given the notoriety of everyone's favorite cluster, Silicon Valley. Economists essentially agree that colocation of firms in the same industry can produce powerful synergies. Some of these contribute to efficiency, like increased market power, matching jobs with specialized workers, shared information, and provision of special services. But other, intangible advantages generate growth. The most important of these are knowledge spillovers, information networks, and the culture and infrastructure that enhance entrepreneurship. Thus, an economic cluster is greater than the sum of its parts. In theory it should create the dynamics for self-renewal and sustained growth.[32]

The relationship between economic clusters and university innovation is both obvious and somewhat wishful. Certainly there is an important link between the excellence of university research and the industry clusters that have developed in the San Francisco Bay Area, or around Austin, Boston, and San Diego. For biotechnology, in particular, studies show that clusters form and grow around academic leaders. But the existence of powerful clusters also draws new firms away from other localities.[33] Universities by themselves can do little to foster clusters or economic growth: the impact of their innovations will depend heavily on the capacity of the surrounding milieu to anchor and assimilate these technologies.

University spin-offs would seem to offer the promise of contributing to cluster formation, and hence to the capacity to absorb innovations. Insofar as they represent nascent, science-based technologies, these firms are possible seeds of new industry clusters. Some of their characteristics support such dreams—radical breakthroughs, young technologies, and decentralized industries. However, the long gestations of these firms might preclude possibly the most important trait—the ability to grow large fast. Nevertheless, the association of university spin-offs with cluster building, even in theory, elevates their significance for economic development. Not only do these firms represent contributions to the economy in their own right but, under the best of circumstances, they also conjure a vision of the cornucopia of growth.

## The Innovation Track for Corporate R&D

In the vast mosaic of corporate R&D, universities supply relatively few pieces. However, those pieces can fill important spaces, from solving practical problems to exploring the possibilities for far-reaching future innovation. To appreciate the roles university research plays in corporate innovation, one needs to consider its contribution to the entire mosaic.

In 2004 U.S. industry spent almost $200 billion on R&D—64 percent of the nation's total expenditures. In addition, industry performed another $26 billion of R&D for the federal government. This spending was heavily weighted toward product development. Industry's own expenditures represented 12 percent of the nation's basic research, 54 percent of applied research, and 82 percent of development.[34] This pattern is consistent with the basic strategy of corporate labs to keep the seedbed of innovation and product development within the firm. Accordingly, contracts for research with universities are the obverse of this pattern, consisting of almost 70 percent basic research. The basic research that corporations perform internally tends to be concentrated in central laboratories, sometimes with strategically located satellites. Otherwise, corporate R&D is quite decentralized, and more so since the post-1990 reorganizations. The purpose of those changes was to bring innovation closer to manufacturing processes, suppliers, and consumers, which are now recognized as important sources of potential innovation. These R&D activities are heavily applied or developmental, aimed predominantly at the incremental improvement of products. Thus, industry "consumes" the gamut of R&D, mainly from internal sources, but also shops selectively for external inputs.

During the 1980s and 1990s, universities were a growing part of those external inputs. Real corporate spending for research more than tripled from 1980 to 2000, stimulated by government programs and the expansion of new and old research-intensive industries. Real corporate spending for university research more than quadrupled during these decades, reflecting its growing importance. For universities, industry support rose from 4 to more than 7 percent of the total. Around 2000, however, this trend experienced a sudden reversal, for reasons that have yet to be explained. (See Figure 2.1.)

Corporate spending for R&D is fairly sensitive to the economy. Thus, a slowing growth in corporate research spending from 1991 to 1994 reflected a recession and its aftermath. Corporate R&D then continued its upward trajectory, rising 69 percent by decade's end (in constant dollars). Total corporate research was affected more severely by the recession of 2001 than it had been 10 years before. The brunt of the reductions hit the software and telecommunications industries, and small to medium-sized firms in particular seemed to reduce R&D spending. By 2004, despite rising corporate profits, spending for R&D was 6 percent lower than in 2000.[35] Industry support for university research exaggerated this pattern, falling 10 percent below the 2000 level (constant dollars) by 2004 before turning up once more in 2005 (Figure 2.1).[36] This drop was unprecedented in a half century of National Science Foundation (NSF) record keeping. The economic slowdown does not appear to be a sufficient explanation for such a dramatic weakening of university-industry research.

The literature on both management and innovation has stressed that in the knowledge economy firms should satisfy an increasing portion of their

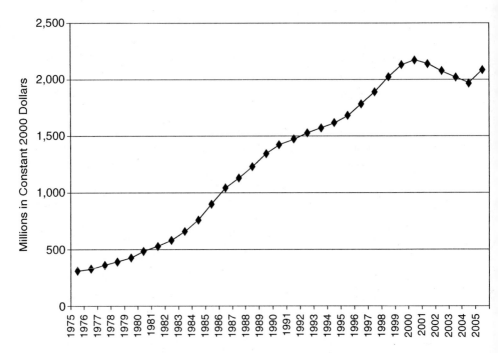

**Figure 2.1.** Industry Funding of University Research, 1975–2005 (in 2000 dollars).

knowledge needs from external sources. The complexity of science-based technologies as well as the testimony of industrial scientists corroborates the difficulty of any single lab providing for all its own knowledge needs. In addition, the advantages of focusing on core competencies and the increasing potency of networks for knowledge acquisition point to greater outsourcing of R&D by industrial firms.[37] Experience appears to support these views. From 1993 to 2003 external R&D grew at nearly twice the rate for internal R&D in U.S. industry, and it exceeded $10 billion by the latter date.[38] Over two-thirds of this research was performed by other for-profit companies. However, independent nonprofit laboratories increased their research support from industry more rapidly than universities during the 1990s, and they retained this volume after 2000. Thus, universities are the only sector that has been losing share of outsourced industrial R&D since 2000. The upturn in industry-sponsored research in 2005 underlines the persistent need for university contributions to industry R&D. However, the loss of share indicates a keener competition for industry research dollars.

Five years is a short span for identifying historical trends, but this stark reversal of the pattern that prevailed throughout the 1980s and 1990s calls for explanations. Reasons for the change most likely lie on both sides of this relationship. In industry, the implications of the reorganization of corporate research continue to unfold, and most likely were affected after the turn of the century by increased concerns for financial performance, accompanied by a foreshortening of developmental horizons. In the years after 2000, industry expectations for R&D foresaw contraction of both internal and external investments.[39] In universities, the very factors that have encouraged the nurturing of small tech companies may be inhibiting cooperation with large corporations, particularly the emphasis on patenting and intellectual property. In addition, competition for research dollars has grown, providing corporate labs with greater choice.

The discussion that follows probes these and other factors affecting university-industry research relations. We look first at contrasting patterns of corporate R&D in several industries, and then at the various means by which industrial and academic researchers interact. Universities still have a vigorous relationship with corporate research and innovation, although one persistently afflicted by underlying tensions.

## Universities and Corporate Knowledge Needs

The modern study of innovation asks how firms acquire the knowledge on which innovation is based and how they appropriate the value of that knowledge for proprietary gain. These knowledge flows are misleadingly called "spillovers," even though knowledge is more often deliberately extracted. Universities, given their role of advancing fundamental knowledge, have received special attention in these inquiries. From this industry perspective, university contributions vary on one dimension by the multiple ways universities disseminate knowledge, and on another dimension by the different needs across industries for what universities supply. Understanding of this interaction relies heavily on two surveys of industrial research laboratories, one conducted at Yale in the early 1980s and the second at Carnegie Mellon a decade later.[40]

Both surveys found university or public science to be "somewhat to very important" for a majority of large industry groups, and that importance seemed to have increased in the 1990s.[41] In general, utilization of university research increased with firm size, with the exception of biotechnology start-ups. There was great variety in what fields were relevant to which industries. Among basic disciplines, chemistry alone was widely utilized; biology was exploited heavily only by the drug industry. The authors did not consider that this evidence signaled the unimportance of basic science, but rather that its contributions were mediated through more applied fields. Most industries drew predominantly from engineering, materials science, computer science, and (in the Yale study) agricultural sciences. On the issue of appropriating and protecting knowledge assets, both studies documented the minor role played by patents in the majority of industries. Pharmaceuticals again were the outlier, but most other industries placed greater emphasis on first-mover advantages and (for processes) trade secrets.

Table 2.1 provides a breakdown of the ways industrial labs apprehend the usefulness of public (or university) research. The most highly valued contribution that universities make to industry is through public science—publications and presentations at meetings. The next most valuable contribution comes through personal contact—consultants and recent hires, which also facilitate informal interactions. Contract research and cooperative research were considered important by only about one-fifth of respondents. And patents and licenses were rated as valuable by the smallest percentage of respondents, which is consistent with a corporate strategy of developing IP in-house.

Despite the modest rating in these findings, contract research plays an important role for both industry and universities—and, by implication, the same could be said for cooperative or collaborative research in university-industry research centers or consortia. These purportedly different sources interact in substantial ways. Contract research can lead to consulting or, more likely, vice versa. Hiring graduates can facilitate both these activities, as well as informal or personal contacts. Industry frequently contracts for university research in order to build relationships with key scientists rather than to obtain specific findings. Patenting and licensing are also connected with other knowledge flows, although perhaps less directly. Patents sometimes result from consortia projects, and university inventors tend to have ongoing relationships with industrial licensees. Perhaps the chief message of Table 2.1 is that research forms one channel among multiple, interrelated knowledge flows. Moreover, even these patterns blur the distinctive modes whereby knowledge is acquired and applied in different industries.

**Table 2.1** Importance for Industrial R&D of Sources of Public R&D Information

| Information source | % Rating important |
| --- | --- |
| Publications and reports | 41.2 |
| Informal interaction | 35.6 |
| Meetings and conferences | 35.1 |
| Consulting | 31.8 |
| Contract research | 20.9 |
| Recent hires | 19.6 |
| Cooperative R&D projects | 17.9 |
| Patents | 17.5 |
| Licenses | 9.5 |
| Personal exchange | 5.8 |

*Source:* Wesley M. Cohen, Richard R. Nelson, and John P. Walsh, "Links and Impacts: The Influence of Public Research on Industrial R&D," *Management Science* 48 (2002): 1–23.

The pharmaceutical industry, which has shaped university practice in matters of intellectual property, is an outlier in several respects. Besides relying on patenting and maintaining close relations with basic biological research, the industry draws more heavily from external sources than any other. In 2003 it devoted more than 17 percent of its R&D budget to contracts outside the firm, more than three times the average.[42] A good portion of these contracts support clinical trials, which are unique to the industry. This situation also reflects the powerful effects of the biotechnology revolution superimposed since the 1970s on the research traditions of large pharmaceutical firms.

The pharmaceutical industry is a prodigious performer of R&D. The $39 billion it expended in 2005 is nearly equal to the total research expenditures for all U.S. universities. Moreover, after 1970 that figure grew steadily by 12 percent per year, although the pace has been closer to 8 percent since 2000. Only one-quarter of these expenditures is devoted to "prehuman/preclinical" activities where research (rather than development) takes place.[43] "Big Pharma," as these enormous multinationals are called, has had close ties with university research since the 1930s, but this relationship has been used far more to develop new drugs than to invent them.

Today, pharmaceutical scientists are probably the most academic of corporate researchers. That is, most have PhDs and participate in "public science" through conferences, meetings, and journals. Big Pharma consequently has multiple ties with universities covering all forms of interaction. Contract research tends to fall within three broad categories. Clinical trials take many forms, but most are tightly structured and rigidly controlled to assure validity across different patients and different sites. University health centers appear to welcome this revenue, but have little scientific input once the design is set. A good deal of research activity emanates from the mutual interest of corporate and academic scientists in common molecules or compounds. This interaction generates research contracts and "material transfer agreements," which play a large role in this field. Big Pharma tends to be demanding about IP in these transactions, fearful of allowing any claims against its property or products. Finally, these companies have entered into some extended partnerships with select universities, aiming to further basic scientific understanding in strategic areas. Such commitments have been one possible entrée for Big Pharma into biotechnology.

For the last generation pharmaceutical firms have struggled to adapt to the biotechnology revolution. The companies and their labs were built around chemical analysis (small molecules), and hence were distant from the intellectual wellsprings of biotech (large, protein molecules), culturally as well as geographically. They have consequently had difficulty recruiting biotech scientists to corporate labs, and have been laggards in the intense competition for biotech advances. They have compensated by establishing some multiyear, multimillion-dollar contracts with a few universities. Merck has entered a series of partnership agreements with Harvard Medical School and MIT; and Pfizer, besides closing a chemistry-based laboratory in Ann Arbor, signed a $100 million agreement with The Scripps Research Institute and opened a "biologics" laboratory in San Francisco.

The inability of Big Pharma to get in on the ground floor of biotech has meant that the U.S. industry developed through small start-up firms. Although a handful of these early firms grew into large corporations themselves (still not Big Pharma size), the most remarkable feature of this industry is that the relentless advance of fields such as genomics and proteomics has resulted in ever more new, research-based firms. Instead of following the normal pattern for new industries, namely, firm proliferation followed by consolidation into larger firms, biotech companies have continued to proliferate, developing a symbiotic relationship with Big Pharma and the larger biotech corporations based on division of labor. These firms now constitute a vital source of innovation and drug development for the older, larger firms, and a distinct sector of the industry. Still, a remarkable feature of this industry is the centrality of university science. In an analysis of biotech patent activity from 2002 to 2006, 11 U.S. universities were in the top 24 (organizations with more than 100 patent families), compared with 10 corporations.[44]

The typical biotech firm was launched on the basis of discoveries in university laboratories, and most continue to have close relations with academic research. Their chief task is performing highly specialized applied research aimed at developing proprietary technologies.[45] Their own IP is their most valuable asset, but that value can only be realized when a workable product is at least in sight. Furthermore, those proprietary technologies are less likely to be consumer products like drugs than inputs to therapeutic processes controlled by larger corporations. The vast majority of these firms are small and unprofitable. According to the CEO of Genentech, biotech is "the biggest money-losing industry of all time": since 1976 when Genentech was founded, the industry "has lost $90 billion. . . . [F]or most of the 1,300 to 1,400 companies—300 or 400 of them public— this is a money-losing enterprise."[46] These losses must be covered through venture capital or the proceeds from selling stock. The market structure of the biopharmaceutical industry thus concentrates innovation and technical risk in this sector, along with speculative financing. Rewards come from developing a real product and usually result in movement up the food chain—being absorbed by a larger firm either through outright purchase or licensing and marketing agreements. The biopharmaceutical industry has thus evolved a large commercial sector, drawing on multiple sources of funding, that has become an intermediary between academic research (in universities or independent laboratories) and the development and sale of health products.[47]

In the electronics and computing industries an entirely different pattern has evolved for acquiring and incorporating new knowledge. Although this field is based on science and technology, fierce competition has favored internal generation of knowledge and few academic ties. These industries have the lowest percentage of externally contracted R&D (1.4 percent). As they developed, they depended heavily on manufacturing expertise rather than scientific breakthroughs. Speed was rewarded; patents had limited value, often serving merely to slow down competitors. Intel, for example, long resisted establishing a central lab, keeping its R&D staff relatively small and closely focused on semiconductors and microprocessors. According to its legendary founder, Gordon Moore, it operated on the principle of "minimum information": that is, Intel engineers attacked problems with intuition as far as possible, and resorted to deeper analysis only when these informed guesses failed. Originally it derived much new technology from industrial sources, notably Bell Labs. More recently, however, "Intel looks to universities for much of the basic research of interest to it." By 2007, Intel was supporting research projects at 150 universities in 34 countries. Some Intel projects were leveraged further through faculty proposals for government grants on related topics (testimony to the pervasive role played by public science). Its chief scientist expected universities "to play an increasingly major role in the longer-term research topics," including novel forms of collaboration (discussed below).[48]

Indeed, closer cooperation with university science would seem to be the long-term trend. At Hewlett-Packard a product-oriented research lab was gradually reconfigured to occupy the middle ground between basic university research and internal product development. It has devised a "partnership continuum" that extends from traditional kinds of support toward an ideal of "holistic engagement" with universities. Disk-drive maker Seagate Technologies, coping with data storage demands that posed increasingly difficult scientific challenges, created a new research center in Pittsburgh in order to work with scientists at Carnegie Mellon University.[49] Still, the university's role in this industry faces inherent limitations. For example, Moore considered it "impossible for universities to afford the equipment required to support work with state of the art semiconductor technology."[50] For these needs, Intel and other manufacturers turned to industry consortia, especially SEMATECH. Launched in 1986 with federal subsidies to revitalize the U.S. semiconductor industry, SEMATECH is now an international consortium focused on several aspects of semiconductor manufacturing. It performs precompetitive research that each company can utilize in its own manner for manufacturing its distinctive product line. This arrangement is typical of the electronics industry, where leading firms have resorted to cooperation to push the science-technology frontiers in industry-wide organizations. But even here the university role is growing: SEMATECH finalized agreements in 2007 to establish new operations in conjunction with the College of Nanoscale Science and Engineering of the University at Albany (discussed in Chapter 3).

Another electronics consortium also has university ties: the Microelectronics Advanced Research Consortium, or MARCO, is a wholly owned subsidiary of the Semiconductor Research Corporation, associated with the Defense Advanced Research Projects Agency (DARPA), and funded by the Department of Defense, the Semiconductor Industry Association, and semiconductor suppliers. This labored description identifies the numerous interested parties for this technology. MARCO supports four major labs, at Berkeley, Carnegie Mellon, Georgia Tech, and MIT, each with multiple participants—altogether a complex information system with specific activities at each node. At Berkeley, for example, the Gigascale Systems Research Center aspires to create a chip containing one billion transistors.[51] The Semiconductor Research Corporation was originally established in 1982 as the university research arm of the Semiconductor Industry Association. In the 1980s it established "centers of excellence" at several universities for longer-range, precompetitive research, and it currently sponsors four separate programs that harness different aspects of university capabilities. Hence, a good deal of information technology (IT) research is sponsored by this nonprofit corporation rather than individual companies.[52] Universities are highly relevant to the information technology industry, but in quite different ways from biotech.

The strong-patenting regime practiced by universities is incompatible with the IT industry for two reasons. First, the industry has evolved from producing single products to complex systems, which might embody thousands of patents. As explained by the Hewlett-Packard vice president for university relations, "due to the large number of patents in a typical IT product, companies will not pursue royalty-bearing licenses with universities." Second, the pace of innovation in IT has accelerated the product development cycle as well as product lifetimes. The patenting system, and indeed the whole process of university invention followed by technology transfer, is too slow for this industry. Instead, it seeks collaborative relationships in which emerging technology can be incorporated into the firm's continual process of innovation.[53] The industry has evolved extremely complex organizational forms in order to found and fund "neutral" sites where precompetitive research can address major future challenges in ways that will subsequently be developed independently by competing firms.

The materials industries present a third pattern for utilizing university research. Chemistry was the first academic discipline to develop direct links with industry, and these exchanges thrived throughout the twentieth century. The sophistication of materials science and engineering merely added more channels to this knowledge flow. "Better living through chemistry" was long DuPont's slogan; and firms in metals, plastics, and glass could have added, "better products too." Compared with drugs and electronics, materials technologies advance at a more languid pace, making access to cutting-edge science a less critical factor. In addition, these firms largely sell commodity materials to manufacturers. The use of more advanced, and more expensive, materials is often constrained by the pricing limits of the final products into which they are incorporated. In working with universities, materials firms have tended to favor informal arrangements and long-term relationships. These are often established with individual scientists and their laboratories, and result in combinations of consulting, contract research, lab support, gifts in kind, supporting or hiring students, and the catchall from Table 2.1, "informal interaction." These firms are uncomfortable with some charges for indirect costs, university demands for intellectual property, and above all the prospect of running royalties. Their profit margins are too narrow, they argue, to shave off percentages of royalties for a small university contribution to their own far-larger efforts.[54]

The materials industries in many ways typify university relations with innovation in mature manufacturing corporations. Changing conditions in the twenty-first century have both favored and obstructed those ties. A research director at Dow Chemical spoke for these industries in observing that Bayh-Dole and university patenting have made "U.S. universities . . . substantially less attractive as research partners for companies. As U.S. universities focus on controlling intellectual property and maximizing their revenues from licensing inventions they have become more like competitors than partners to companies that sponsor research with their faculty and students."[55] Industry resents having to pay twice—once for the research and a second time to use university-patented findings. They object that this arrangement ignores the far-larger industry investment in perfecting and developing a product. When lawyers for both sides negotiate contracts, legal costs can exceed the value of the research project. Another negative is the time required for these negotiations, on average more than five months. Yet industry often needs timely answers to research questions. It has become increasingly common for research agreements to be scuttled over IP negotiations. Such an impasse, moreover, can poison a relationship: "long after a single negotiation has failed, the reluctance to participate in other areas of support such as gifts, grants, endowments, research contracts, consulting arrangements, and others lives on."[56] As a result of these irritations, industry reports contracting for less research at U.S. universities than they would otherwise, and has become more receptive to seeking knowledge from other partners.

On the other hand, not everyone believes this relationship is deteriorating. Scaling back investment in industrial labs has caused firms to tap university resources. Dow Chemical, for example, now has universities perform materials characterizations that were formerly done in-house. Air Products and Chemicals and DuPont, among others, have embraced the doctrine of "open innovation"—looking to external sources to supplement internal R&D. Air Products has concluded general "alliances" with at least three universities. Focused partnership agreements are becoming more prevalent: for example, those between DuPont and MIT to study biological materials, and between Rohm and Haas and Virginia Tech for elastomers.[57] In both cases the companies sought university expertise in a precompetitive topic area that would contribute to future product development. In these situations, IP issues are more easily resolved, often with nonexclusive, royalty-free licenses. These kinds of situations are becoming more common as industry seeks access to emerging science-based technologies in which expertise is in limited supply. For materials firms, nanotechnology is the most salient example.

Nanoscale science and engineering promises enabling technologies that will be applied to the life sciences, electronics, and materials. For the first two, relations with universities largely conform to the patterns for those industries. That is, start-up firms are developing nanoscale applications to biotechnology in areas like drug delivery; and in semiconductors the connection between nano and SEMATECH has been noted. For materials, some of the simpler applications of nanotech have already reached the marketplace, primarily coatings with novel properties. However, more advanced and more remarkable applications lie in an indeterminate future, and the structure of the industry that will deliver them is uncertain as well. At this stage, universities are very much involved in shaping that future. Like biotech, nanotech's advancement rests heavily upon basic science and requires inputs from the multiple disciplines that can be found in large research universities. It also may rely more heavily on patents than any previous enabling technology.[58] In terms of research equipment, it depends totally on very expensive instruments and facilities. To date, NSF has supplied much of this infrastructure at universities, and recipients have had little difficulty attracting the industrial partners that NSF insists upon. The California NanoSystems Institute at UCLA likewise recruited corporations from the three relevant industry groups as supporting partners.

University scientists have perceived a sharp dichotomy in the field: "you have the large companies . . . who are keeping an eye on what's developing . . . and working on some technical developments themselves"; "and very young companies looking to try to engineer some of these materials into real products."[59] In other words, at this early stage nanotechnology seems to be evolving toward a structure similar to biotechnology, where a great deal of product innovation and technical risk is concentrated in start-up companies, mostly university spin-offs. Moreover, also like biotech, this commercialization is concentrated around those universities that lead in nanotechnology research.[60] Already enough of these companies have gone public to provide a basis for an exchange-traded nano fund.[61] But no Amgens or Genentechs have emerged, and the huge profit potential of key biotech discoveries seems to be lacking. Instead, the more successful among the nanotech firms will most likely partner with large materials corporations. Air Products, for example, established a toehold in the field by forming a partnership with one such firm, proclaiming "the keys to successful nano projects are alliances and partnerships."[62] Corporations may well be looking to universities for learning but to the start-up sector for more relevant technologies.

## University-Industry Research Relationships

From the perspective of the industrial lab, the utilization of external knowledge and technology is intended to complement the internal process of innovation. The highly specialized staff are often resistant to external inputs—the "not-invented-here" syndrome. Maintaining relations with universities frequently requires an internal champion to remind the lab of the longer-term advantages of these partnerships. Without support from management, the greatest barrier to tech transfer can be the culture of the corporate lab. Thus, assimilating external knowledge is a challenge faced by all industrial R&D labs. Exacerbating this obstacle is the sensitivity of lab operations to costs. R&D by itself represents a large fixed cost with a somewhat precarious status in company budgets. External expenditures are evaluated by price as well as contribution. At one representative firm, projects up to $50,000 could be readily authorized, research contracts under $75,000 were preferred, projects over $100,000 were "painful," and those above $250,000 had to prove their worth to management.

Cost is only one among many considerations when firms decide where to seek R&D services. U.S. universities are storehouses of expertise and a pretty good deal as well. A typical small, low-risk project might support a doctoral student for a year (cheap labor) and a sliver of the professor's time (a bargain for access to a professor's knowledge and lab). Often such projects are used to maintain a working relationship with a scientist whose research is valued by the company. By comparison, contracting for a portion of a full-time scientist at a national laboratory or an independent research corporation might cost more for personnel and have higher indirect costs. However, the nature of the research, more than costs, determines these choices. A greater challenge to U.S. universities in this respect is the growth of industry-sponsored research outside the United States. Domestic corporations have taken research offshore for a variety of reasons. When making location decisions, firms seem to balance four factors—markets, costs, quality, and protection of intellectual property.[63]

Conducting R&D in emerging countries—principally China and India—is motivated most strongly by the desire to have a presence in those booming economies. The actual R&D tends to be focused on local products and markets, although both countries have developed centers of scientific excellence and undoubtedly will develop more.[64] Costs are lower in these locales, but protection of IP can be problematic, especially in China. High-quality research at a very low cost is also available in Russia as a result of special programs intended to sustain scientists after the fall of the Soviet Union. For some topics, researchers with very different backgrounds have an additional value in bringing fresh perspectives or new ways of seeing problems.

Still, companies are far more likely to place basic research in developed countries. The paramount consideration here is research quality, and in most cases this means connections with universities and university faculty. Higher costs are not a deterrent when the objective is obtaining access to the best scientists and engineers. This is clearly the great strength of the United States, although by no means does it have a monopoly. One attraction of universities in other developed countries is that they make no claims on IP from industry-supported research. Sans the IP hassle, research agreements are easier to negotiate. Sensitivity to this issue probably varies by industry but has clearly intensified. According to one research manager in materials, "this much more favorable treatment of IP is causing companies to do more of their sponsored research abroad."[65] For all industries, it is safe to say, U.S. universities face heightened competition for corporate research support.

The pattern of commissioning offshore research is consistent with that for the support for domestic university research. In general, when industry seeks access to basic research, it looks to partner with high-quality universities and faculty. When more applied forms of research are the object, nearby universities are likely to be more convenient and cost-effective.[66] This relationship describes a continuum rather than a dichotomy. Firms can and do seek solutions to their research needs anyplace in the world. However, access to the latest thinking in cutting-edge fields is invaluable for large, research-based corporations that depend on their technological edge. Often these firms are less interested in specific research results, but simply wish to maintain relationships with key researchers. Local universities, on the other hand, seem to prove more accommodating for the near-term problems of nearby industries. Most firms probably pursue both strategies. Many examples could be given of mutually beneficial relationships between regional firms and universities, usually involving more than research. However, given the dispersed operations of multinational corporations, little of the economic fallout from any single university-assisted innovation is likely to remain near home. A survey conducted at Penn State, the largest public performer of research for industry, found only one-fifth of support coming from Pennsylvania companies, and another fifth from the six contiguous states. Moreover, the farther the sponsoring company was from Pennsylvania, the larger the average grant size, with contracts from international corporations averaging more than twice the median size of $62,000.[67] For the bulk of industry-sponsored research at major universities, globalization is the rule.

When considering industry-sponsored research at universities, it is important to keep in mind both the differences across industries, described above, and the related pathways, listed in Table 2.1, by which industry obtains knowledge. Within this complex picture, two general trends are evident. First, the modest, discrete research grant ($50,000 to $75,000) continues to be a kind of baseline for industry contracts for academic research. The reasons for this are the cost considerations explained above coupled with a need for multiple, dissimilar knowledge inputs. Second, the prevalence of larger-scale, longer-term, cooperative arrangements appears to be growing. These arrangements take multiple forms under sponsorship from governments, universities, industry groups, and single corporations. Many of these agreements are of long standing, but their increasing numbers represent an effort by corporations to tap more directly the economic relevance of academic science.

The discrete research project is the most common way in which industry obtains external knowledge, particularly from universities, but it may be the least studied aspect of this relationship. In theory the goal is quite simple. As stated by Air Products, "industry views university research as one of many tools it may wish to use to maintain a competitive edge. The goal is to get the best research results for the lowest possible investment. The value of the research is in its extraction of commercial value from those results. . . . Industry views university collaboration as a stepping-stone to help augment the innovative ideas of its own scientists."[68] However, when Air Products took the additional step of formally evaluating the contributions of its external research projects, the criteria it developed were anything but simple.

Air Products' scheme provides insight into what a firm expects to gain from supporting university research.[69] The company distinguished four levels of external research projects: fundamental studies; learning or evaluating external technologies; assimilation of external technologies to internal uses; and applications or process development. Expectations obviously differed for each type, but all were rated according to ten criteria, which can be summarized as follows:

*New ideas or new expertise or skills* (two criteria): the highest scores were
   given to scientific advances or "world-class" understanding likely to be
   derived from basic research.

*Time or net R&D saved* (two): these criteria measured the value of the
   contribution to internal R&D in terms of development time or
   person-years saved.

*Access to existing IP or generation of new IP* (two): this emphasis underlines
   the company's ubiquitous concern for IP.

*Long-term access:* this criterion refers to building relationships with other
   organizations and hence access to their capabilities, measured in dollar
   value and given greater weight (five possible points versus three for
   other criteria).

*Program emphasis:* evaluated as offensive (highest) or defensive, critical or
   noncritical; also given greater weight (five possible points).

*Commercial impact:* measured as the dollar volume of resulting sales or
savings.
*Technical leverage:* the overall contribution to technological advancement.

The Air Products exercise illustrates the general point that external research
enhances the capabilities of internal R&D.[70] It contributes to efficiency (time
and R&D saved), intellectual capital (new ideas and expertise), access to the
resources of other organizations, and technical leverage. In terms of outputs,
it may produce new IP and increased sales, but in this case income is one
factor, not the bottom line. R&D labs see their role chiefly as strengthening
the company's competitive position, leaving subsequent financial consequences to other corporate divisions. Otherwise, the stance is aggressive in
terms of seeking to extract advantageous information from other organizations. The managers who implemented this evaluation found proximate
benefits. The 42 projects they evaluated each saved on average two person-
years of effort. They anticipated using this exercise to improve the effectiveness of external research even further, but the process apparently proved too
cumbersome to continue. Since the chief benefits from external research are
merely inputs (stepping-stones) to a much larger process, companies have
generally rejected formal evaluation as inefficient and possibly misleading.[71]

The Air Products exercise reveals the multiple dimensions of each research project, and confirms the status of the discrete project as the baseline
for university-industry research. The explicit inputs listed by Air Products
are not likely to be realized through "informal interaction" or "personal exchange" (Table 2.1). Public science, in the form of publications and meetings, is obviously an important supplement to industry R&D and can be particularly useful for identifying potential research partners, but cannot by
itself yield technological advantage.

Companies have two alternatives to discrete grants, but they appear to
use them selectively. Instead of a formal research agreement, firms often
make gifts to universities, designated for a particular scientist or laboratory,
with the understanding that it will support research or a student in a specific area. These arrangements are usually based on an established relationship and mutual understanding. However, a research-related gift must include no deliverables and be otherwise disinterested. The trend in corporate
funding has run strongly in the direction of greater focus and more explicit
links with benefits for the corporation.[72] Accountability and targeting tend
to discourage transactions like research gifts.

Consultants offer a way to avoid university entanglements and the IP problem entirely. Consulting by its very nature is highly individualized, and for that reason probably depends heavily on personal relationships. The scant evidence on the topic suggests that consultants are used most often for specific purposes—assisting with the completion of projects or addressing problems.[73] Consulting thus plays an important role, but not one that rivals the greater breadth of purpose of discrete research projects.

The second general pattern has been for industry to establish larger and more sustained research relationships with universities. In the past, these arrangements arose haphazardly as universities formed consortia to accommodate industry interests in specialized fields. Beginning in the 1980s, governments promoted collaborative research as a means of encouraging technology transfer. The removal of antitrust restrictions in 1984 allowed industry associations to create cooperative research organizations like SEMATECH. Since the late 1990s, corporations have increasingly followed a second approach: independently concluding extended partnerships between individual firms and universities. All these approaches are designed to further the deeper kinds of ongoing collaboration advocated by the IT industry, but appreciated throughout the corporate world. The last form allows collaborations to be tailored more closely to each corporation's objectives.

The largest effort to promote collaborative research has been the NSF program for Engineering Research Centers (ERCs). From 1985 to 2006 NSF supported 43 successful centers in two generations of awards (see Chapter 3). ERCs are proposed by universities according to NSF guidelines. Industry partners pay a nominal membership fee to participate, and may commission additional research projects. This formula appeals principally to large corporations with R&D labs.[74] An evaluation of industry experience with ERCs found anticipated benefits that were essentially the same as the inputs to R&D identified by Air Products—most prominently, new ideas and expertise, but also access to university knowledge and facilities and relevant new technologies.[75] Similarly, actual benefits realized were strongest for knowledge transfers and weakest for tangible outcomes, like products or patents. When participating firms rated the factors related to those benefits, the most important were all associated with connectedness—either the closeness of ERC activities to those of the firm or the firm's ability to assimilate ERC results. This critical finding reveals a limitation of this model, since consortia organized by universities or government are likely to approximate, at best, the specific interests of companies.

Despite the overall favorable assessment of ERC contributions, evaluators found that "industry support for consortia-based fundamental engineering research is fragile."[76] Firms participated because the low membership fee provided access to millions of dollars of state-of-the-art engineering research and facilities. But that research, available to all members, did not provide the competitive advantage that companies sought. Nor are companies necessarily consistent in their aims. One ERC explained, "companies have chosen to withdraw based on the shortening of their time horizons. Simply stated, companies and their timeframes change quite often, with some companies coming and going."[77] For universities, the tenuous nature of industry commitments represents the weak reed of consortia arrangements.

From the perspective of universities, consortia are in many ways an ideal arrangement for supplying research to industry. Consortia are usually established in specialized areas of fundamental scientific or engineering research—the strength of universities. They provide a select group of faculty and students with infrastructure, support, and interaction with real-world problems. Thus, they are accretive to university learning and to economic relevance. For industry, consortia appeal predominantly to research-based corporations, which ration their investments for this kind of generic research. Smaller companies, in particular, tend to focus their R&D narrowly on achieving tangible results, and can spare few resources for longer-term enhancements.[78] This dichotomy is reflected in IP policy. Consortia usually grant nonexclusive, royalty-free licenses (called NERFs in the tech transfer world) to their affiliates for any patents emerging from the research. NERFs are well suited to the practices of large corporations, which meld these patents with their own IP and above all wish to avoid royalties; but smaller companies rely heavily on exclusive licenses to protect their technology. The success of consortia ultimately rests with the mutual benefits derived by both parties, but here the fragile economics reflect the limited price that industry will pay for rather intangible benefits. Thus, consortia generally need some form of subsidization to overcome the fragility of this relationship.

UC Berkeley provides an example of independent action taken by a university to improve the economics of its consortia. It recognized the benefits to research and teaching of developing specialized areas of inquiry and of having direct connections with industry, but also felt a need to improve campus relations with industry. After a 2005 task force review, Berkeley lowered its indirect cost rate for consortia members from the regular 52 percent to 20 percent. The lower rate may represent a form of subsidy, but the campus expects the consortia to engender good will, gifts, and subsequent research relationships. IP terms are determined separately for each program. Berkeley's actions are representative of university efforts to cement longer-term relationships with industry.

Industry has sought this same end. Science-based corporations have increasingly pursued arrangements to tap more deeply into basic research in strategic areas and to transcend the limitations of discrete research projects. Their goals are a combination of gaining foresight into possible future technologies, enriching the capabilities of their own research staff, and accelerating their capacity to act upon relevant discoveries. The ideal would be a mode of continuous collaboration so that companies not only had access to cutting-edge research, but could assimilate it seamlessly into their own R&D. One overriding objective is to secure access to partners engaged in state-of-the-art research, whether universities or government labs. Generically, these efforts can be called "partnerships." Companies have taken different routes to such partnerships and have achieved different degrees of seamlessness.

The "alliances" of Air Products represent one step in this direction. They include master agreements to cover the usual contractual issues and are designed to provide a basis for long-term relationships. Air Products has established alliances with Penn State, UC Santa Barbara, and Imperial College London. Boeing has relationships with some 300 universities and more extensive, ongoing ties with about 40, half of which are in the United States. However, for research designed to open new frontiers in an 8- to 15-year time frame, it has established "strategic partnerships" with seven universities—Caltech, Carnegie Mellon, Illinois, MIT, Stanford, Cambridge, and the Indian Institute of Science. These partners receive $500,000 annually for at least five years to investigate specific areas. The universities can retain any IP, but Boeing gets a NERF.[79] IBM too has relationships with virtually every major university, but about 20 of these links have the special designation of "collaborations." In these, an IBM scientist is assigned to work directly with a university investigator, thus promoting staff development and a long-term relationship beyond any project results.

Perhaps the most far-reaching partnership model has been implemented by Intel, which has inverted the usual pattern of collaboration by creating its own labs adjacent to key universities to foster joint research.[80] Dubbed the "open collaborative research model," the centerpiece is a master agreement designed to avoid the usual conflict over IP rights. Research is open and publishable; patents are not an expected outcome, but any that arise are licensed on a nonexclusive basis. Labs were opened in Berkeley and Seattle in 2001. A Pittsburgh lab followed in 2002, and moved into the Collaborative Innovation Center on the Carnegie Mellon campus in 2005. The directors of the labs are faculty from computer science departments at the respective universities who take three-year leaves of absence to fill that position. They can use this highly unusual arrangement to focus intensively on "mutual skill sets." Other university scientists are welcome to participate, encouraged in some cases by Intel support for their graduate students. An Intel scientist serves as codirector of each lab and takes responsibility for communications with the company. Intel regards these labs as windows on the future. As the Berkeley director put it, "when you have collaborations going on with . . . the best universities in the world . . . you will hear about every important new research concept."[81] Research projects are aimed not at Intel's core manufacturing technologies (the role of SEMATECH), but at exploring future markets for Intel products. In probing frontier areas, such as intensive computing in distributed systems (Pittsburgh), the aim is no different from that of purely academic research.

Partner universities praise the Intel labs as valuable assets. Their presence increases the critical mass of expertise in subfields of computer science. They also expand the facilities available for certain kinds of research. The Intel labs particularly value the participation of students as a resource in themselves, but also because working with Intel can encourage future ties. At Berkeley, Intel scientists also teach courses on campus in their specialties. Intel's open collaborative model appears to offer considerable leverage to both parties. Intel is able to enhance the breadth and depth of its advanced research; and each university receives access to resources that increase the size and effectiveness of its computer science program. In Pittsburgh, moreover, collaboration has steadily expanded. The University of Pittsburgh and its medical center signed open collaborative agreements, and participation at Carnegie Mellon has spread well beyond the computer science department.

The open collaborative research model has been mutually beneficial because its aims are congruent with academic research. Intel finds the participation of students particularly stimulating, and the combination of professors and students together, as a result of their funding, especially "powerful." Since its founding, the Pittsburgh lab has assisted with eight doctoral dissertations and filed for zero patents.[82] Even so, initiating and sustaining the right chemistry for this kind of collaboration can be problematic. A fourth Intel lab at the University of Cambridge was closed in 2005, partly for lack of participation. The model itself may not translate to other industries either, but the principles probably would. To tap into the best of university research, industry must accept the academy's terms of open, publishable research on theoretically challenging themes without competition over IP rights.

More commonly, companies have made large investments to promote singular lines of research at individual universities. Such agreements first appeared in the 1970s and became more frequent during the biotech boom of the early 1980s. Industry predilection for long-term commitments seemed to wane in the 1990s, but reappeared at the end of that decade. The motives were familiar: to establish lasting relationships with the highest-quality academic research, to anticipate the next generation of innovation, and to inform internal R&D. In some of the earlier partnerships research targeted specific areas, and this is still the case with most biopharmaceutical partnerships; but recent agreements have been broader, aiming more at fundamental discoveries that will point the way toward future products and markets.

Among universities, MIT has led all others in establishing these more comprehensive industry partnerships. After forming its first "strategic alliance" with Amgen in 1994, MIT concluded seven more such agreements from 1997 to 2000. Each called for $3 million to $5 million of annual research, usually for five years.[83] According to then-president Charles M. Vest, such long-term agreements were based upon challenging research— "bottom-up faculty and company interest and commitment." Partnerships provided both sides with benefits that transcended normal university-industry interactions: "all of these partnerships engaged multiple academic departments, and indeed multiple schools, and all ended up with significant educational objectives—development of new courses and pedagogy, as well as student support." Faculty participants found these relationships to require "high maintenance," but they were also a valued source of new ideas. MIT extends its normal policies to partnerships, namely, university ownership of IP and open publication of research results. An underlying concern was nevertheless present that working so closely with industry might bring distortions to academic research. However, when the Institute surveyed the faculty in 2002, "no one could site [sic] an instance in which they believed it actually had."[84]

Such partnerships were by no means easy to establish or maintain, even for MIT. The original impetus owed much to a corporate relations officer recruited from industry. His efforts were strongly supported by President Vest, who felt that MIT had relied too heavily on federal sources for research support and needed fresh stimulation from industry. Nonetheless, the most productive partnerships were based on preexisting "deep relationships," while those lacking such long-standing ties experienced greater tension. At least three partnership negotiations fell through for various reasons. Thus, besides basic agreement among scientists over aims and research objectives, partnerships require a commitment from the highest corporate officers, and even then MIT's partnerships were vulnerable to changes in leadership or corporate fortunes.[85]

The shortcomings of these generally successful partnerships pale in comparison with the most notorious—and misunderstood—partnership of this new era, that between the former agricultural R&D unit of Novartis Corporation, located in La Jolla, California, and the UC Berkeley Department of Plant and Microbial Biology (PMB). This dismal tale sheds light on how major partnerships should and should not be structured.[86]

The most unusual feature of what became known as the Novartis Agreement was that the initiative came from the Berkeley department, not industry. PMB felt that the resources available to plant science were not adequate to keep pace with the revolution in molecular biology. In 1997 it set out to find a single industrial partner for a research alliance. The agricultural unit of the giant Swiss pharmaceutical corporation Novartis made the most attractive response to the department's proposal, and lengthy, secret negotiations produced the collaborative research agreement signed in November 1998.[87] Novartis promised $25 million over five years, two-thirds for research and one-third for general support. A joint research committee, consisting of three university members and two from Novartis, would determine the allocation of research grants on the basis of short faculty proposals. Participation was voluntary, but those who did participate, and their students, agreed to allow Novartis to vet their work 30 days prior to submissions or presentations. Novartis received the right of first refusal for roughly a third of *all* inventions disclosed from the department. If it wished to obtain rights to any of these discoveries, it had to follow the usual procedures with the technology licensing office. Only the provision giving the company first pick of findings other than those it directly supported seemed to go beyond the normal terms of industrial partnerships. However, the magnitude of the agreement raised the specter of industry domination of a distinguished academic department.

The announcement of the agreement touched off a storm of controversy that continued to build. Much of the criticism was based on uncertainty, not just about the terms, which long remained unclear, but especially about how they would work out in practice. Matters like secrecy, delay in publication, implications for graduate students, the presence of Novartis scientists in the department, its influence over research agendas, and of course IP all raised legitimate questions that were taken up by the academic senate and other bodies. For those philosophically opposed to working with industry—a widespread persuasion at Berkeley—these uncertainties were conflated into scenarios that threatened academic freedom, shared governance, or the integrity of research and teaching. Paranoia was heightened further by the connection with genetically modified organisms—an objective of research at both Novartis and PMB—during the height of concern over "Frankenfoods." This animus outlasted the duration of the agreement. Even an independent evaluation, subsequently expanded into a book, slighted the benefits of the partnership while repeating the innuendo of critics.[88]

In the event, none of the conjectured threats to academic integrity materialized and, for whatever reason, PMB thrived with the infusion of Novartis funds. Research funding from non-Novartis sources doubled by 2002 (making Novartis grants just over one-quarter of the department total). PMB acquired new research tools with these funds. Scientific publications increased. The Novartis fellowships permitted the recruitment of more and better graduate students. And, contradicting fears of diminished teaching, PMB offered more classes than previously. Rather than any diminution of freedom of research, faculty found Novartis grants less restrictive and open to more creative approaches than proposals to federal agencies. In sum, it was business as usual at PMB, only better. The Novartis Agreement was a sweetheart deal for Berkeley, but it was not a good partnership.

One of the original attractions for both sides was the possibility of mutual collaboration. Each had complementary expertise and infrastructure in related subject areas. True collaboration held the promise of advancing learning for all participants. However, developments on both sides scuttled these possibilities. At Berkeley, both internal critics and an avalanche of negative publicity poisoned the atmosphere. The original agreement had foreseen ongoing collaboration through creation of a Novartis laboratory near the Berkeley campus and the appointment of Novartis scientists as adjunct members of PMB. Given the prevailing suspicions, Novartis personnel were scarcely welcome on campus, and in fact none ever worked there. Building the projected lab, which might have yielded Intel-like synergies, was seriously considered in 1999 but then abandoned. On the Novartis side, the corporation had envisioned the partnership as contributing to its research horizon of 10 or more years. But corporate reorganizations scrambled even its short-term outlook. During the years of the Novartis Agreement, the corporate lab in La Jolla changed ownership twice and was phased out of existence in 2002.[89]

The Novartis lab possessed a proprietary genomic bioinformatic database, as well as advanced instrumentation for studying gene expression. To use these resources, Berkeley scientists had to sign nondisclosure agreements (similar to standard material transfer agreements), but then received free access. Eleven of the 23 faculty participants to the agreement, along with their students and postdocs, signed and used the Novartis resources to perform investigations not otherwise possible. In addition, PMB scientists and postdocs attended annual retreats in La Jolla with their corporate counterparts, retreats that they reported to be of value. But few benefits flowed in the other direction. Novartis and its successor found four of the invention disclosures from PMB sufficiently interesting to exercise options. After paying $170,000 for patenting costs and licensing options, the company exercised none of these licenses.

In terms of collaboration and potential innovation, the Novartis Agreement represents an opportunity lost. Two sets of highly qualified scientists with complementary research assets might have formed a larger critical mass and been able to drive advances in plant biotechnology; but this did not happen. The extra funding and freedom afforded the Berkeley scientists were a windfall while they lasted, and no doubt furthered individual research agendas. However, the basis for enduring university-industry partnerships should be mutual benefit—quid pro quo. The critics naively assumed that the *quid* Novartis sought was a tangible product, a lucrative patent or another genetically modified organism. But the real goal, at least originally, was greater learning that could feed into the internal R&D process and help it prepare for future markets and products. Still, this kind of mutually beneficial learning is difficult to accommodate within an academic department.

In this respect, the seeds of failure of the Novartis Agreement lay in its origins. PMB recruited Novartis to resolve its own predicament, and thus could not avoid the corporation-in-the-department dilemma that rightly agitated critics. Partnerships would seem to require some degree of separation from the teaching and degree-granting core of universities. This can be accomplished through consortia, centers, or institutes, or in the case of Intel, separately organized labs. The strategic alliances at MIT involved such units but also were linked with departments and schools. Most important, separation should allow participation to be strictly voluntary, for faculty and for students. The separation of financial accounting precludes the kinds of jealousy and backbiting that occurred at Berkeley over finite university resources, like lab space. And separation also permits meaningful participation by the corporate partner.

These lessons may have been learned. After this tumultuous marriage dissolved, both parties found their way to the partnership altar again in 2007. Berkeley joined with energy giant BP to create the Energy Biosciences Institute, which is discussed in a later chapter. The relevant feature here is that this partnership was structured as a separate institute, where faculty from numerous departments, including PMB, and BP scientists will perform their own and collaborative research. The corporation will be on campus for purposes of collaboration, but entirely removed from the academic core. Novartis concluded a 10-year, $65 million agreement to create the Novartis-MIT Center for Continuous Manufacturing, actually a virtual center in which MIT scientists and Novartis researchers will work in their own laboratories but collectively focus on developing processes for the continuous manufacture of drugs—a potentially valuable improvement over the prevailing batch method of production. In both cases, corporations wished to harness university expertise for challenges that spanned multiple fields and could scarcely be tackled through discrete grants. Although results will not be known for years, organizational arrangements in both cases seem consistent with productive partnerships and quite unlike the ill-fated Berkeley-Novartis pact.

Relations between university research and industry in the twenty-first century present a kind of paradox. On one hand, corporate spending for university research has diminished after more than two decades of absolute and relative expansion. On the other hand, university research appears to be playing an ever-greater role in stimulating the innovation that is vital to U.S. industry in a global economy. The picture that has emerged from this chapter explains how these two trends coexist. Innovation based on scientific and technological advance has increasingly followed two different tracks: one for oligopolistic corporations with huge internal R&D labs, and another for small firms and university spin-offs that seize single innovations and attempt to develop them into marketable products. At the same time, the principal conduit of university-industry research exchange, traditional discrete research projects, appear to be inhibited by industry dissatisfaction over the terms of trade, namely, provisions for IP, and by increased competition from foreign universities, independent and federal labs, and some of those same science-based spin-off companies. If these three phenomena are considered for purposes of analysis as separate sectors, each presents a different challenge to universities.

Universities generally have sought to increase their economic relevance in all three of these sectors. They have felt particular pressure to increase the number of spin-off firms, as will be evident in the next two chapters. Spin-offs contribute to the local economy, can be remunerative for the institution, and are conspicuously toted up on economic development scorecards. From the perspective of innovation, though, spin-offs represent a unique spillover from academic research; they embody inventions that might not otherwise be made available to the economy. This is more than enough reason to justify the extra efforts and subsidies that are now being institutionalized to lead these fledgling firms through the "valley of death."

However, the very procedures for patenting and licensing that undergird the founding of new firms have been a growing impediment to traditional research relationships outside of the life sciences. It is not immediately evident why this long-standing tension has worsened in recent years—whether reorganized tech transfer offices became more assertive or industrial R&D labs more focused on near-term product development. Here the salient issue is the loss of potential research by U.S. universities to domestic or international competitors. This is not to suggest that universities should necessarily become more accommodative of industry wishes. Corporations, given the opportunity, can be overbearing in their demands for IP concessions and narrowly tailored research. But most universities appear to favor expansion of industry-sponsored research, and given current trends this will require adjustments to current practices that few universities seem willing to entertain.

Large corporations maintain both extensive and intensive relations with university research. Extensively, they may sponsor limited research projects at literally hundreds of universities and other research facilities worldwide. These contacts create an information network touching an enormous array of expertise that can feed the innovative capacity of internal corporate R&D. In this arena, U.S. universities compete with other research performers. However, corporations have an incentive to support multiple nodes in order to maximize the power of the information grid, and this goal as much as anything explains why their contacts have been widening. Intensively, these corporations have been making large, multiyear investments in research partnerships that will significantly advance innovation in targeted areas. For the most part, these agreements are highly congruent with university research and public science. That is, they are usually consigned to an appropriate research unit; mutually satisfactory IP provisions are negotiated for the entire relationship; research is usually basic or long-term applied and thus consistent with academic science and engineering; student participation is encouraged; and the collaboration is accretive to learning for both partners. These kinds of collaboration are most effective when industry's goals are pegged to future innovation, either in products, processes, or markets. When industry seeks to learn from basic research, partnerships with universities can be readily arranged, and common objectives are likely to be achieved. Thus, the payoff from these partnerships is not so much in the findings as it is in the doing, and as such represents a unique contribution of academic research to the enhancement of corporate innovation.[90]

This kind of equilibrium, however, cannot be easily reproduced. The upheavals in corporate R&D since 1990 illustrate the relativity of long-range research perspectives in the business world. In the twenty-first century, intense pressures for bottom-line results would seem to be balanced against the imperatives of sustaining future competitive advantage through innovation. Long-term investments in basic research for many firms depend on an underlying optimism about the future of the economy and the company, which in turn depend largely on the current financial outlook.

There is uncertainty on the university side of the equilibrium as well. Corporations seek partnerships to tap into the most advanced academic research. U.S. universities represent an enormous reservoir of expertise, and a fairly broad one as well when individual specialties are considered; but cutting-edge thinking on the most consequential future challenges is concentrated in a handful of institutions. Thus, corporations seem to be bidding ever-larger sums to secure relationships with these coveted partners. A common reaction to the Novartis Agreement was that Berkeley's academic eminence might protect it from exploitation, but it set a bad precedent for less prestigious institutions that could be more easily corrupted. But corporations do not spend $25 million to share in the research of less prestigious universities. There are inherent limitations to partnerships both in industry's willingness to invest and universities' capacity to accommodate them. Nevertheless, if the pressures for corporate innovation and the salience of research-based technologies are allowed to drive the growth of industry-supported research, this dimension of the economic relevance of universities should increase as well.

# CHAPTER 3

# Policies for Technology-Based
# Economic Development

Every modern government regards the health of the economy as a legitimate area of concern, although how or how much governments ought to intervene in economic affairs to promote healthiness is a perennially debated topic. Government policies for economic development comprise a vast territory with varying topography. The part of this terrain that most affects universities consists of technology-based economic development, now known as TBED, which covers activities related to scientific or technological innovation. In the land of TBED, the same distinctions pertain between the two tracks of innovation arising from corporate R&D labs and from small entrepreneurs.

In terms of policy, actions of the federal government differ greatly from those of the 50 states. Federal research agencies have created incentives for universities and firms to collaborate in the pursuit of innovation, but they are less concerned about retaining tangible benefits within particular regions. In the states, where retention is the biggest concern, TBED policies consequently tend to be slanted toward the smaller technology-based firms.

Universities generally play only a minor direct role in the universe of economic development policies, but they are key actors in facilitating innovation. To this end, state policies to harness university research for purposes of economic development have grown in number, size, and scope in the twenty-first century.[1] The effects of these policies on economic activity may be hard to detect, confounded as they are with myriad other conditions, but the impacts on universities are more evident.

## Science Federalism

Since World War II, the predominant funding of scientific research by agencies of the federal government has reflected a national consensus on federal responsibility for supporting the advancement of basic scientific knowledge and furthering knowledge of human health, space, energy, agriculture, and especially defense. This arrangement has been characterized as science federalism.[2] Although the terms and depth of the federal commitment have fluctuated, its basic features have not only remained unchallenged, they have shaped the roles of other stakeholders in American science. This is particularly true for universities, which have consistently performed roughly half of the nation's basic research. And it also applies to the states, which, despite their critical role in sustaining universities, have long been a junior partner in science federalism.

The federal government initially took the lead in encouraging technology transfer from universities to industry. Federal research agencies and legislation have consistently sought to encourage linkages between R&D spending and the utilization of potential findings by industry since at least 1980. Regulatory obstacles were eliminated by the Bayh-Dole Act (1980), the 1982 creation of a centralized appellate court for patent cases (the Court of Appeals for the Federal Circuit), and the exemption of industry research consortia from antitrust laws (1984). In 1986 the national laboratories too were directed to establish mechanisms for technology transfer. These changes redirected or allowed research institutions to pursue a more aggressive role in industrial innovation.

Federal agencies also created programs and provided funding for universities to collaborate with firms. Legislation in 1982 directed federal agencies to devote a small portion of their extramural research funding to support research by small businesses (Small Business Innovation Research, or SBIR). The original program was primarily aimed at stimulating technology development in small businesses, but over time these efforts became more germane to universities. The 1992 reauthorization of this act doubled the scale of the set-asides (from 1.25 to 2.5 percent) and added a new program with a smaller set-aside (0.3 percent) called Small Business Technology Transfer (STTR). These latter awards required businesses to collaborate with nonprofit partners, which in many cases would be universities. Since then, both programs have grown in step with the growth of federal R&D, and Congress enacted further provisions to induce states to encourage participation (2000).[3] The rapid growth of patenting and spin-offs has made these awards increasingly relevant for technology transfer. Universities now actively promote partner applications for STTRs, and SBIRs have proved particularly effective for aiding university entrepreneurs.[4] Most of these competitive awards go to a handful of states, with California and Massachusetts doing particularly well, as shown in Table 3.1. The number of awards in a state reflects the base of fledgling science-based firms and thus is sometimes used as an index for entrepreneurial activity. Massachusetts stands out for the number of grants awarded as a proportion of the number of small businesses in the state.

Federal agencies have also sought to narrow the gap between basic science and industrial innovation. Among the funding agencies, the National Science Foundation (NSF) has taken the lead in influencing the organization and culture of university research. One of its most consequential initiatives has been the creation of centers for collaborative university-industry research. In addition to bringing resources to universities, these center

**Table 3.1** Top States in Number of SBIR (2005) and STTR (2004) Awards, Share of Awards, and Awards per 1,000 Small Businesses in the State

| State | N | % | SBIRs[a] |
|---|---|---|---|
| California | 822 | 19.66 | 1.19 |
| Massachusetts | 513 | 12.27 | 3.58 |
| Virginia | 249 | 5.96 | 1.69 |
| Colorado | 206 | 4.93 | 1.70 |
| Maryland | 206 | 4.93 | 1.88 |
| Texas | 201 | 4.81 | 0.53 |
| New York | 190 | 4.54 | 0.25 |
| Total | 2,387 | 57.31% | |

| State | N | % | STTRs[a] |
|---|---|---|---|
| California | 135 | 16.03 | 0.20 |
| Massachusetts | 112 | 13.30 | 0.78 |
| Virginia | 48 | 5.70 | 0.33 |
| Texas | 45 | 5.34 | 0.12 |
| Colorado | 42 | 4.99 | 0.35 |
| Pennsylvania | 34 | 4.04 | 0.14 |
| New York | 32 | 3.80 | 0.07 |
| Total | 448 | 53.21% | |

[a] per 1,000 firms

grants, awarded competitively through peer review, are signals of academic quality. Current favorable attitudes about cooperation with industry and collaborative research can be credited in part to the "culture change" induced by these NSF mandates for centers and other programs.[5]

These efforts date from the 1970s, when the NSF launched what would become the Industry / University Cooperative Research Centers in the following decade. This enduring program is relatively small in terms of federal funding, but it is primarily intended to leverage industrial participation and support for university-based centers. Each center affiliates several firms and one or more universities. During the 1990s, in its second decade of operation, the program was judged to be successful in producing quality science, imparting relevant knowledge to firms, and providing students with career-relevant educational experiences.[6] In 2007 there were 38 active centers based in U.S. universities, in addition to 14 operating centers that no longer receive NSF funding. This program has inspired other initiatives at the NSF, in particular a less successful version involving state governments that was terminated in the late 1990s.[7]

In 1985 the NSF launched a program for Engineering Research Centers (ERCs), which provided extended support to universities for large focused projects of collaborative research. In many respects a much more ambitious program, ERCs responded to concerns about the estrangement of academic and industrial engineering, aiming to make engineering research and education relevant to the needs of industry. The ERCs were envisioned as a way to instill long-term change: centers were (and still are) funded for up to 11 years to develop large-scale research and education programs. The overarching goal has been to promote activity in "engineering systems" through the formation of cross-disciplinary teams of university researchers and industrial partners.

Evaluations of the ERCs have found appreciable impacts, both in the creation and dissemination of knowledge and in indirect organizational and cultural changes in universities. Universities exhibited increasing acceptance of planning to guide large-scale research programs, of interdisciplinary research and education, and of cooperation with industry. They also altered internal policies and regulations governing the evaluation of faculty work to accommodate the team-based, cross-departmental activities of scientists and engineers participating in ERCs.[8] Firms found affiliation with ERCs beneficial, particularly for access to cutting-edge research and expertise. Characteristic of the logic of innovation in large firms described in

Chapter 2, corporate affiliates valued ERCs for access to generic ideas and know-how. When asked about future directions and priorities, they wanted the centers to continue to focus on fundamental investigation.[9]

Rutgers University's Center for Structured Organic Particulate Systems, awarded in 2006, exemplifies the spirit behind ERCs. The center addresses the needs of the pharmaceutical, food, and agrochemical industries, which all use organic materials in their products. The center performs fundamental research in areas where tangible discoveries with clear potential applications might be expected. As its principal investigator explains, "Today's products and processes were often developed through costly and time-consuming experimentation. We want to uncover more of the science behind these products and the engineering that goes into making them, so companies can get them to market faster, cut costs and eliminate waste."[10]

That these reactions occur in the world of academic engineering is not surprising, given the "hard applied" nature of the field and its problem-solving orientation. Analysts express concern, however, that the NSF stipulation that "graduated" centers be self-supporting may hinder further industrial investment. Federal support allows firms to benefit from subsidized research and educational activities while paying a relatively modest membership fee. Absent this incentive, graduated centers may be torn between more targeted and short-term activities that individual firms would be willing to support and more academic topics that appeal to the faculty.[11] In 2007, 22 funded centers and 21 graduated centers were operating, most of them in leading research universities.[12]

Subsequent NSF programs incorporated some aspects of the ERC model, particularly the expectation that universities pursue large-scale, multidisciplinary research in science-based technologies in collaboration with industry. Among these programs, the Science and Technology Centers (created in 1987), Materials Research Science and Engineering Centers (1994–), and Nanoscale Science and Engineering Centers (2001–) all require industrial partners. Altogether, these programs devoted $216 million in 2006 to 81 centers, typically involving partnerships among multiple academic and other institutions.[13]

The Materials Research Science and Engineering Centers illustrate how the NSF has shaped the organization of university research and education programs in ways that would probably not have occurred otherwise, certainly not on the same scale. The latest in a series of federal investments in materials research, the Materials Centers organize scientists from fields such as physics, chemistry, mathematics, biology, materials science and engineering, and other engineering disciplines into interdisciplinary groups. They also include a range of activities beyond scientific investigation, such as education and outreach programs, interactions with industry, and the management of specialized research facilities.[14]

In a recent assessment commissioned by the National Academy of Sciences, the Materials Centers were found to support excellent basic research, although it was hard to distinguish activities that occurred inside and outside the centers. Scientists draw on multiple sources of funding and infrastructure in the course of their work, including the centers. The assessment committee of distinguished scientists from leading universities identified these centers as a necessity in the current environment of corporate R&D and international competition, but expressed concern over the relatively weak ties established with firms thus far.[15] Reflecting the orientation of the centers toward basic science, the assessment committee recommended that the program incorporate the goal of industrial interactions more clearly in the review process, without losing sight of fundamental research as the key contribution of the Materials Centers to technological innovation. Not surprisingly, the Center on Polymer Interfaces and Macromolecular Assemblies based in Stanford (in partnership with UC Berkeley and UC Davis) was singled out among these centers for its fundamental research and its close working relations with the IBM Almaden Research Center, which undoubtedly reflects the university's culture and tradition, as well as those of IBM.[16] Among the education and outreach activities, "the most significant and well-documented contribution . . . is the preparation of future researchers at all levels"—a pure academic outcome.[17]

These NSF centers have fostered the diversification of research and educational activity by stimulating programs that cut across traditional departmental lines. One common theme among all center programs is the emphasis placed on training new scientists differently, allowing for early contact and experiences with multiple scientific perspectives and sometimes with industrial researchers as well. The National Institutes of Health (NIH) and the Department of Defense have also funded centers that emphasize generic research and formal collaborations with industry.[18]

Federal agencies have thus provided general encouragement and specific programs for tapping the economic relevance of university research. Science federalism has not, however, supplied the single ingredient that states prize most highly—the stimulation of economic activity within their borders. Specific federal programs to assist states to harness science and technology have largely foundered. In the late 1970s Congress directed the states to create "science and technology commissions," but federal funding did not follow. The NSF State/Industry University Cooperative Research Center Program was also dropped. Such federal initiatives usually covered only a portion of the costs, and states proved reluctant to commit their own funds to federally designed programs.[19] Instead, states have acted independently to design and implement their own science and technology (S&T) policies.

## Research and Economic Development in the States

Following the lead of federal policy, states too have created instruments to induce research collaboration between universities and industry. S&T policies have become a permanent fixture of state governments since the 1980s, but their impact and relevance for universities have varied enormously. States had funded university science before the 1980s, but in that decade, state S&T programs became more closely aligned with economic development strategies.[20] New York launched centers for advanced technology at public and private universities, and New Jersey established centers of advanced technology. By 1990, 144 university-industry research centers had been established in 22 states. However, in the new decade enthusiasm for such initiatives cooled considerably. This type of program was aimed chiefly at local corporations and was intended to complement their internal R&D. But for state politicians, these admittedly long-term investments did not appear to be creating local jobs. Indeed, as described in the previous chapter, corporations too were questioning the productivity of their internal R&D organizations during these years. Nationally, TBED policies drew back from university-based research and instead offered services directly to businesses, especially for manufacturing.[21]

The reevaluation of state S&T policies in the early 1990s diminished the role of universities.[22] Above all, state S&T policies are fundamentally economic development policies. The nature and circumstances of these policies largely follow from this fact.

State S&T policies are embedded in a broader set of alternatives or "paradigms" of state economic development. Until the 1980s, states' efforts were predominantly based upon negotiations with individual firms to attract or retain their operations, often revolving around tax abatements, grants, or infrastructure improvements that would lower their operating costs. This paradigm is known as "industrial recruitment" (and derided as "smokestack chasing") and has been severely criticized as an ineffectual, zero-sum game. Since the 1980s, the "entrepreneurial" paradigm has emerged as a growing force, and here the clearest connections are displayed between economic development policy and S&T programs. The entrepreneurial paradigm seeks to promote economic growth by supporting local entrepreneurialism through mechanisms such as incubator facilities, technical assistance programs, provisions for venture capital, and funding for R&D. The strategy of many entrepreneurial state policies is thus one of promoting "endogenous growth"—achieving economic development internally by assisting local industries to develop and expand. Despite criticism of smokestack chasing, industrial recruitment persists alongside entrepreneurial approaches.[23] For all the emphasis on universities as agents of economic development, state policy in this area is a much broader effort encompassing a multitude of stakeholders, kinds of programs, and possible destinations for state investments.

These policies may ebb and flow depending upon the place of TBED among the governor's priorities, pressure from interest groups, and the efforts of "policy entrepreneurs." Policies affecting universities tend to be discretionary and hence subject to such forces. The relative unpredictability of the shape and survival of S&T programs beyond the electoral cycle was a factor in the 1980s and 1990s. New governors and legislators brought different priorities that displaced TBED initiatives; state budget deficits sometimes required a slashing of discretionary programs; and changing preferences regarding the format and clientele of S&T allocations could redirect investments.[24] The periodic dismantling or reorganization of state S&T agencies has been symptomatic in the past; however, since around 2000 the increasing institutionalization of S&T programs in the states promises to prolong these programs beyond the terms of governors and legislators.[25]

States can choose from a broad range of approaches that have different bearings on university functions and roles. The most salient distinction is between "upstream" policies, which strengthen the research capacity of universities through infrastructure, strategic faculty hiring, or other forms of targeted support; and "downstream" programs that seek to assist the development of new technologies into marketable innovations. The former is clearly a long-term strategy that complements the R&D of existing high-tech industry and may spawn new industries. The latter is a shorter-term approach that envisions job creation through the success of new and fledg-ling technology firms.[26] Upstream policies are most beneficial to universi-ties, enhancing their capabilities in faculty, research, and graduate educa-tion. Downstream policies provide less direct benefits, such as assisting the development of spin-off firms or supporting economic development organi-zations.

Both upstream and downstream policies are best judged in the long run. Because their impacts are often diffuse and hard to determine, measure-ment of results has proved challenging. Worse, the vested interests that op-erate these programs have little desire for close scrutiny.

Interests are central to politics and policy making. How and by whom these policies are generated often determine their nature. Large firms are likely to view universities as a source of basic research and skilled gradu-ates, and they have an interest in programs that enhance the quality of those outputs. Universities naturally applaud such programs as well. State officials, on the other hand, hope for more tangible gratification from pro-grams in the form of new businesses and job creation. Downstream pro-grams are also most appreciated by the wider economic development community, including early-stage investors, technology trade associa-tions, and the myriad local or regional economic development organiza-tions.[27] More recently, several regional and national foundations have thrown their weight behind upstream strategies to bolster university re-search in strategic fields.

During the 1980s the reigning ideology of economic competitiveness and technology transfer was conducive to upstream policies, but the disillusion-ment of the early 1990s favored downstream programs. In the second half of the 1990s, steady economic expansion accelerated into the "dot-com bubble" at the end of the century. Innovation once again was hailed as the savior of U.S. industries and the best hope for the economy. Reflecting this new mood, the National Governors Association published reports in 2000 on "Building State Economies by Promoting University-Industry Tech-nology Transfer" and "Using Research and Development to Grow State Economies."[28] States reacted as well with new upstream policy initiatives, while also emphasizing the creation and commercialization of intellectual property.[29]

A boost to this wave of TBED policy came in 1998, when states negotiated the Master Tobacco Settlement Agreement with the principal cigarette manufacturers, creating a large, judicially imposed tax on smokers.[30] The settlement produced an enormous annual windfall of around $6 billion at a time when the economy was booming and state coffers were uncharacteristically full. Many states chose to invest some portion of these funds in biomedical research. Some states were familiar with this territory, since the biological and biomedical sciences already received the largest share of state support by the mid-1990s: in 1995, 38 percent of all state-funded R&D performed by universities was in these fields.[31] These investments were also linked with commercialization as part of TBED strategies, reflecting the zeitgeist and the burgeoning biotech industry. Rapid advances in genomics and biotechnology assured the eagerness of universities to invest in those areas as well. In subsequent years states, their coffers now emptied by the recession of 2001, occasionally redirected the tobacco lucre into general funds; but in the longer term more states made additional funds available to bolster biomedical research.[32]

Since 2000, states have devoted conspicuous upstream investments to areas strategic to science-based technologies. They have recognized the competitive nature of these fields and the crucial role of cutting-edge research as the basis for innovation, intellectual property, and industrial advantage. Individual programs supported the hiring of "star" professors and the creation of centers of excellence. The rubric "centers of excellence" covers a variety of arrangements, many antedating 2000. However, states like New York and Georgia have intensified these investments since that date. The most audacious commitment was made by California in 2000—$400 million of state funding for the California Institutes for Science and Innovation (Cal ISI, discussed below). These initiatives aimed at fostering "technology creation": establishing the conditions in universities for research oriented toward commercially relevant discoveries and innovation.

States now profess to be eager above all to develop "clusters." Michael Porter and others have popularized the notion that the most robust and enduring form of economic advancement occurs through the concentration of firms in the same industry.[33] The logic of building clusters has required both downstream and upstream approaches to TBED—the creation and nurture of new firms and the intensification of knowledge assets. Clusters by definition require both numbers and density, but beyond this consideration spin-off and early-stage firms are presumed to be the natural vehicles for innovation and job creation.[34] Endogenous growth strategies of the new century have been targeted to such neophyte firms through the creation of "innovation zones," the establishment of business incubators or "entrepreneurial development centers," and the provision of venture or seed capital. Universities are expected to play a key role in forming or anchoring clusters, at least for technology-based industries.[35] New York, New Jersey, and Pennsylvania, for example, created their respective innovation zones around universities. New York has made a huge investment in nanotechnology R&D at Albany, with the intention of building a nanoelectronics cluster (discussed below).

States have also attempted to capitalize on federal R&D funding priorities, most notably in the biomedical sciences. The federal government doubled the NIH budget between 1998 and 2003, although its growth since that date has been meager.[36] Still, in 2006 the NIH had a budget of $28.6 billion and made by far the largest commitment to academic research among federal agencies. In the same year, 27 states provided nearly $400 million in annual research funds for the biosciences alone. Forty-four states invested in infrastructure for biomedical research, and 15 had faculty development programs. These substantial upstream investments were accompanied by an equally vigorous expansion of downstream commitments. Twenty-three states operated commercialization funds, and twice that number had programs to support emerging new firms. Twenty-one states allocated money for pre-seed or seed capital, and 27 could offer venture capital. In addition, 43 states had business incubators for bioscience firms.[37] Thus, states invested in both the quantity and quality of academic bioscience with explicit expectations of economic returns.

From the viewpoint of the states, upstream programs promise payoffs through enhanced federal research grants, regardless of economic impact, thanks to the largesse of NIH funding. However, many observers, including NIH director Elias Zerhouni, fear that such expectations are overly optimistic. While the NIH research budget is immense, it has barely grown since the doubling was completed in 2003. But there has been no slowing in the expansion of biomedical research capacity. Research space was on schedule to grow by 26 percent from 2003 to 2008, with further expansion on the drawing board. There has been a corresponding increase in biomedical researchers, including an intensifying scramble to hire so-called "star" professors. Some of the state strategies described below are betting that they can succeed against these odds.[38]

Finally, states have developed substitute S&T policies to address the federal failure in stem cell research. In a dubious effort to reach a compromise acceptable to Christian fundamentalists and the scientific community, President George W. Bush limited federally funded research on stem cells to a small number of preexisting cell lines. As scientific interest in stem cell research grew, along with popular hopes for miraculous regenerative therapies, these approved cell lines proved entirely inadequate for research needs. This situation created an opportunity for the states to fill a critical void in human health research, and possibly to gain an advantage in the subsequent commercialization of a potentially lucrative medical technology. California was the first to act in 2004, when voters approved Proposition 71 to sell $3 billion in bonds to support stem cell research for 10 years. This initiative established the California Institute for Regenerative Medicine to coordinate and lead this huge effort. Other states responded with projects of their own. New Jersey, with a pharmaceutical industry as large as California's, established a research grants program in 2005 and also broke ground for the Stem Cell Institute of New Jersey. It also became the first state to actually award funding for research projects.[39] By 2007 New Jersey was joined by Connecticut, Illinois, and Maryland. Democratic governor Eliot Spitzer brought New York into the stem cell arena as well when he took office in 2007.[40] Other states have legislation pending and can be expected to join this club whether or not a change in federal policy or a scientific breakthrough alters this situation.[41]

Unlike previous state S&T policies, these efforts mimic the federal role of technology creation rather than technology development for local industries. Moreover, unlike previous state support for research that was entrusted to universities, these new initiatives will require the dispensing agency to evaluate research proposals, like NSF or NIH. Besides the California Institute for Regenerative Medicine, three other states have taken this path or intend to do so. Science Foundation Arizona was established in 2006 and is described below. Following an emotional appeal featuring cyclist and cancer survivor Lance Armstrong, Texas voters in 2007 approved by a 3:2 margin a constitutional amendment authorizing $3 billion in bonds to support cancer research over 10 years. Details of implementation were sketchy: an institute will be created and presumably will employ some form of peer review to disburse research grants to the Texas medical universities, which specialize in this field. At the end of 2007, a task force appointed by New York governor Eliot Spitzer recommended, among other measures, the creation of an "Empire State Innovation Fund." Following the pattern, the $3 billion fund would provide 10 years of peer-reviewed grants for research in universities "that holds significant promise for economic development."[42] Scientific peer review is a delicate process that has already experienced difficulties in California. The federal agencies provide a robust model, but it remains to be seen how well the states will be able to imitate it. Still, direct state funding of research grants is a telling sign of inadequacies in the scale of federal science support, given the mounting competition for research funds, and in its targets, given state demands for economic impact.

In contrast to the university-centered policies of the 1980s, current state S&T policies contain an explicit component for the commercialization of discoveries. Hence, when universities accept this form of support for research, new faculty positions, or infrastructure, they also commit to economic development aims. Most state universities consider such commitments to be an explicit extension of their public service mission, and private universities have embraced this mission as well. Current state S&T policies thus reinforce, if not intensify, university efforts to commercialize intellectual property and spin off new firms.

Support for state TBED policies appears to be gaining momentum. For example, in 2006 the National Governors Association sponsored studies and meetings around its "Innovation America" initiative, led by Arizona governor Janet Napolitano. A task force also included academic proponents of closer university engagement with state economic development and industry partnerships, such as Arizona State University president Michael Crow, Rensselaer Polytechnic Institute president Shirley Ann Jackson, and Georgia Tech president G. Wayne Clough. From the corporate sector, high-tech giants Intel, DuPont, Symantec, Microsoft, and eBay were represented. Innovation America enjoined states to commit to a "comprehensive innovation policy" that included investments in education in science, technology, engineering, and math (STEM) fields; innovation-based economic policies; and, pivotally, a new compact with postsecondary education.[43]

A key report from this project, *Investing in Innovation*, differs strikingly from previous exhortations from the National Governors Association in ways that seem to reflect the TBED experience of the individuals who led the project.[44] It advocates an explicit and aggressive approach to promoting high-quality upstream research, and it specifically warns against the weaknesses in state policies that have just been discussed.

The report advocates building university research prowess in areas where states possess competitive advantages so that higher education and industry "can excel jointly."[45] It endorses an approach favored by consultants of analyzing industry types, or clusters, within a state in terms of relative size (percentage above or below national norms) and relative growth rate (above or below average). Clusters that are above average in size and growth become the first targets for R&D investments. Bolstering the strength of university research in these areas is most likely to produce spillovers—employment and economic activity—that are captured within the state. Secondarily, states are advised to look among fast-growing clusters of below-average size, which could offer strategic opportunities to identify niches and build comparative advantage in expanding industries. Above all, the report endorses searching for world-class research talent and making the investments required to obtain it. More than previous policy prescriptions, these recommendations link research excellence directly with jobs through analyses of actual employment patterns.

The National Governors Association guidelines for implementing such strategies reflect a sophisticated grasp of the history of state S&T efforts. Since these are inherently long-term investments, they need to be supported by dedicated funds rather than uncertain annual appropriations. Earmarked tax revenues or bond revenues are two ways to do this, and tobacco settlement funds have also served this purpose. Also essential is the involvement of the four sectors—universities, industry, government, and the nonprofit sector. Intermediate bodies can facilitate such interaction, but the true key is buy-in from the relevant actors and active collaboration in projects. Enlisting expertise is a further injunction; policies should be set and managed by experts in this field, not by political cronies. Finally, the report stresses that progress must be accurately measured across the entire range of impacts. This can be accomplished more readily in collaborative efforts across sectors than in programs delegated to state bureaucracies. By invoking examples drawn from several states, *Investing in Innovation* reflects the evolution of state TBED policy in the twenty-first century.

## Research Policy in Four States

States differ in their approaches to investing in science and technology for economic development. Inherited capacity from historical investments in research institutions, the structure of the state economy, and the business strategies of the industrial sector all shape the competitive position of states, regardless of the predilections of state policy makers at any given time. The following sections examine four states with aggressive S&T policies focused on universities. California and New York, the two largest state economies, have made outsized investments in their academic and industrial R&D bases. Georgia and Arizona, by comparison, are midsize economies striving to improve their economic performance and elevate their position in the knowledge economy. As summarized in Table 3.2, California and New York are among the national leaders in economic performance and indicators of research activity, both academic and industrial, whereas Georgia and Arizona have mixed standings.

Each of these states has pursued a distinctive approach for incorporating universities into a TBED policy. California, the national leader in academic and industrial research, has made huge upstream investments in science-based technologies without benefit of an overarching strategy, but with confidence that these actions will redound to the benefit of its high-tech industries. New York too has wagered vast sums, but these commitments stem from a tradition of active state intervention in TBED. New York has combined old-fashioned industrial recruitment with a TBED strategy focused on nanotechnology. Georgia has evolved a set of nationally admired policies largely from initiatives that originated in the private sector, but quickly spanned government, academia, and the nonprofit sector. Arizona, through rational policy planning, has formulated a "roadmap" in an ambitious effort to generate economic development based chiefly on investments in the biosciences.

**Table 3.2** National Ranks of Arizona, California, Georgia, and New York in Measures of State Economies and R&D Activities

| State | GDP/capita 2006 | Percent change GDP 2003–2006 | Academic R&D 2005 | Industrial R&D 2004 | Industry-funded academic R&D 2005 |
|---|---|---|---|---|---|
| Arizona | 36 | 26 | 21 | 21 | 16 |
| California | 9 | 7 | 1 | 1 | 1 |
| Georgia | 26 | 48 | 12 | 22 | 10 |
| New York | 4 | 6 | 2 | 7 | 5 |

*Source:* National Science Foundation and calculations by the authors.

*California*

With the Institutes for Science and Innovation and the Institute for Regenerative Medicine, California has one of the most extensive, and certainly the most expensive, state policies for linking academic research and economic development (Table 3.3). The institutes resulted from a concerted effort of entrepreneurial individuals to influence state investments in TBED, following their own agendas and political acumen. The political culture of California has created an open field for such "policy entrepreneurs," advocates inside or outside government "who are willing to invest their resources—time, energy, reputation, money—to promote a position in return for anticipated future gain."[46]

For economic competitiveness, California is the envy of other states. It is home not only to Silicon Valley, possibly the most prolific agglomeration of high-tech industry, but also to similar clusters from Sacramento to San Diego. California leads all other states in absolute measures of high-tech performance, including formation of and employment in high-tech businesses, patenting, and especially venture capital. Its high-tech economy generates a comparatively high per capita income, but the state is a laggard in educational attainment and poverty rates.[47] Despite its achievements rel-

**Table 3.3** Selected TBED Initiatives in California

| Initiative | Year | Nature |
|---|---|---|
| California Institutes for Science and Innovation (Cal ISI) | 2000 | Four institutes funded by state and matching funds, based at multiple University of California campuses |
| Institute for Regenerative Medicine (CIRM) | 2005 | State-funded nonprofit institute supporting stem cell research, first grants in 2007 |
| Energy Biosciences Institute | 2007 | Joint university-industry research institute at UC Berkeley, in collaboration with the Lawrence Berkeley National Laboratory and the University of Illinois at Urbana-Champaign, supported by BP p.l.c. and state contribution |

ative to other states, California too feels pressure to sustain growth in its huge and rather volatile economy.

California's advantage in the new economy lies in part in the unique qualities of its flagship university. The University of California's 10 campuses (counting newly created Merced) perform one-eleventh of the country's academic research and harbor many of the most distinguished academic programs. This prominence is owed partly to the genius of Clark Kerr in building out the system and negotiating the hegemony of UC under the "Master Plan," partly to (generally) generous state funding that reflects state pride in academic leadership, and partly to the university's unique structure.[48] The California Constitution accords the university separate status under the authority of the board of regents. This authority is exercised by the university president. Since Kerr's time, the University of California Office of the President, known locally and perhaps symbolically as UCOP, has evolved into an enormous central bureaucracy that serves as an intermediary between state government, regents, and the individual campuses. The campuses are buffered further by the university-wide academic senate, which defends academic freedom, promotes high academic standards, and virtually prohibits outside interference with academic matters. In practice, then, the campuses have a great deal of autonomy, and, with the explicit encouragement of the senate and UCOP, they have consistently used their freedom to strive for academic distinction. The UC, on one hand, has the size and coverage to serve as an instrument of state policy, which can be implemented through UCOP. On the other hand, the autonomy of the campuses preserves a powerful orientation toward national and international disciplinary communities, regardless of other incidental tasks.

Economic relevance has always been present at the University of California. Never a high priority, it has often been more feared than welcomed. The strong connections between agricultural departments at the Davis campus and California agribusiness have long been a target for criticism. Partly because of such connections, however, UC was early in organizing its own patenting office. Nevertheless, through the 1980s intellectual property was handled clumsily from a central office, while most patent disclosures emanated from Davis and the medical campus at San Francisco. The prevailing mentality was to protect the family jewels rather than stimulate economic activity.[49] This attitude was evident in the controversy over the Novartis Agreement discussed in Chapter 2. But each UC campus has its own culture. Favorable attitudes and practices with regard to industry emerged at UC San Diego in the 1980s, sparked by the burgeoning biotech and telecommunications clusters, and eventually inspired the state's only true TBED initiatives.

In 1985 UC San Diego chancellor Richard C. Atkinson began exploring possible ways to help reinvigorate the local economy, which had been highly dependent on the defense industry. His efforts linked the university with the local economic development agency and the university's distance education unit to form CONNECT, an organization designed to stimulate interaction between scientists in the university and local high-tech firms and to provide other services to these inchoate industry clusters. The organization was particularly successful in fostering social networks across the university, local scientific institutes, and the entrepreneurial community. It sponsored forums for scientific presentations by both academic and industry researchers, and financial forums to connect new or prospective firms with sources of capital.[50] As a self-supporting organization with few funds, CONNECT was a decidedly downstream operation, facilitating the commercialization of technology through firm formation, tapping capital, networking, and providing essential services to fledgling firms. The organization is credited with assisting the rise of San Diego as a new-economy powerhouse. San Diego developed the largest concentration of wireless firms and the third largest number of bioscience firms. A third of its biotech firms were started by UC scientists. The entrepreneurial community now refers to the region as "wireless valley"; indeed, the proliferation of high-tech firms, the vitality of social networks, and the growth of supporting legal and financial services are not unlike conditions in Silicon Valley.[51]

When Atkinson assumed the presidency of the University of California in 1995, San Diego clearly stood out as the UC campus most in tune culturally and programmatically with economic development. Atkinson brought this same spirit to his new post and made it one of his goals to increase the contribution of UC research to the California economy. His first initiative was the creation in 1996 of the Industry-University Cooperative Research Program. Now called Discovery Grants, this program matches industry support for selected, peer-reviewed research projects at any UC campus. Originally limited to biotechnology, it soon expanded to include electronics and communications. The university initiated this program with a commitment of $3 million, and the state added another $5 million. The university's support has remained at $3 million, while the state's has grown to more than $20 million. With industry support, Discovery Grants now account for more than $50 million, or about one-sixth of UC's industry-supported research. Thus, Atkinson's university policy has become a state policy, implemented through UCOP, and making a contribution to TBED.[52]

The California Institutes for Science and Innovation (Cal ISI) mentioned earlier were inspired by two policy entrepreneurs from the same San Diego milieu: Richard A. Lerner, president of The Scripps Research Institute, long involved with CONNECT, and advisor to the governor; and John Moores, a San Diego software entrepreneur and member of the board of regents. They agreed in late 1999 on the desirability of creating large research institutes for university-industry collaboration in fields that would contribute to California's new economy.[53] Lerner presented this idea to Atkinson and Democratic governor Gray Davis, who both favored it. With the state's booming economy and overflowing treasury, economic development was hardly the governor's foremost concern, but the institutes would be welcomed by high-tech industries and the governor had consistently favored the University of California. For Atkinson, the institutes rekindled his initial, but now overshadowed, policy thrust toward research collaboration with industry. Davis proposed $300 million for the institutes in his January 2000 budget message, and Atkinson managed the development of proposals through UCOP. After two rounds of peer review, three multicampus institutes were announced before year's end.

The three winning proposals emphasized aspects of biotechnology, nanotechnology, and information technology. A fourth institute was subsequently created (with another $100 million) to apply information technology to problems of society. The state's $100 million contribution to each largely covered the capital costs of launching the institutes, and had to be matched by at least $200 million from other sources—the campuses, federal grants, but mainly industry. Given the scientific prowess of the sponsoring units, their potential for scientific productivity can hardly be doubted. And given the initial matching contributions from industry, the integration of this research with industry also seems assured.

The four Cal ISI combine a focus on strategic science-based technologies with UC scientific strengths, particularly in the physical sciences and engineering. The California Institute for Telecommunications and Information Technology (Calit2), based at UC San Diego and including UC Irvine, is focused on technologies underlying the Internet, including wireless. The California NanoSystems Institute, based at UCLA and also including the established nanotechnology group at UC Santa Barbara, encompasses a wide range of nanoscience—nanobioscience, nanoelectronics, and mechanical and fluid nanosystems. The California Institute for Quantitative Biosciences, based at the new Mission Bay campus of UC San Francisco and including UC Berkeley and UC Santa Cruz (as well as Lawrence Berkeley National Laboratory), aims to apply the quantitative approaches of physics, chemistry, and engineering to the understanding of biological systems. The Center for Information Technology Research in the Interest of Society, based at UC Berkeley but also encompassing research at the Davis, Merced, and Santa Cruz campuses, is perhaps the most diffuse, with a mission to apply information technology and engineering to eight areas of social concern.

Characteristic of the bipartisan support for TBED at the state level, Republican governor Arnold Schwarzenegger announced continued funding for Cal ISI with unstinting praise: "as a leader in developing new technologies, California will reap tremendous rewards for our economy and environment from this investment in our innovation infrastructure."[54] If the Cal ISI are able to live up to this gubernatorial hyperbole, it will be due to the design and execution of this policy. The institutes represent the epitome of upstream research, but they have been designed to assure a continuous interface with industry. Furthermore, Atkinson, who was director of NSF (1977–1980), used peer review by outside experts in choosing the final institutes. They consequently reflect the strength and comparative advantage of UC's deep pool of academic talent. Finally, the UC system was ripe for stimulation of its interaction with industry. Despite the previously mentioned pockets of collaboration, UC science has been predominantly oriented toward federal patrons, and below average in research support from industry. Tilting that balance in the direction of collaboration, innovation, and applications had few drawbacks and many potential rewards.

This formula underscores the successful bid of UC Berkeley researchers (along with partners at the Lawrence Berkeley National Laboratory and the University of Illinois) for the British Petroleum (BP)–supported Energy Biosciences Institute. The British energy giant has pledged an astounding $500 million of support over 10 years for research into biofuels.[55] The sponsors describe the institute as the world's first lab dedicated to the long-term production of clean fuels. Recognizing the importance of this initiative, Governor Schwarzenegger pledged $40 million to build a new research facility for the institute, thus making it an element of state S&T policy. The consortium led by UC Berkeley researchers asserted their leadership in this area of growing economic import, as it was selected over other prestigious American and British institutions.[56] The new Energy Biosciences Institute facility will house laboratories for Berkeley faculty, who can conduct research funded from any source, and space for BP to rent for its own research. With fresh memories of the recent Novartis controversy, Berkeley's administration quickly dismissed comparisons between the two deals, highlighting that multiple units will be involved in the Energy Biosciences Institute and that the company will have no editorial control over research, except in the case of proprietary information.[57] This ambitious investment is a direct result of the scientific leadership of UC Berkeley, amplified by the contiguous Lawrence Berkeley National Laboratory.

California's stem cell initiative arose from different motives. The state supports three "Special Research Programs" that fund biomedical research on HIV / AIDS, breast cancer, and tobacco-related diseases. These health-related programs were originally instigated by policy entrepreneurs.[58] The California Institute for Regenerative Medicine (CIRM), irrespective of its economic potential, belongs with this category. The policy entrepreneur in the case of CIRM was Robert N. Klein, a real estate developer with a personal interest in the potential therapies promised from human embryonic stem cell research. Klein largely financed the campaign that placed Proposition 71 on the ballot in November 2004, and fought to achieve its approval by California voters by a 3:2 margin. Like the Special Programs, CIRM's specific goal is to develop actual therapies, but this initiative was extraordinary in terms of the scale, the financial arrangements, and the structure of the resulting institute. Proposition 71 authorized a staggering $3 billion in general obligation state bonds, which would yield $350 million in annual funds for research at California institutions for 10 years. It established CIRM as a separate state agency (with Robert Klein as the initial head of its governing board). The entire project was challenged by lawsuits from other special interests and controversy over the disposition of potential economic benefits. In a unique concession, CIRM included provisions for the state to share in any payoffs from blockbuster therapies. CIRM launched its first grant competition in 2007. For universities, stem cell research requires separate facilities as long as the federal prohibition remains in force. However, Stanford, the University of Southern California, and the UC campuses at Irvine and San Francisco have all made such investments in preparation for the CIRM bonanza.[59]

California's major TBED efforts have built upon an established and outstanding research infrastructure that, aside from Stanford and possibly Caltech, has had a checkered history with local industries. The state's endorsement of university-led initiatives such as the Discovery Grants and the Energy Biosciences Institute has strengthened UC's links with industry. Also rooted in university-industry collaboration and focused on innovation, Cal ISI and CIRM are ambitious upstream investments that will likely have a prominent place in their fields for years to come. Curiously, such initiatives have arisen not from careful analysis or strategic thinking on the part of the state or UC, but from the mobilization of political and economic resources by policy entrepreneurs. The peculiarities of the California political culture allow private entrepreneurs to advance policies that can trump gubernatorial and legislative priorities.[60]

### New York

As an active state in terms of TBED programs since the 1980s, New York illustrates the evolving patterns described above. The political culture of the state has long condoned prodigal spending for all manner of economic stimulation. Since 2000, S&T policies have spawned upstream and downstream programs for universities and corporations (Table 3.4).

With the second largest state economy and the third largest population, New York has numerous workers in high-technology sectors, although they represent a fairly low proportion of the total. New York City's forte is business and financial services, as well as entertainment, media, and the arts.[61] Its glamour presents a glaring contrast to declining upstate manufacturing regions still struggling to adapt to the restructuring of the U.S. economy. Renewing the upstate economy while fine-tuning the downstate one has been an ongoing policy challenge.[62]

The long administration of Republican governor George E. Pataki (1995–2007) gradually came to embrace TBED, ultimately committing New York to stimulating high-technology industries through state programs. The New York State Foundation for Science, Technology, and Innovation (NYSTAR) was formed in 1999/2000 with a $130 million budget, replacing the previous Science and Technology Foundation. Governor Pataki stated that NYSTAR would "help make New York the nation's premier center for technology-based economic growth in the new millennium."[63] Such faith apparently took some time to develop. There had been proposals in 1997 to eliminate programs established by previous governors: the Centers for Advanced Technology (CATs) as well as downstream programs such as the Re-

**Table 3.4** Selected TBED Initiatives in New York

| Initiative | Year | Nature |
| --- | --- | --- |
| New York State Foundation for Science, Technology, and Innovation (NYSTAR) | 2000 | State office linked to the governor, consolidated previous science and technology foundation |
| Centers for Advanced Technology (CATs) | 2000 | Funding for university research and infrastructure since 1983, extended under NYSTAR |
| STAR Centers (Strategically Targeted Academic Research) Gen*NY*sis (Generating Employment through New York State Science) | 2000 | NYSTAR-run programs for capital investments in university research infrastructure |
| SEMATECH International North | 2002 | Announced, R&D lab of semiconductor industrial consortium |
| University at Albany College of Nanoscale Science and Engineering | 2004 | First college of nanotechnology, core of the Albany Nanotech R&D complex |

gional Technology Development Centers (RTDCs) that provide assistance to small and medium-sized technology manufacturing firms.[64] These programs nevertheless survived: NYSTAR incorporated the CATs and eventually expanded the number of centers to 14; it also became the coordinator of the 10 RTDCs.[65]

Since 2000, NYSTAR has placed its stamp on a series of new initiatives to fund academic infrastructure in selected science-based technologies: the "Centers of Excellence," "STAR Centers" (Strategically Targeted Academic Research), and "Gen*NY*sis" (Generating Employment through New York State Science). These programs primarily funded activity related to biotechnology-biomedicine, computer and information technology, and advanced materials and nanotechnology. Every research university in the state received some funding from one or more of these programs. SUNY campuses at Albany, Buffalo, and Stony Brook obtained 10 of these centers, in some cases building significant research facilities, such as the Albany

Center for Functional Genomics. Private universities too benefit from these programs for economic development. For example, Rensselaer Polytechnic Institute (RPI) received state funds to enhance the research infrastructure of its large new facility for the biosciences.

The lineage of New York's contemporary programs is traceable to the 1970s, before TBED policies had become fashionable or known by that acronym. Back then, RPI sought to assert leadership in uplifting American manufacturing, starting from its home base. Under the presidency of George Low (1976–1984), the highly entrepreneurial and politically connected former NASA director, RPI strove to replicate what it perceived to be the Silicon Valley formula. The university organized corporately funded interdisciplinary research centers, tried to create "steeples of excellence" among its academic programs, and built a technology park with a business incubator (a first in academia). The assumption underpinning Low's plan was clearly derived from the Stanford story: a close relationship between the university and locally grown firms could elevate the stature of the institute and contribute to regional prosperity. One of Low's signal achievements was to secure support for the Center for Industrial Innovation, a large research facility to house industry-related research programs. Low's impressive lineup of partnering corporations probably helped in obtaining a $35 million interest-free state loan for the facility.

Despite Low's success in raising the profile of RPI, benefits to the local economy from university-based initiatives proved elusive. The region lacked an entrepreneurial infrastructure to retain sizable technology firms. The migration of brains and promising companies to other regions exposed the "slipperiness" of RPI's surroundings.[66] Moreover, the emphasis on high-technology manufacturing behind Low's efforts met the needs of established companies such as GE and IBM that faced increasing international competition in the 1970s and 1980s, but did not provide RPI with distinctive capabilities to attract the next generation of information technology and software corporations.[67]

The state decision to fund RPI had an important collateral effect: the creation of the Centers for Advanced Technologies. A program that could spread the wealth among other institutions was a political necessity for RPI's funding proposal to pass muster.[68] The CAT program, in operation since 1983, has been considered effective despite the caveats about evaluations of such programs.[69] An outside study in the early 1990s estimated that the state's $61 million investment in the nine CATs had yielded between $190 million and $360 million in measurable economic returns.[70]

With their emphasis on university-industry collaboration and the leveraging of state funds, the CATs were representative of the state advanced technology programs of the 1980s.[71] Each university research center designated as a CAT was given up to $1 million in state funding for 10 years, with a required 1:1 match from other sources. After the fifth year, the required match increased gradually up to 2:1 by the end of the funding period.[72] Centers were therefore expected to be increasingly productive in research and collaboration with industry. At the end of a decade of state support, CATs had to compete for redesignation. The design of the program clearly stimulated researchers to seek out grants and contracts, but also created strains as centers tried to achieve the program's objectives. The need to find the matching funds encouraged CATs to pursue the kind of sizable grants and contracts that only large firms could provide, despite the objective of the program to emphasize collaboration with New York industry, and small and medium-sized businesses in particular. Large corporations have greater capacity to support CAT research programs, but the economic fallout from these programs may not be retained in the state.[73]

The CATs nevertheless established a relationship between the state and its universities that has been sustained. State funding encouraged several institutions to build research programs oriented toward industrial innovation. The later programs fulfilled university expectations for receiving state support for economically relevant initiatives, and also provided an outlet for state investments in key economic areas—and electoral districts.

The TBED coalition among universities, state government, and industry has had the greatest impact on the Albany region. Since 2000, the University at Albany has aggressively sought to develop a local nanotechnology industry. The origins of this effort date back to the 1980s when President Vincent O'Leary at Albany and President Low of RPI persuaded the state to purchase an abandoned industrial site for a joint bioscience research park. This cooperation sparked additional collaboration in atomic physics. Perhaps more important, the public-private partnership amplified the influence of the two universities in the state legislature.

A key development took place in 1993, when the University at Albany obtained support for a CAT on thin film technologies. Led by Professor Alain E. Kaloyeros, this center served as a focal point to develop a critical mass of researchers in nanotechnology. The center built research programs and relationships with firms in computing technology (nanoelectronics) and biology (bioelectronics). In 1997 the CAT moved to the new Center for Environmental Sciences and Technology Management, largely funded by the state through a $10 million economic development grant.[74] The building was designed to foster innovation by accommodating university scientists and industrial partners in close proximity. The unit seized the opportunity afforded by state support for a high-technology agenda in general, and the interest in creating a semiconductor cluster in "Tech Valley" in particular. The state later funded a $10 million expansion to house a pilot manufacturing facility for new-generation computer chips. In 2000, a new $15 million grant assisted further expansion for a 300mm wafer facility.[75] This design and pilot manufacturing technology represented the latest technical advances in computer chip making and proved to be a valuable resource for industrial users.

Albany gained recognition at the national level as well with its designation as part of the National Interconnect Focus Center program, organized by the Semiconductor Industry Association, the Defense Advanced Research Projects Agency, and semiconductor equipment suppliers. Again, the hand of the state was present through $5 million in support (over five years) to back the focus center.[76] Before the end of its first decade, the Albany center received an additional boost. In 2001, the state and IBM provided $50 million and $100 million, respectively, for the establishment of a NYSTAR Center of Excellence in Nanoelectronics. The funding was used to strengthen the R&D infrastructure in a way that would be relevant to the nanoelectronics industry—and IBM—by adding a major "Nanofab" with a 300mm wafer integration facility. Besides the governor, the university counted on the political support of Senate Majority Leader Joseph Bruno and Speaker of the House Sheldon Silver.[77]

With the new research infrastructure sprawling around the Center for Environmental Sciences and Technology Management—dubbed the Albany Nanotech complex—the university sought additional industrial partners and state support. Counting on the governor's sustained support for a semiconductor-nanotechnology cluster in the capital, Albany Nanotech redeemed the state from its failed attempt to attract SEMATECH to the Capital Region in the 1980s by landing SEMATECH International North. This international consortium was announced in 2002 with projected investments of $405 million, making Albany a center of nanotechnology for the semiconductor industry. Further achievements required further state investments: $225 million was pledged for the two operating nanofabrication facilities composing the Albany complex; $75 million was allocated to a third, to be completed in 2008; and $310 million was invested to recruit the SE-MATECH unit and a research lab of Tokyo Electron.[78]

The convergence of economically relevant university science, industrial partnerships (most notably with IBM), and ample state support set the course for further developments. The government-university partnership was highlighted in the announcement of the University at Albany's new College of Nanoscale Science and Engineering in Governor Pataki's 2004 State of the State address.[79] A first in the nation, the college became the academic epicenter of the Albany Nanotech complex. Counting on the available infrastructure, the college is an attempt to redefine an academic unit to meet the mandate to work with industry and foster TBED (see Chapter 5). Other partnerships were established successively, involving several multinational firms in the semiconductor industry. Moreover, Albany Nanotech successfully attracted a number of major research institutes involving industrial consortia and joint ventures, including the International Venture for Nanolithography, the Center for Advanced Interconnect Science and Technology, and the Institute for Nanoelectronics Discovery and Exploration.[80] These R&D ventures add to the critical mass at Albany Nanotech and, by demonstrating industrial interest in the infrastructure developed there, validate the state's policy.

If this impetus is sustained, Albany may bring to fruition the regional industrial identity of "Tech Valley." However, these efforts to revitalize the Capital Region are neither unique nor original. Not only must Albany compete with other regions, such as Austin, but it also needs to overcome the legacy of its inability to retain new firms. Interestingly, Albany Nanotech is another university-led attempt in the Capital Region to gain comparative advantage in manufacturing, yet of a different sort. Albany is arguably at the cutting edge of building technological capacity for the next wave of advanced manufacturing, which does not depend on a large workforce but on highly skilled workers. The Albany enterprise has been partially credited with influencing IBM's decision to remain in the state and open its new factory in East Fishkill in 2002, and again in 2006 when Advanced Micro Devices decided to build a new $3.2 billion factory in Saratoga County.[81] These feats have understandably been claimed as successes of the nascent nanotechnology "cluster" at Albany, even though state and local government provided massive subsidies of the traditional kind to secure the plants. Between grants, tax breaks, and other incentives, $900 million was pledged to the IBM plant and $660 million to AMD's. The question that remains for the next several years is whether the R&D infrastructure for nanotechnology at Albany will be sufficient to sustain entrepreneurialism and create the desired cluster dynamics.

TBED policy in New York has benefited from the active promotion of state government, industry, and academic institutions. As difficult as it is to translate science into the plainer and shorter-term political language of job creation, the state pledged significant funding for upstream initiatives during the Pataki administration. The succeeding Spitzer administration apparently aimed to intensify this thrust, assuming the recommendations of the Commission on Higher Education reflected the wishes of the departed governor. The previously noted $3 billion Empire State Innovation Fund is motivated by a shrinking research share at the state's universities and an attendant diminished economic impact. The commission also recommended improvements in the quality of the public systems, the State University of New York and the City University of New York, which could only be accomplished through substantial investment of public funds.[82] New York appears committed in theory to the premise that academic quality is the indispensable complement to technology-based economic development.

### Georgia

In 2007 the State Science and Technology Institute, the central organization for TBED practitioners, presented its first "Excellence in TBED Awards." In both categories relevant to universities—"expanding research infrastructure" and "commercializing research"—honors were awarded to the Georgia Research Alliance (GRA), for their Eminent Scholars program and VentureLab, respectively.[83] This was scarcely a surprise; since its formation in 1990 the GRA has spearheaded widely admired approaches to state TBED. The GRA unites universities and firms around the common interest of strengthening a scientific infrastructure that supports research-based innovation in the state. Since 2000, additional programs have emerged from and around the GRA (Table 3.5).

Georgia's economy reflects a tension between the legacy of a stagnant industrial and agricultural base and the concerted moves made in the past 25 years toward greater investments in science and technology and research-based enterprises. While the Atlanta region has epitomized the New South

**Table 3.5** Selected TBED Initiatives in Georgia

| Initiative | Year | Nature |
|---|---|---|
| Georgia Research Alliance (GRA) | 1990 | University-industry-government partnership |
| VentureLab | 2002 | GRA program to nurture new science-based firms |
| Georgia Electronic Design Center (GEDC) | 2004 | Georgia Tech-based university-industry research center |

with its strength in technology and selected business sectors, the contrast with development elsewhere in the state has become more apparent.[84]

Georgia has pursued an active TBED policy since the 1980s. When it lost to Texas in the competition to attract the Microelectronics and Computer Consortium in 1984, business leaders and the state government launched a movement to enhance the state's competitiveness. A study urged the state to invest in scientific capacity to face the challenges posed by the knowledge economy. The Governor's Research Consortium was created to support university-based research centers in selected areas through the end of the decade. While it followed general trends in state S&T policy at the time, this initiative proved more important for the reactions it provoked than for the centers it established. Influential business leaders in Atlanta were disappointed with the impact of the centers. They enlisted the presidents of Georgia Tech, the University of Georgia, and Emory University in an effort to create greater university-industry collaboration, to connect academic science with industrial development. This alliance added three more institutions—Georgia State, Clark Atlanta, and the Medical College of Georgia—and in 1990 created a nonprofit organization eligible for public and private funding, the Georgia Research Alliance. With the establishment of the GRA, the business community and the universities forged a permanent cooperative arrangement with the state to make investments in scientific capacity and infrastructure, to enhance university-industry interactions, and to augment collaboration among the state's universities.[85]

The GRA is a model public-private S&T partnership. It was envisioned as an organization run like a business, yet dependent on the state for the funds it would invest. Participating firms contributed the operating costs for a small staff, and GRA founders soon secured from the governor $100 million to disburse over four years. State funding has continued at that level. In 2006 the GRA invested $27 million of state funds. Perhaps the most remarkable feature of the GRA has been the consistent state funding to a nongovernmental organization. This arrangement is no doubt facilitated by the political and economic clout of the GRA trustees, who include representatives of major Georgia corporations and the alliance universities. Independence from state politics was sought from the start, but the alliance still served the governor in an advisory capacity while remaining at arm's length. Given the state's conservative political culture, the nongovernmental status of the GRA seems to have worked in its favor. It has buffered the GRA from the usual political pressures to include less research-intensive institutions in its programs and to decentralize funding geographically away from Atlanta.[86]

From the beginning, the goal of attracting scientific talent to the state was pivotal to the GRA strategy. The Eminent Scholars program is the centerpiece of this effort. It provides half of the funds to support and equip new professorships. The proposing university provides the other half, usually from industrial sources interested in the scholar's area of research. Consequently, universities work with industry to identify individuals and subjects for these positions. Thus, Eminent Scholars have connections with industry from the outset. Permanent $1.5 million endowments are created for each of these positions. Part of the attractiveness of the Eminent Scholars program rests on the supplementary investments made in research infrastructure, which allow universities to set up labs and centers for the recruited faculty. The GRA has emphasized a few selected areas for investments, currently nanotechnology, biosciences, and advanced communications and computing.

Finding individuals who fit the profile and arranging for matching support have been ongoing challenges. The initial appointments took an average of three years to arrange, although more recent Eminent Scholars have been recruited in less than two years. But the results have been visible. Since 1993 the program has invested over $350 million in salaries and infrastructure. As of 2006, the six participating universities had recruited 54 Eminent Scholars.[87] These positions are concentrated at Georgia Tech (17) and the University of Georgia (14). From the start, universities were supported in their areas of strength, such as advanced communications technology at Georgia Tech and applied genetics at the University of Georgia. The GRA has emphasized strategic investments in quality and building sufficient scientific depth to generate meaningful impacts. With the emphasis on hiring faculty stars, the Eminent Scholars program has helped attract established scientists who enhance the reputations of their university's academic programs.

The Eminent Scholars program and the several components of the commercialization programs received almost half of GRA investments in 2006. The remaining funds, $14 million, were invested in research infrastructure. These awards are made with the same strategic purposes, namely to promote commercialization or attract substantial federal grants. Such funds have been instrumental in establishing 18 Centers of Research Excellence, sometimes involving Eminent Scholars, as well as facilitating partnerships with industry.[88]

VentureLab is the centerpiece of GRA's technology transfer programs. Launched as a pilot program at Georgia Tech in 2001, its strategic mission is facilitating the transition from research discoveries to early-stage enterprises. It provides three kinds of services for entrepreneurs: technology assessment, to determine the most feasible strategy for commercialization; connections with experienced entrepreneurs or managers serving as VentureLab Fellows, for advice; and commercialization grants, to support research leading to product development. VentureLab thus assists the most problematic stage in the commercialization of academic discoveries. Successful projects emerge as operating enterprises and move on to one of several business incubators.

The GRA has helped elevate the stature of Georgia's research and nurtured a culture of collaboration among universities and industry. Above all, the GRA epitomizes university responsibility for implementing state innovation strategies. The model represents a striking division of labor. The state provides the funding, in this case through the governor's office. The GRA staff, supported by private donations, screens and approves awards. All the initiatives originate from the alliance universities and embody some combination of promise for academic excellence, federal funding, and commercial impact. In 2006, for example, the University of Georgia lured from Germany one of the foremost experts in poultry vaccines, including avian flu, to an Eminent Scholar's chair. Poultry is a $5 billion industry in Georgia. Other Eminent Scholars have obtained NIH centers in nanomedicine and cancer research. Two of Georgia Tech's Eminent Scholars study optoelectronics. The GRA has measured its success in terms of federal grants won by

Eminent Scholars or Centers of Excellence, private investments in these units, spin-off companies, partnerships with Georgia companies, and new jobs. Academic-industrial connections and underlying research activity have created momentum in selected technological areas where the state seeks a competitive advantage.

Georgia's push into broadband technology is perhaps the best example of the impact of GRA initiatives.[89] Started in 1999, the Yamacraw initiative united the GRA, universities, business leaders, and state agencies for the goal of building a cluster around Atlanta in broadband communication systems, devices, and chips. Riding on the wave of the dot-com boom, proponents secured a commitment of $100 million from the state over five years. State funds were pledged to create over 80 faculty positions, build a university-industry research center (with a new building), expand the pool of graduates in the field, support commercialization activities, and market Georgia's industrial broadband technology identity. A specific goal was the creation of 2000 new jobs in this industry, which were pledged by the companies that joined the center. The Yamacraw Design Center was created in 2000, with much faculty recruitment taking place at Georgia Tech's departments of computer science and electrical engineering. In some ways Yamacraw was an eminent scholars program writ large and focused on a single industry. However, the strategy was dealt a blow by the 2001 depression in the telecommunications industry, which slowed state and especially industry investments.

In 2004 the center was renamed the Georgia Electronic Design Center (GEDC). The GEDC has become the self-styled academic leader in "mixed-signal technology." With a growing volume of federal and industrial support, the center still draws on the resources of GRA's infrastructure and commercialization programs. A new strategy enticed industrial partners with the creation of testing and prototyping "testbed" facilities for near-market technological development. GEDC has five "focus areas" of relevance for industrial partners: agile optical/photonic, cognitive radio, RFID/wireless sensor, and mixed-signal and multi-gigabit wireless. Occupying a building at Georgia Tech's Technology Square, a mixed-use complex near the center of Atlanta, the center has attracted corporate R&D labs to colocate in the area and work in close collaboration with its researchers. Samsung Electro-Mechanics, Pirelli Labs, and Nokia Siemens Network have R&D operations on and around the center facilities. In 2007, the center counted 250 faculty scientists and had about 50 corporate and government members.[90]

The rise of Yamacraw-GEDC as a university-industry research center ex-emplifies the deep involvement of Georgia Tech in economic development. With a long history of engagement in regional affairs and the centrality of economic development as an institutional mission, the institute is considered an active partner of the state in TBED. Its entrepreneurial culture is expressed in numerous interdisciplinary research centers like GEDC that forge research relationships with governmental agencies and firms. Unlike the older Georgia Tech Research Institute, a major performer of applied research with a specialist staff, GEDC embodies the contemporary paradigm of tying academic science and core university faculty to innovation-oriented research projects. Moreover, Georgia Tech has internalized most of the functions of a TBED agency through units such as the Enterprise Innovation Institute, a statewide economic development organization that provides business assistance services, and the Advanced Technology Development Center, a high-tech business incubator. Hence, Georgia Tech is arguably the chief enabler of the GRA and other university-related economic development initiatives. Although it has appreciably benefited from them, its leadership has undoubtedly helped to implant economic relevance at other Georgia institutions. Tying economic relevance to the aspiration to rise as a preeminent technological institution, Georgia Tech has markedly improved its research capabilities and academic reputation. It is among the elite public universities that have risen relative to their peers in quality and prestige over the past decade.[91]

In 2003, Georgia launched its Centers of Innovation, a program that seeks to attract business investments in particular industries to several regions of the state. There are centers in aerospace, agricultural technologies, life sciences, marine logistics, and information technology. These centers, like others of their kind, are essentially intermediary organizations that tailor their approaches to the characteristics of their locales and the targeted industries. They attempt to link the agents in the state's innovation system, assisting entrepreneurs and firms to obtain federal R&D funding and access relevant resources in the state, including the research universities.[92] In a rather standard approach, the centers address the development needs of regions outside booming Atlanta. In its bridging role, this program benefits from the S&T infrastructure built through the GRA.

The relationship between universities, industry, and the state of Georgia has undergone substantial change since the 1980s. The state's political culture and the unique qualities of Georgia Tech have contributed to the emergence of a policy infrastructure that is separate from the state bureaucracy and relies on a partnership between the public and private sectors. More than most state policies, this alliance has allowed Georgia to channel investments into targeted areas among selected institutions. The GRA has forged stronger ties between the academic and industrial sectors, and has offered the state a ready conduit for investments in TBED. It has also served as a catalyst for other initiatives that draw on the cumulative investments in scientific capacity.

*Arizona*

Around 2000, a consensus began to emerge among Arizona's political, business, and higher education communitie; around the desirability of investing in research and technology in order to stimulate and upgrade the state economy. Surprisingly, that effort soon came to focus on the biosciences, where, as some critics noted, the state was a comparative laggard. The lone medical school, at the flagship university in Tucson, had only become active in research in the 1980s. Yet by 2007, through deliberate planning, public investments, and private-sector support, Arizona appeared to be on its way to establishing Phoenix as a bioscience hub.

While the population and economy of Arizona have experienced consistent rapid growth, the state has been an underachiever in the quality of employment and personal income.[93] TBED had long been viewed as a remedy for this predicament through the creation of high-wage jobs. Arizona was one of the first states to adopt cluster-based economic development programs in the early 1990s. The premise at the time was that clusters were keys to economic development and that dedicated organizations would enhance the vitality of such clusters. A decade later, cluster organizations had been formed for seven high-tech industries (aerospace, bioindustry, environmental technologies, information technologies, optics, plastics / advanced materials, and semiconductors / electronics), but state initiatives had done little to advance them.[94] Worse, technology transfer efforts at the University of Arizona were hobbled by hostility toward research in the state board of regents and an adverse judgment of several million dollars in a disastrous intellectual property suit.[95]

The atmosphere in the state seemed to change in 2000 when Arizona voters gave a ringing endorsement to TBED by passing Proposition 301 (Table 3.6). This measure raised the state sales tax by 0.6 percent for the next

**Table 3.6** Selected TBED Initiatives in Arizona

| Initiative | Year | Nature |
| --- | --- | --- |
| Proposition 301 | 2000 | Increase in sales tax to fund economic development initiatives |
| Arizona Bioscience Roadmap | 2002 | State plan to focus TBED on bio science |
| Translational Genomics Research Institute (TGen) | 2002 | Public and private funds raised to recruit nonprofit research institute |
| House Bill 2529—Research Infrastructure Bill | 2003 | Allocated funding for university-based research infrastructure |
| House Bill 2477—Arizona 21st Century Competitiveness Initiative Fund | 2006 | Provided state funds to be awarded by Science Foundation Arizona |
| Science Foundation Arizona | 2006 | Public-private partnership that allocates public funding for university research |
| Phoenix Biomedical Campus | 2006 | Opening of University of Arizona's Medical School in Phoenix in partnership with Arizona State University, located with other research organizations |

20 years, and dedicated the extra funds to activities related to economic development. Some funds were directed to improving the public schools, and the rest created an "Economy Initiative Fund" to be coordinated by the board of regents. Each of the three state universities was allocated "Technology and Research Initiative Funds" to be used for purposes of technology transfer according to each university's own priorities. Thus, like Georgia, Arizona entrusted universities with considerable responsibility for shaping TBED policy. Revenues from Proposition 301 soon exceeded $50 million annually, with the University of Arizona and Arizona State University (ASU) receiving around $20 million each. The state's third university, Northern Arizona University, has significantly expanded its role in research and economic development as a result of these funds and subsequent initiatives.

The University of Arizona used its bounty to create the BIO5 Institute, a unit for integrating research in agriculture, medicine, pharmacy, basic science, and engineering. It also supported information sciences, optics, and water sustainability. The Office of Economic Development received about $1 million for tech transfer support. ASU originally distributed its Proposition 301 funds across bioscience fields; however, these commitments became part of a more ambitious plan in 2002, when Michael Crow became the new president. The arrival of Michael Crow, in fact, was just one of three developments in 2002 that launched Arizona into an unprecedented statewide commitment to economic development based on the biosciences.

Early in that year, leaders from across the community met to discuss a project for stimulating biotechnology research in Arizona. The scientist and policy entrepreneur who prompted this meeting—native Arizonan Dr. Jeffrey Trent—sought an institute for translating advances in genomics into medical therapies. Although he had talked with the universities, his idea was backed by Governor Jane Dee Hull, who appointed a Bioinitiative Task Force. Its twofold goal was to attract to Phoenix the headquarters of the International Genomics Consortium and to establish an independent Translational Genomics Research Institute, known as TGen, an endeavor with a price tag of $80 million. Remarkably, this sum was raised in several months with support from across the community: local corporations, individuals, and health care providers contributed; the Native American community pledged $5 million; the Flinn Foundation and Virginia G. Piper Charitable Trust donated $10 million and $5 million, respectively, and more importantly took an enduring interest in bioscience-based economic development. The city of Phoenix donated land that became the Phoenix Bioscience Center (soon the cornerstone of the Phoenix Biomedical Campus), and the state added commitments of $30 million.[96] Phoenix not only secured a foothold in genomics research; it contracted bioscience fever.

In April 2002, the governor, mayor, and a host of community leaders spent a weekend visiting the National Human Genome Research Institute at the NIH. That same month, the Flinn Foundation commissioned the Battelle Memorial Institute to conduct a multiyear study of how to develop the biosciences in Arizona. The "Bioscience Roadmap" that Battelle presented at the end of the year recognized the state's late start and underrepresentation in this field. However, it argued that the powerful growth momentum of the biosciences made them the target of choice, and that Arizona could exploit strengths in related fields such as electronics and optics to identify and develop niche specialties. Three "near-term technological platforms" were identified for initial emphasis: neurosciences, cancer therapeutics, and bioengineering. Explicit steps were outlined for achieving a significant ramp-up in NIH research grants and creating the conditions for the subsequent commercialization of bioscience research.[97]

When Michael Crow assumed the presidency of Arizona State in July, he could scarcely have asked for an audience better primed for his message. In his inaugural address he called for the creation of a "New American University" that would be deeply embedded in and engaged with its cultural, socioeconomic, and physical setting. For ASU this meant greater involvement with the community and the economy. As vice-provost of Columbia University, Crow was responsible for numerous initiatives in tech transfer and commercialization. He brought to Phoenix the same vision of the efficacy of university science and technology for generating innovation and economic growth. His first endeavor in university entrepreneurship was the launching of the Biodesign Institute, which sought to vastly enlarge bioscience research by integrating biotechnology with existing strengths in computer science and engineering.[98] Arizona State employed a mix of its own funds, Proposition 301 revenues, and the allocation from the subsequent research infrastructure bill to erect and staff the first two buildings of a four-building complex (see Chapter 5). By 2007 the institute had 10 operating centers that drew upon nanotechnology and sensor technology as well as genomics.[99]

In 2003, despite a $1 billion deficit in the state budget, the legislature endorsed an important component of the Bioscience Roadmap by passing a research infrastructure bill (House Bill 2529). Supported by the governor, the speaker of the house, and the business community, the bill pledged a total of $440 million solely for building and enhancing research facilities.[100] Such funding was a handsome complement to Proposition 301 revenues: Arizona State channeled its allocation toward five research facilities, including the Biodesign Institute; the University of Arizona invested in the BIO5 Institute facility; and Northern Arizona University funded its component of the Roadmap, the Strategic Alliance for Bioscience Research and Education.

Not all aspects of the Roadmap received public approval. Given the mounting support for TBED and the favorable views of Arizona residents on the economic benefits of science and technology, the defeat in 2004 of

Proposition 102 came as a surprise. The proposition sought to allow the state universities to accept equity in private firms, like their peers in other states and as called for in the Roadmap. With the backing of the governor and legislative leaders from both parties, the bill had little organized opposition, but was turned down by 52 percent of the voters.[101] Proponents contended that the problem originated with the Arizona Constitution, which prohibits the state from owning equity in private companies. Opponents framed the issue as state intervention in the free enterprise system, potentially leading to favoritism and corruption, and celebrated the vote as a victory for free-market capitalism.[102]

Despite this setback, Arizona's bioscience efforts continued to gather momentum. In 2006, three regional associations of corporate CEOs combined to form Science Foundation Arizona (SFAz) and to support its operating costs. Specifically inspired by the Arizona Bioscience Roadmap, the foundation was dedicated to advancing research and commercialization in the state. Organized as a nonprofit organization, the foundation is truly a public-private endeavor. Concurrently, the legislature approved the "Arizona 21st Century Competitiveness Initiative Fund" (House Bill 2477), providing $35 million in the state budget to support research and infrastructure in the biosciences and designating the Science Foundation to award the funds.[103] Indeed, the approved bill resulted from consultations among legislators and business leaders concerning the format and focus of the proposed state efforts in the biosciences, couched as "Innovation Arizona" by the governor earlier in the year.[104] The foundation has employed the state funds in a variety of ways to support education and research programs selected through peer review. About half of the funds were intended to support "strategic research groups" that would engage in collaborative research involving industry and/or having the potential to attract major federal grants.

The foundation was modeled after Science Foundation Ireland, which has been acclaimed as a success in mobilizing science for Irish economic development. William Harris was recruited from Science Foundation Ireland to lead SFAz. A distinguished chemist well versed in the challenges of promoting collaborative research, he had previously directed the Science and Technology Centers program during a long career at the NSF.[105]

In its structure and aims Science Foundation Arizona resembles the Georgia Research Alliance. Like the GRA, it reflects a public-private consensus regarding steps needed to fuel the growth of high-tech industry in the state, and it too has the authority to award moneys from the public treasury, in this case through peer-reviewed grants. The foundation is a striking example of the priority given to research in Arizona's TBED policies. The state's below-average share of federal research dollars was identified as a shortcoming in the Roadmap, and the foundation (again like the GRA) has accordingly emphasized grants having the potential to attract additional federal support. However, whereas the GRA's ongoing funding has come from the governor, the continuity of the SFAz programs will depend on the legislature for continuing allocations.[106]

Additional developments in 2006 contributed to the growing density of bioscience-related organizations and programs. The University of Arizona collaborated with Arizona State University in opening an extension of its medical school in Phoenix, at what is now the Phoenix Biomedical Campus. Perhaps a tardy development for the nation's fifth largest city, the medical school would seem to be an inescapable complement to the city's growing bioscience and biomedical infrastructure. In addition, the Virginia G. Piper Charitable Trust announced the largest gift in the state's history: $50 million to support the establishment of 10 chairs related to research on personalized medicine. Universities will be responsible for salaries and labs for these professors, and the Trust's award will support research and graduate education. This gift was followed by an additional commitment of $45 million by the trust and the Flinn Foundation to establish the Virginia G. Piper Center for Personalized Diagnostics in conjunction with TGen and the Biodesign Institute. These are impressive gifts by any standard, but perhaps more remarkable for being available to public universities with little history of philanthropic support. Clearly, these developments would have been unlikely without the momentum generated by the Bioscience Roadmap.

At the end of 2006 Battelle delivered a progress report on the Roadmap to date. In evaluating multiple measures, the consultants deemed "substantial progress" to have been achieved on six and "progress" on ten; three were "not yet implemented."[107] In keeping with the strategy of research leading economic development, the most impressive progress was made on building research infrastructure, garnering federal grants, and inducing collaboration among universities that had seldom collaborated before. Progress was more grudging in building a "critical mass of bioscience firms," although steps were taken to encourage and assist the formation of new firms. In any case, a four-year window can scarcely provide an adequate picture of the ten-year journey envisioned in the Roadmap. Only one year later this lesson was painfully brought home.

An informal appraisal based on 2006 data showed Arizona failing to meet key goals. Funding for bioscience research weakened in 2006, for unspecified reasons, but most likely reflecting Arizona's neophyte status in the intense competition for static NIH funds. This result left Arizona trailing, rather than beating, the averages for growth since the Roadmap commenced. This slight shortfall brought out the skeptics. Charges were again raised that the state had no competitive advantage in biotech, and thus was engaged in a futile quest. Fairly impressive job growth was deprecated with charges that, except for PhDs, biology jobs pay the least of all the sciences.[108]

Speed bumps are probably inevitable on journeys like the one charted by the Roadmap, especially if metrics are reported faithfully. In fact, the overall thrust of this Battelle report was "upbeat." Since 2002, research spending on academic bioscience increased 35 percent—one percentage point below the national average, but a substantial absolute rise. Viewed more widely, the Roadmap would seem to have provided the centerpiece of a planned approach to TBED policy making that has produced positive results overall.

Since 2000 the state's scientific establishment has been realigned to impact future economic activity. Perhaps least expected, the civic culture seems to have become engaged with a commitment to advancing science and science-based industries. The state has made generous appropriations to the overall effort, but public-private partnerships and support from philanthropic sources have certainly expanded the achievements. Another cultural transformation has engulfed the universities, which have emerged from their stovepipes to engage in multiple collaborations. Arizona State has been the instigator for some of this interaction, and the chief beneficiary as well by virtue of the emphasis on Phoenix as a bioscience hub. Collaboration nevertheless appears to have become generalized, which enlarges both scientific and commercial possibilities. Finally, progress can be measured simply by the proliferation of new scientific institutions (see Table 3.6): the Biodesign Institute, the Translational Genomics Research Institute, the International Genomics Consortium, the joint Phoenix Biomedical Campus, and Science Foundation Arizona.

These last achievements were hardly incidental. Arizona recognized that scientific research is an "industry" in itself, anterior to potential spillovers. The policy design that emphasized basic research in the biosciences succeeded in its initial phase in creating thriving institutions as well as increasing the flow of federal funds. Longer term, there can be little doubt that Arizona has developed niches in the biosciences, not to mention other science-based technologies. Future progress may be difficult, but these achievements provide a foundation for development that did not exist in 2000.

The state policies described in this chapter are a product of the most favorable climate for the expansion of university research since the post-Sputnik years. At the center lies the currently unshakable belief that the future economic weal of the nation will depend on science-based innovation. Such sentiments are amplified by some indefatigable cheerleaders like the National Governors Association, the Council on Competitiveness, and the Business Higher Education Forum. At the state level, this scenario is translated into a seemingly desperate struggle to gain advantage, or at least stay abreast, in a rapidly changing global economy. These anxieties are apparently shared by the general public which, when given the opportunity to register its feelings, has usually voted to support state spending for research linked with enhanced economic competitiveness. Under these conditions, governors and legislators have had powerful inducements to sponsor or support measures for TBED. Universities have aptly exploited these conditions by developing their own strategies to benefit from state interest in science and technology.

The trajectories of the four states analyzed here differ notably in the way policies came about, their shape and form, and the level of financial commitments made to them, but all are predicated on augmenting and harnessing the economic relevance of university research. In judging these policies, three obvious issues arise: What has been the economic impact of these policies—their ostensible aim? What lessons for state science and technology policies can be inferred from these cases? And, the specific concern of this book, how have state initiatives affected universities?

Given that state economies are enormous, unwieldy entities, it is by no means certain that any of these research-led policies will advance the relative gross state product, or even improve a state's rank on the New Economy Index.[109] Upstream policies are by definition long-range investments, and they all are focused on circumscribed parts of the economy. In such cases empirical proof of economic impact is elusive. Instead, a case can be made from the abundant circumstantial evidence presented above, buttressed by more general studies documenting the economic consequences of university research.[110]

The aim of most of these state initiatives was to augment the performance of university research, and the short-term payoff has been increased research expenditures in the targeted areas. Spending for research produces the same kind of multiplier as other forms of economic activity. An Arizona study found that each dollar of research spending generated an additional $1.35 in sales and $0.87 in wages.[111] Economic impact studies for other locales have yielded similar results. Moreover, building research capacity—infrastructure coupled with high-quality faculty—has the additional advantage of attracting external grants, especially from the federal government. The programs in Georgia and Arizona explicitly sought to deploy state spending in ways that would bring additional federal dollars. The GRA has been particularly effective in winning federally supported centers. One of its Eminent Scholars leads a multimillion-dollar NIH Nanomedicine Development Center, and another, the poultry vaccine expert, has spearheaded an effort to obtain a National Bio and Agro-defense Facility. Arizona's inchoate initiatives augmented federal and NIH funding in the state, even if only approximating average gains.[112]

Research produces other valuable outputs, namely knowledge and human capital. Human capital is a slippery element in the economic development equation, not least because it is eminently mobile. Research activity augments the human capital of researchers, their students, and laboratory workers. However, the ability of regional industry to benefit from this asset depends on the absorptive capacity of the local economy, with mature industrial clusters being particularly efficient in utilizing human capital. The original Yamacraw plan was a human capital strategy, based on the generation of graduates and jobs in broadband. Similar motives underlie the Albany nanotechnology college and the new Phoenix medical school, both of which are intended to build human capital for their respective clusters through research and education.

The central aim of these upstream policies has nevertheless been knowledge creation, fundamental and technical, and subsequent knowledge spillovers. The existence of knowledge spillovers has been discussed in Chapter 2, but the issue for state policy has always been their locus. The formation of spin-off companies based on research discoveries tends to occur locally, and encouraging this kind of innovation has consequently been an important goal of state policies. The Georgia Research Alliance claims a strong record here, with more than 125 start-ups associated with units it has funded, including 25 from the laboratories of Eminent Scholars. In Arizona, the Biodesign Institute has made spin-off companies an explicit priority, and has already produced a few in its short history. All told, Arizona generated 33 bioscience start-ups since the Roadmap was announced (2003–2006).[113] Mere numbers, of course, do not reveal the vitality of these companies nor their indebtedness to state subsidies. Rather, the existence of multiple firm foundings is circumstantial evidence that knowledge spillovers are having the desired impact on innovation by spawning small, science-based firms.

For the corporate track of innovation, the most cogent evidence comes from the behavior of firms. The association of firms, generally fastidious about research spending, with university research centers is the most credible testimony to the centers' economic value. The largest prize for states is the actual recruitment of corporate plants and laboratories. New York has landed the largest fish with a combination of investments in nanotechnology infrastructure and old-fashioned industrial subsidies. California too had to provide state support to seal the deal with the BP Energy Biosciences Institute. However, in both cases the scientific base was the sine qua non. The Electronic Design Center at Georgia Tech has had success in attracting industrial partners, many of which have established contiguous research facilities. Industry has also provided matching funds for many of the Eminent Scholars. Corporate participation in the Cal ISI is somewhat more opaque, though all those institutes have corporate affiliates with some degree of involvement. Both Cal ISI and the Albany nanotechnology complex targeted the corporate track of innovation, with anticipated spin-off activity as a possible secondary outcome. More generally, studies have found that university research has a positive effect on corporate research within the same region. Hence, knowledge spillovers resulting from state policies that target the knowledge base of local industries ought to be captured disproportionately by those same industries.

This last point raises the issue of effective state strategies for TBED. The four state cases examined here were selected to represent significant examples of the twenty-first-century trend toward upstream investments. Regardless of previous TBED initiatives, each significantly expanded the states' investments since the turn of the century. California and New York, as the largest state economies, were able to make enormous commitments toward these policies. Georgia and Arizona, as midsize states, executed more deliberate approaches. Each state's policies reflected its distinctive political culture—citizen initiatives in California, extensive state intervention in New York, tacit understandings among sectors in Georgia, and planning in Arizona. Across these different styles, some tentative conclusions can be drawn about effective practices even at this early date.

One critical element of strategy is whether or not to target TBED investments. All four states in fact implemented programs with and without specific targets. New York targeted nanotechnology support for the computing industry in Albany, but its numerous other TBED programs spread state dollars widely across regions and fields. Georgia presents a more focused approach. The Yamacraw project chose broadband for its target, but as it evolved it had sufficient flexibility to coalesce around the specialties of the Electronic Design Center. At the same time, the Eminent Scholars program was pursuing a market-based approach, in which universities negotiated with the private sector to arrange and propose prospective appointments. Although confined to three broad areas, each chair represented existing support for an economically relevant field. The success of both approaches suggests that there is more than one way to identify productive investments. Arizona pursued a more conventional route of employing consultants and analysis to select bioscience as a target. The choice was questioned in some quarters, given the state's initial weaknesses, but the methodical approach of the Roadmap afforded additional legitimacy. On the other hand, the universities were allowed to choose relevant investments with Proposition 301 and infrastructure funds.

California made a huge targeted investment in stem cell research, with results that will not be known for years. The Cal ISI represent a different kind of commitment. Although economic relevance was the underlying rationale for these institutes, no clear design for their potential contribution was ever specified. Rather, it seemed to be assumed that research results would naturally spill over into the state's extensive high-tech industries and that the benefits for industry would warrant continuing corporate support in the future. These were not unreasonable assumptions for the world's eighth largest economy.

Since upstream programs are only as good as the research they produce, a second critical factor is how to assure academic excellence in TBED policies. For the most part, these initiatives rely on universities to guarantee academic quality. For implementation of the Cal ISI, for example, a peer review process was employed by UC president Atkinson, a former director of NSF. The UC campuses developed proposals that reflected their academic strengths as well as potential economic impacts. The four institutes that were selected were thus certain to embody high academic standards. University vigilance to uphold quality standards was also assumed in Georgia, Arizona (Proposition 301), and New York. The one nonuniversity example, Science Foundation Arizona, upholds quality by vetting proposals through peer review. For top universities, like the UC campuses, prevailing standards of excellence should prove sufficient. For others, though, boosting quality may be a challenge. In general, hiring new faculty should improve quality: by scanning the country, or the world, for faculty candidates, universities should be able to identify scholars who will bolster their academic standing. This is particularly true when new, state-of-the-art facilities are included, as they were in Arizona and for Georgia Eminent Scholars. Absent these conditions, such programs may be less effective. New York's NYSTAR sponsors a faculty development program that is available to public and private institutions. It seeks the same type of faculty as GRA Eminent Scholars, but on less attractive terms: awards are for just five years with escalating matching requirements, and no support for research infrastructure is included. While undoubtedly helpful to universities in given situations, this program is not designed to drive major senior appointments.[114] To date, New York's state-administered programs have been less focused on academic quality.

Not all upstream investments in TBED are directed to universities. Pure research laboratories have also benefited from state initiatives, with expectations that their discoveries will also yield innovations for the economy. The recruitment of the Translational Genomics Research Institute to Phoenix was seen to be a catalyst for energizing the biosciences in Arizona, as was the recruitment of SEMATECH International North to boost semiconductor research in New York. For certain, independent laboratories like Scripps will receive a good share of California's grants for stem cell research. Florida initially based its TBED strategy on what might be called "wetlab chasing." In 2003 it announced more than $500 million in subsidies to bring an eastern branch of San Diego's Scripps Research Institute to the state. Since then, large state subsidies have been employed to recruit three additional biomedical laboratories. Expectations for these ventures have been more extravagant than those for universities in terms of federal funding, spin-off firms, intellectual property, and future royalties.[115] Investments of this sort can assure the implantation of top-quality research, which Florida believes will produce ample economic returns. Investments in economically relevant university research may not be able to emulate the focused specialization of a Scripps or a SEMATECH, but they can offer greater impact on students and cross-fertilization with adjacent fields.

Universities have joined these state initiatives enthusiastically precisely because of the institutional benefits they can bring. In some cases, state programs have caused universities to do things they would not have done on their own—to collaborate, for example, with institutions that are bitter rivals in other fields of endeavor, like athletics. States have hardly acted alone; however, especially in the new century, they have been leading actors in the movement toward economic relevance supported by federal science agencies, foundations, donors, and universities themselves. Still, states have a unique moral authority over public universities, and they often exert a similar influence over private institutions when it comes to popular causes like economic development. The next two chapters examine the impact of these commitments on universities: First, expectations for economic relevance have placed increasing pressures and responsibilities on the units responsible for handling discoveries and intellectual property (Chapter 4). And second, the endeavor to address potentially relevant subject matter, especially science-based technologies, has penetrated to the academic core (Chapter 5).

# CHAPTER 4

# Patenting and Licensing University Technologies

Universities' experiences with patenting and licensing vary widely. Consider the differing circumstances of two anonymous universities.[1] At a top private university with a large and long-established technology transfer office (TTO), relations between faculty inventors and the licensing professionals responsible for converting their discoveries into potentially valuable patents are cordial and transparent. Faculty readily disclose their inventions, confident that knowledgeable officers will work with them to determine the feasibility of patenting and possible strategies for marketing. The TTO, experienced with the uncertainties of this process, draws upon the best available advice and is often willing to commit to the expense of a patent application for high-risk prospects. The open attitude also translates into flexible approaches to commercializing intellectual property.

At the institutional foil, a major public research university, a small and relatively inexperienced TTO struggles to accomplish these same tasks. The overburdened staff has a more bureaucratic relationship with faculty inventors. Long delays and uncertain outcomes make faculty reluctant to become involved with patenting. Distrust is mutual, as the TTO suspects faculty of scheming to secure the rights to their own inventions. Unable to give full attention to all disclosures, the TTO seeks to focus its limited resources by identifying and pursuing potential "big hits," though without apparent success. The TTO's own need to generate supporting revenue distorts the ways it negotiates licenses and structures compensation for faculty inventors.

As might be expected, the two universities have quite different results for patenting and commercializing innovations, despite having comparable numbers of scientists and engineers. The private university receives three times as many annual disclosures and issues five times as many patents. It also concludes four times as many licensing agreements and has far greater licensing revenues—which also help to sustain its excellent services. The lesson of this rather unfair comparison does not reside in the organizational models, but rather in the cumulative organizational learning and adaptation that affect the creation of intellectual property (IP) and its translation into commercial products.

The "technology transfer office" is used here to designate the variously named units at every university that are responsible for patenting, licensing, and IP in general.[2] These offices all perform four principal tasks: receiving disclosures of potential inventions from faculty, staff, or students; evaluating disclosures to determine what steps, if any, should be taken to commercialize; conducting the patenting process, including arrangements with patent attorneys; and handling all phases of licensing, from finding licensees to negotiating agreements to subsequent enforcement.[3] These responsibilities do not encompass all forms of university technology transfer, as explained earlier; but the TTO represents the sole portal through which university-generated knowledge is converted to intellectual property and a potential input to economic activity.

Few universities equal the smooth and effective operations of the private exemplar; and few are as hapless as this public one. Most fall somewhere in between, and probably have room for improvement. Moreover, because of annual data published by the Association of University Technology Managers (AUTM), they are acutely aware of their relative performance. However, any attempt to increase the throughput of IP confronts both the limits of scientific discovery and the ambiguous charge of TTOs themselves.

TTOs face the challenge of mediating between two organizational fields with antithetical cultures. Residing within universities, they derive their raw material (inventions) from academics who are motivated primarily by the advancement of knowledge, and they convert that material into intellectual property that must be marketed in accord with the competitive conditions of commerce. They seek to strike a balance of mutual interests among these divergent ambitions. Reflecting this Janus-faced position, most report to the VP for research but others to the VP for business operations. Their contribution to economic relevance is usually endorsed rhetorically in institutional documents, but ignored or resented in many precincts. Lacking a true home in the academic structure, they are treated like auxiliary enterprises and expected to pay their own way.

Most universities define the mission of the TTO as making the benefits of university discoveries available to the public. This vague rationale contains an important element of truth. Many of the earliest academic patents were filed only after serious debate over implications for the public good.[4] Countless examples could be offered of university inventions that now save lives or enhance creature comforts. The logic of the public-good rationale is precisely that of the Bayh-Dole Act: inventions must be owned so that the return on investment will justify the cost of developing them into commercial products. This reasoning is valid for many, if not most, academic discoveries, which tend to require extensive development (discussed below). However, some of the most lucrative academic patents, like Cohen-Boyer and other research tools (see Chapter 2), have asserted ownership, and a corresponding rent, for processes that would have been used as much or more had they been in the public domain.

In the conflicted world of academic patenting, TTOs justify their existence through their contribution to local economic development, their service to the faculty, and the need to generate income for the university and inventors. A large survey of TTOs found little agreement over the priorities accorded to these goals.[5] This result reflected not a confusion of purpose, but the multiple pressures that TTOs experience today.

Contributing to economic development is the local dimension of the public benefit mission, and its prominence has risen with that of technology-based economic development (TBED) generally. Findings that economic spillovers from university research tend to fertilize local or regional industries are particularly evident for IP—the TTOs' particular domain. Inventions that cite university patents tend to originate in those same regions, and the same is true for patents citing published university research.[6] The role of academic inventors is undoubtedly a factor in localization, since their unique knowledge is best communicated face-to-face. This would be especially true for spin-off firms based on university patents. Partly for this reason, efforts by TTOs to encourage spin-off companies have grown markedly in recent years.

Serving the faculty is also a prime mission of TTOs. A relatively small number of academic scientists have strong inclinations to patent. These individuals are not only characterized by their inventiveness, but they are among a university's most talented and valued professors.[7] An effective TTO is consequently an asset, if not a necessity, for recruiting and retaining entrepreneurial faculty. Conversely, TTOs depend heavily on the good will of faculty (and to a far lesser degree of staff and students) to bring disclosures to their attention.

These two missions provide a strong rationale for universit es to support TTOs regardless of any income they might generate. In fact, most universities downplay this as a part of their mission. However, the public associates patenting with dollar signs and largely assumes that institutions engage in patenting above all to make money. One could scarcely deny this motive, whether or not any "profits" are realized. Still, the desire to maximize revenue seems apparent when TTOs devote their limited resources to patents with the largest income potential, instead of widely serving all faculty inventors; or when they pursue potentially lucrative claims regardless of likely expensive legal challenges. Actual licensing revenues are highly skewed. For most AUTM universities, revenues from IP either do not cover the cost of operating the TTO or do not allow it to operate at an optimal level. Hence, one critical purpose of licensing revenues is supporting the TTO itself. This situation is virtually unavoidable for all but affluent universities, since universities are loath to employ general funds from student tuition to create private property, no matter what the reputed public benefits. The scope of operations thus depends in large measure on the amount of income generated. Yet under current conditions, income may depend on the scope of operations. The nature of this paradox will become evident when the entire range of TTO operations is traced.

## Creating and Selling Intellectual Property

In the vast and growing U.S. patent system, universities play a minor role. Although the proportion of academic patents has been rising, such patents represent only about 2 percent of all standard "utility" patents. This contribution is concentrated in a few areas among the hundreds of patent classes. Table 4.1 collapses the 45 largest classes of academic patents, or three-quarters of the total, into principal fields. From the perspective of innovation taken in Chapter 2, the university contribution looms larger. Some 16 percent of all biotechnology patents and 9 percent of drug patents were awarded to universities in 2003. Other fields are more difficult to disentangle, but academic patents tend to be overrepresented in the fields listed in Table 4.1.

University patenting thus occurs chiefly in specific parts of the institution. Biotechnology—patents in molecular biology, microbiology, and organisms—cuts a wide swath through the life sciences, and may or may not be linked with drug development. Surgery belongs with medicine, but may also have

**Table 4.1** Utility Patents Assigned to Universities by Field, 2001–2003
(45 largest classes of academic patents)

| Field | Classes | Patents | % of academic patents |
|---|---|---|---|
| Biotechnology | 2 | 1,852 | 19.0 |
| Drugs | 1 | 1,832 | 18.8 |
| Chemistry / Chemical Engineering | 12 | 1,710 | 17.6 |
| Electrical Engineering / Computer Science | 11 | 689 | 7.1 |
| Materials | 7 | 586 | 6.1 |
| Surgery | 5 | 567 | 5.8 |
| Optics / Physics | 5 | 517 | 5.3 |
| Other | 2 | 192 | |

*N*=9,742.

*Source:* "U.S. Colleges and Universities—Utility Patent Grants, Calendar Years 1969–2003," U.S. Patent and Trademark Office.

ties with bioengineering. In physical science and engineering, interdisciplinary areas are prominent. Discoveries in materials draw upon chemistry, physics, and/or engineering. The many facets of electronics likewise may partner with those other disciplines. Apparently, science-based technologies, which confound disciplinary borders, are the wellspring of university invention. For universities, the potential for patenting will depend importantly on the amount of activity in these fields.

Technology transfer can be measured in several ways. Besides the number of patents granted, the AUTM collects data on invention disclosures, patent applications, and start-up companies, as well as the number of licenses executed, the number yielding income, and the amounts. Institutions tend to rank differently on each measure. Licensing income is the most skewed, since it reflects the serendipity of a handful of lucrative discoveries. Disclosures may be furthest removed from actual IP, but are possibly a good indication of faculty participation in tech transfer. "Utility" or full patents provide a strict measure of a university's overall tech transfer effort, because they must pass three screens: First, invention disclosures are screened by the TTO to determine whether or not to seek a patent. Second, two-thirds of new applications are for provisional patents, which allow a year to identify potential licensees. Third, if this important second screen is passed and an application for a full patent is made, there remains the gauntlet of the U.S. Patent and Trademark Office (USPTO) itself. This process can easily take three years or more. Hence, the patents awarded to a university in a given year represent past streams of research.

Table 4.2 lists universities in declining order according to the number of patents issued to each in calendar years 2001–2003, compared with a decade earlier. These 38 universities represent 54 percent of academic patents in 2001–2003. The differences in magnitude are substantial, varying by a factor of five from 1st to 38th position. However, while the advantages of the top schools are enduring, the overall rankings are not. This is not just because university patenting has been growing, but because of the way it has grown.

Much of the initial writing about university patenting noted the "cumulative advantage" of the patenting leaders, and cast some doubt on the capacity of late starters to ever catch up.[8] However, patenting is not a zero-sum game: the success of some schools has no bearing on how many inventions any other school might patent. Indeed, Table 4.2 reveals a jumble of different patterns. What stands out, however, is the general increase in the rate of patenting since the early 1990s. Twenty-four of these institutions averaged fewer than 15 annual patents during those years, and some academic leaders were well below that level.[9] Looking back further to the early 1980s reveals how dramatically patenting behavior has changed. Among the late starters, Michigan counted just four patents in 1983–1985, Chicago two, North Carolina and Maryland one, and Princeton and Penn State none. This variability suggests that some universities fulfilled their capacity to patent, while others harbored unfulfilled potential. However, capacity and potential are difficult to determine for university technology transfer.

For patents and other measures of intellectual property, the productivity of universities has increased greatly since the early 1980s. That is, outputs of IP grew more rapidly than inputs, such as research expenditures or faculty scientists, at least until the late 1990s.[10] A university's potential for generating IP depends on the interaction of four factors. First, the amount of research occurring in the patent-rich fields: not all research yields patentable discoveries, but the fields identified in Table 4.1 are clearly most likely to do so. Second, the quality of academic scientists and engineers: discoveries on the cutting edge of highly competitive fields do not come easily, hence the institutions in Table 4.2 are all strong academically, with the top patent holders being recognized academic leaders.[11] Third, the degree to which faculty culture

**Table 4.2** Utility Patents Issued in 2001–2003 and 1991–1993 to Universities with 75 or More Patents in 2001–2003

| University | 2001–2003 | 1991–1993 | University | 2001–2003 | 1991–1993 |
|---|---|---|---|---|---|
| MIT | 387 | 338 | U Minnesota | 111 | 90 |
| Caltech | 373 | 97 | Georgia Tech | 111 | 43 |
| Stanford | 273 | 149 | U Maryland | 109 | 39 |
| UC San Francisco | 243 | 54* | North Carolina State | 108 | 62 |
| U Wisconsin | 236 | 145 | Princeton | 103 | 28 |
| Johns Hopkins | 231 | 78 | UC Davis | 100 | 22* |
| Columbia | 166 | 42 | U Iowa | 94 | 24 |
| U Michigan | 161 | 61 | U Utah | 92 | 38 |
| Cornell | 155 | 116 | U North Carolina | 87 | 28 |
| Penn State | 154 | 23 | U Chicago | 82 | 6 |
| UC Berkeley | 153 | 34* | U Pittsburgh | 82 | 36 |
| UC San Diego | 153 | 34* | Yale | 82 | 30 |
| U Florida | 152 | 114 | Northwestern | 81 | 20 |
| Michigan State | 137 | 43 | Rutgers | 79 | 42 |
| Duke | 136 | 27 | Washington U | 79 | 58 |
| U Pennsylvania | 126 | 78 | U Southern California | 76 | 36 |
| UCLA | 126 | 28* | New York U | 76 | 38 |
| Harvard | 120 | 31 | U Kentucky | 75 | 18 |
| U Washington | 120 | 34 | Iowa State | 75 | 91 |

* estimated

*Source:* "U.S. Colleges and Universities—Utility Patent Grants, Calendar Years 1969–2003," U.S. Patent and Trademark Office; University of California. *Annual Report: Technology Transfer Program, 2001, 2002, 2003.*

encourages entrepreneurial activities among scientists and engineers varies widely across institutions. Finally, the size and effectiveness of the TTO can be an independent factor.

In their quest for economic relevance, universities can and do attempt to optimize these four factors. Building academic quality is obviously most difficult, given resource constraints and competition for talent, but externally funded programs to hire star faculty are designed precisely to build talent in economically relevant fields. The upstream state policies described in Chapter 3 aim to fortify and stimulate research activity in those areas that yield discoveries and patents, and this is also true of many of the university strategies examined in Chapter 5. Faculty culture is difficult and slow to alter, but, as will be seen, universities attempt to encourage entrepreneurship among their faculties. In the final analysis, however, the TTO is the variable most readily manipulated, and often the focus of university efforts to increase the generation of IP.

The connection between patenting and the kind of academic quality reflected in publications, peer recognition, and scientific prestige is loose but firmly established.[12] Many academic patents (and most nonacademic patents) occur in applied fields like engineering, agriculture, or medicine. However, a large number of academic patents stem from science-based technologies (Table 4.1), frequently the result of cutting-edge research. Federal agencies are the chief supporters of such research. The large center and enabling grants that propel these fields are predominantly won by distinguished universities, which employ the nation's most talented scientists and engineers. Such research is the seedbed of invention, and this probably explains why leading private universities, which are better suited to invest in quality, generate somewhat more IP than public ones.[13]

From the beginning of the Bayh-Dole revolution, allegations were rife that commercial activities deflected scientists from fundamental research. Early surveys of biomedical scientists soon belied that fear, showing that scientists with industry ties were more active in publishing and professional activities as well as in patenting.[14] Further research established that in breakthrough fields like biotechnology a limited number of "star scientists" had the esoteric knowledge needed to both advance the field and launch successful commercial ventures. Thus, concentrations of star scientists are linked with the local creation of firms in fields related to their expertise.[15] Even for recent PhDs the relationship between patenting and publishing productivity is strong.[16] Indeed, the correlation between the academic standing of universities and their success in commercialization appears to have strengthened over time.[17] Table 4.2 supports this finding, particularly the prominence of late-starting prestigious universities that did little patenting in the early 1980s.

The brilliance of their scientists does not fully explain why academic leaders also lead in generating IP. Industry seeks out the leading scientists in relevant fields, visiting the most prestigious departments as well as monitoring their contributions to public science. This attention produces a "pull" effect—explicit encouragement to commercialize findings.[18] Top universities also have ready entrée to corporations and entrepreneurs to market their technologies. Their prestige advantage is probably even more pronounced in attracting angel and venture capital for launching new companies. Still, these social factors reflect not only the quality of their research but also the fields in which it is conducted.

The current policies of federal science agencies support an aggressive agenda for advancing science-based technologies, and particularly those having economic relevance. The National Nanotechnology Initiative, led by the National Science Foundation (NSF), is one such effort. Launched in 2000, its funding approached $1.5 billion for 2008. The American Competitiveness Initiative, announced in 2006, aims to double funding for physical science and engineering research in areas underpinning future innovation. Spread across NSF, the Department of Energy, and the National Institute of Standards and Technology (NIST), these funds bolster multidisciplinary investigations in nanotechnology, materials, networking, computing, and, recently, energy-related sciences.[19] Universities have responded by adopting interdisciplinary strategies of their own in order to align their scientific priorities with those of federal patrons.[20] These strategies are analyzed in the next chapter. Here the salient point is that most universities are consciously reshaping their programs around science-based technologies, especially those that generate the most IP.

Faculty culture is often cited as an important variable affecting invention disclosure, patenting, and start-up firms—in other words, the inclination of faculty members to seek out or avoid involvement with commercialization. TTOs in particular are wont to condemn a lack of entrepreneurship on the part of faculty.[21] While individual attitudes may be unpredictable, several broad generalizations seem to hold. Over time, faculty acceptance of commercial involvement has been rising. While a good deal of resistance was evident in the 1980s, faculty attitudes became more favorable in the 1990s and beyond.[22] Not surprisingly, the attitudes of younger faculty are more accepting than those of their older colleagues, socialized in an earlier era. This tendency, however, can also be dampened by the widespread dictum that patenting or start-ups should be postponed until after tenure. Academic origins seem to play a large role. Scientists and engineers trained at hotbeds of tech transfer carry this spirit to their new institutions. Students who spend four years at MIT, by one testimony, are "going to meet twenty people who have started [a company]" and leave with a sense that they can do it too.[23] Faculty members with experience in industry also more readily identify and act upon commercial opportunities. Academic leadership is influential: when department heads and senior faculty are active in technology transfer, younger faculty are more likely to do the same. Finally, as might be expected, the affinity for commercialization is most evident in the patenting fields (e.g., pharmacy, biotechnology, electrical engineering).[24]

## The Role of the Technology Transfer Office

In FY2004, 15,000 inventions were disclosed to U.S. universities, nearly 9,500 new patent applications were filed, and almost 3,300 patents were issued. Some 4,000 new licenses or options were executed, and roughly 9,500 active licenses yielded over $1 billion in gross income.[25] The decisions that are taken in this extended winnowing process are the responsibility of the respective intellectual property or technology transfer offices: namely, extracting invention disclosures from faculty scientists and engineers, determining which disclosures to patent, devising a strategy for commercializing each of the selected inventions, and managing the subsequent licenses. Given the wide variation in performance, the efficiency and productivity of this process have been an intense concern of universities and of scholars who study innovation. What factors determine the output of potentially marketable IP? And what steps can be taken to enhance these outputs, especially the income flows that they produce?

The predicament of TTOs is revealed by a survey that asked directors to identify the most important factor in the success of tech transfer and the biggest obstacle to its progress (Table 4.3). The first three items are to some degree mirror images, while the last items locate success with industrial licensees and frustration with the actions of universities. The involvement of faculty was seen as a key factor both before and after patenting: before, for acquiring invention disclosures; after, for licensing and developing the tech-

**Table 4.3** Factors Affecting the Success of University Technology Transfer

| Most important factor | % | % | Biggest obstacle |
|---|---|---|---|
| Faculty / inventor cooperation | 33 | 25 | Faculty / inventor noncooperation |
| TTO process and deal making | 40 | 31 | Inventor lack of market savvy |
| Technology / market for technology | 12 | 19 | Early-stage, embryonic inventions |
| Contacts, relations with industry | 15 | 11 | Problems of university support / policies |
| | | 14 | Insufficient TTO resources |

*Source:* Farrell Center for Corporate Innovation and Entrepreneurship, Pennsylvania State University, "Technology Transfer Survey."

nology. TTOs not surprisingly rated their own skills at working with all parties and crafting deals as the paramount factor affecting success, and unrealistic expectations and lack of business understanding on the part of academic inventors as the greatest obstacle. Technology that had clear, near-term commercial potential produced obvious winners, but most academic inventions are far from ready for commercialization. Although respondents to this survey were asked to choose the single most important factor, positive and negative, the conditions they identified affect technology transfer at every university.

The process of creating IP begins with the disclosure of a discovery to the TTO. When the Bayh-Dole Act gave universities the right to own IP created with federally funded research, it also created an obligation for university researchers to disclose potentially patentable discoveries. The universities' claims would not, strictly speaking, need to apply to discoveries arising from investigations supported by nonfederal funds, but universities insist upon their ownership of these inventions too. The first responsibility of a TTO, then, is to garner disclosures for all relevant inventions. Here is where their challenge begins.

In one extensive inquiry, TTO directors estimated that less than half of the inventions made at their universities were being disclosed to their offices.[26] Interestingly, this failure to disclose reflected two opposite forms of behavior—avoidance of patenting, and patenting outside the university. Although some academics still have philosophical reservations about patenting, another likely reason for university researchers to avoid filing disclosures is opportunity costs. The work entailed in the entire patent process has been equated (perhaps exaggeratedly) with writing as many as eight scientific papers. For junior faculty, in particular, the prize of tenure depends on publications and grants. For the most productive faculty, those most likely to produce significant discoveries, other considerations weigh against patent commitments. Senior scientists are well compensated for their achievements, intra- and extramurally, and their time is heavily committed. Successful commercialization (and any monetary payoff) requires far more than filing a disclosure. Years of additional involvement are usually needed before royalties, if any, materialize. If monetary returns were the chief motive, this could be a prolonged wager at poor odds.[27]

At the other extreme, a study of faculty patents found that one-third were owned by the inventors rather than their universities.[28] It could not be ascertained whether the universities had declined to patent, releasing these inventions back to the inventors; whether university regulations had been circumvented; or whether the work had been done independently. Some TTOs suspect inventors of submitting incomplete disclosures so that inventions will be released back to them for further development and licensing.[29] Whatever the case, such actions tended to be taken by experienced, entrepreneurial faculty members who were both market-savvy and aware of the value of their inventions.

Of course, many researchers are eager to patent and take advantage of the services of their TTOs. In the life sciences, patenting and professional prestige tend to be complementary, while in physical sciences and engineering, patents are often used to build relationships with firms.[30] Still, if the findings on disclosures are representative, most TTOs face a challenge of harvesting a larger portion of the discoveries being made in their institutions. However, their capabilities are limited. Even large TTOs lack the staff resources to actively canvas for disclosures, and experience suggests that "cold" contacts are not productive in any case. Smaller TTOs are completely dependent on faculty initiative.[31] Universities vary widely both in faculty dispositions to patent and in the degree to which they are encouraged. New faculty sign agreements specifying their responsibility to disclose discoveries, and this obligation is often reinforced in orientations. Some universities now explicitly recognize patenting in promotion and tenure criteria, though this undoubtedly serves more as an encouraging signal than a decisive factor.[32]

Universities go to great lengths to promote tech transfer among the faculty. Some of the most successful universities create positive spin by sponsoring "entrepreneurship day," where exemplars of successful commercial endeavors are exhibited, or by naming and suitably rewarding a "faculty entrepreneur of the year." Such efforts advertise success, and thereby make others mindful of the possibilities of invention and entrepreneurship. Stanford, whose president is a successful academic entrepreneur, offers campuswide entrepreneurship contests and seminars on "How to be a Stanford Faculty Entrepreneur: Role Models and Resources."[33]

Where faculty culture is perceived to be apathetic, universities have increasingly resorted to educational efforts, sending TTO representatives to relevant departments or schools to spread awareness of the patenting process and its implications. They may assure reluctant faculty that "passive patenting," without subsequent involvement, is one alternative. For those who are more favorably inclined, the description of available services is intended to stimulate disclosures. However, the effectiveness of such efforts has limits. The eyes of most listeners no doubt glaze over at compulsory presentations. More commonly, interest is kindled only at the moment researchers realize that they might have invented something, making them suddenly want to learn how to patent. Otherwise, entrepreneurial behavior is strongly influenced by colleagues and by senior faculty, including department heads and deans. The performance and internal reputation of the TTO itself is also a major influence on inventor behavior.

When a disclosure is received by a TTO, its real work begins. It must evaluate both the technology, to determine if it is new, useful, and nonobvious—the criteria for utility patents—and the commercial possibilities, to determine if it is worth patenting. Disclosures in most offices are assigned to individual licensing officers, but decisions about strategy and disposition are sometimes discussed and ratified in group meetings.[34] Here, the skill of the TTO is brought to bear to find an optimal solution to a three-part puzzle—the effectiveness of the technology, the possible involvement of the inventor, and the potential commercial market.

The first challenge is usually the embryonic nature of university inventions. A survey in the mid-1990s found that nearly half (48 percent) of licensed inventions were simply "proof of concept" and another 29 percent offered only a lab-scale prototype. Only 12 percent were close to being ready for practical use. The great majority were far from ready for the market, and an estimated 71 percent consequently required inventor cooperation to advance toward commercialization.[35] Inventors possess "tacit knowledge" far beyond the information contained in a disclosure or a patent application. Such tacit knowledge is indispensable to develop the invention to the point where it can perform useful functions on a commercial scale. The typical disclosed invention, then, requires a lengthy period of uncertain development and more often than not an ongoing commitment from its inventor.

Inventors are indispensable in other ways. Licensing officers usually have some technical background, but they can hardly be expected to fathom the scientific specialties of inventors. They rely instead on inventors to help establish "prior art," against which each invention must distinguish its unique features. Inventors are also likely to have the best understanding of possible commercial use and, especially, firms that might license the technology. When it comes to licensing, the inventor can best explain to a firm the ways an invention might be put to use. The evolution of TTO practice over the last decade has enhanced the importance of these steps.

Beginning in 1995, the USPTO offered inventors the option of filing for provisional patents. At roughly one-tenth the cost and requiring less information, provisional patents protect inventors for 12 months, during which they decide whether or not to file for a full utility patent. This tactic was particularly appealing to universities, given the uncertainty of commercializing academic inventions. They soon began to file provisional patents and use the 12 months to market the inventions to potential licensees, who are then asked to pay the costs of obtaining a utility patent. Provisional patents allow faculty inventors to safely publish sensitive findings, and they also permit further development toward a working product. One result of provisional patents has been an increase in patent filings. Filings have climbed from less than 30 percent of disclosures before 1995 to more than 60 percent of disclosures in 2006. How many provisional patents are later filed for utility patents is impossible to determine. Some universities estimate one-half, but AUTM figures suggest that only a smaller fraction are issued patents.[36] Provisional patenting has nonetheless become a separate stage in the generation of academic IP.

Identifying potential licensees requires a kind of gestalt shift on the part of licensing officers—from faculty preoccupations with technical feasibility ("technology push") to entrepreneurial considerations of marketing possibilities ("market pull").[37] Most TTOs passively advertise their IP on Web sites to bring it to the attention of potential users. Universities create occasions to lure industry to campus, like the annual "Materials Day" at Penn State, and licensing officers pursue contacts with companies at trade shows and conferences. Licensing officers still rely heavily on inventors to identify the companies most likely to have interest in their discoveries.[38] Still, provisional patents offer a fairly small window in which to marry an invention to a license. Hence, the closer the ties with industry, the better the odds of success. However, since such links depend heavily on environmental context, weakness in this area is difficult to overcome.

Success in licensing university IP is associated with three contextual factors: an economic infrastructure of technology-based firms receptive to innovation; access to entrepreneurs and venture capitalists, not so much for capital as for their unmatched savvy for gauging market opportunities; and an experienced, entrepreneurial faculty familiar with the first two factors. Once again, the early-stage nature of university inventions indicates why this is the case.

Large corporations are very selective in taking an interest in embryonic technologies, since it is seldom evident how early-stage discoveries might eventually contribute to their product line and customer base.[39] Universities have always found more willing licensees among small companies and, increasingly in recent years, start-ups. Thus, regions rich in these young, science-based companies more readily assimilate university inventions. In 2006, a fairly typical year, 51 percent of academic licenses were executed by small companies (fewer than 500 employees), 17 percent by start-ups, and 32 percent by large corporations. While TTOs are often able to have multiple firms examine an invention, most commonly only a single firm will bid for it. These firms frequently demand exclusive rights for protection during the lengthy period of development. For start-ups, over 90 percent of licenses are exclusive; for small companies this figure declines to 40–45 percent; and for large corporations, 30–35 percent. A majority of academic licenses are nonexclusive, but since a nonexclusive license might have multiple licensees, probably the majority of academic patents are licensed exclusively.[40] However, the actual situation is complicated by the multitude of possibilities.

Considering that each invention is by definition unique, each IP deal represents a different set of circumstances. Besides being nonexclusive or exclusive, licenses can grant exclusive rights to specific "fields of use." TTOs also sell options on their IP. The arrangements made for any particular invention will depend on the nature of the technology and the uses envisioned by a company. The revenue stream to universities from its IP also has multiple elements. "Running royalties" are most common, consisting of a percentage of sales for the product or service incorporating the IP. In addition,

TTOs negotiate, as appropriate, for issuance or up-front fees, annual or minimum royalty fees, progress or milestone payments, reimbursement for patent expenses, sponsored research, or equity.[41] The various fees, and particularly reimbursed patent expenses, are important for covering direct costs. Running royalties provide more than three-quarters of the gross income generated by academic licenses. They are the preferred outcome by far for TTOs, since they offer the potential of large payoffs from products that sell widely. In a notorious example, or lesson, from the previous era, Indiana University in the 1950s sold the rights to the fluoride additive in Crest toothpaste for $4 million, when running royalties might have netted more than $100 million.[42] For this reason, running royalties are often resented by firms, particularly those that, unlike pharmaceuticals, cannot easily pass along additional costs.

Funds for research are sometimes included in licensing agreements as a way of supporting the continued development of the technology. This arrangement is almost always linked with an exclusive license. Income for research does not pass through the TTO, and is not favored by many offices. However, such arrangements are often more advantageous for inventors than the faint hope of future royalties, and research support focuses them on the continued development of the technology as well. Payments for sponsored research from licensing agreements were roughly $250 million in FY2004, compared with $1 billion from running royalties.[43]

Accepting equity in lieu of monetary payments has been more controversial. Frequently forbidden in the past as a blatant conflict of interest, especially for state universities, the practice has become widespread since the mid-1990s and is now accepted by more than 80 percent of institutions. Accepting equity has the great advantage of preserving the assets of cash-starved start-up companies, thereby improving their chances of survival. Although most deals that include equity are with start-ups, some universities also invest in equity through in-house venture capital funds.[44] Equity deals also detract from the near-term cash flow of TTOs, although they may prove more remunerative for universities in the longer run.[45]

Licensing officers face a critical choice between attempting to license to an existing company and recommending the founding of a new one. At least until the recession of 2001, the number and rate of university spin-offs had consistently risen (see Table 4.4), and in 2006 start-ups executed 17 percent of new university licenses, up from 11 percent in 1996. In large measure this growth was due to recognition of the contribution of spin-offs to economic development. As explained in Chapter 2, university spin-offs probably represent the most distinctive net addition to economic activity by universities because these fledgling companies are based upon and develop a subset of innovations that would otherwise be unlikely to reach the marketplace. Even better, these apples fall close to the tree, largely creating firms and jobs within the region. These characteristics are especially true for firms established by faculty inventors—but those are not the only type of university start-up.

University technologies are also used to start new firms by entrepreneurs, who shop for promising inventions. Investors do the same, but then must also find an entrepreneur to run a new company. A study of start-ups at MIT found roughly equal numbers of firms launched by all three types—academic inventors, entrepreneurs, and investors.[46] But this is surely atypical. MIT's deserved reputation for generating commercially successful innovations no doubt attracts large numbers of entrepreneurs and venture capitalists, creating an unusually powerful "pull" factor. The University of California's 75 percent of start-ups founded by faculty inventors was probably more typical.[47] In both cases, technologies licensed by external founders tended to be closer to market than those of inventor-founders.

The typical start-up company of a university inventor is based on very early-stage innovation or proof of concept. This choice is particularly appropriate when the tacit knowledge of the inventor will be vital over a lengthy period of development. Faculty-led start-ups are also likely to occur in the areas described in Chapter 2: fields that offer strong patent protection during the development process; decentralized industries, where numerous small and fairly new firms can find niches for distinctive products; general-purpose technologies that transcend the usage of single corporations; or radical technologies that might threaten existing products or processes. For similar reasons, start-ups are poor alternatives in fields where economies of scale rule, where patent protection is weak, or where complementary assets are needed for production or marketing.[48]

A lengthy development stage is an ineluctable hurdle for most inventor start-ups. The period from incorporation to the actual sale of product is graphically termed the "valley of death," or more simply the "gap." Investors are seldom tempted until a definite product and business plan are in sight. AUTM reported that 40 percent of new university start-ups were initially supported by venture (18.6 percent), angel (16.4 percent), or corporate (5.5 percent) investments. Of the rest, predominantly those founded by inventors, one-third had personal sources or no external funding, and the rest obtained subsidies, mainly for continued research.[49]

Given the obstacles, plus the adverse selection of inventions distant from the market, it seems remarkable that university start-ups are comparatively successful. AUTM reports that 55–60 percent of university start-ups since 1980 are still "operational," a very high proportion compared with all new companies. Leading universities probably have better records; for example, MIT reports an 80 percent success rate for the same years. However, there are different types of success. Most successful start-ups are acquired by larger companies, often as soon as they have a real product to offer.[50] Thus, the technology is presumably continued without the start-up firm. An unknown number of start-ups become dormant, rather than defunct. Some start-ups are content to garner research grants without ever creating products, becoming "research boutiques" or "technology shops." In fact, while corporations abandon unproductive university licenses rather quickly, inventors have been found to persist far longer. Nevertheless, even if an accurate score could be kept, it would mean little. The real successes are far more significant in terms of economic impact than the apparent failures, which are often cases of little ventured beyond the efforts of the inventor-founder.[51] Even these cases may not be total losses, since the endeavor might have generated research and learning for the inventor and other participants. Perhaps the only clear loser would be the TTO that paid for a patent or accepted equity in the failed firm.

The creation of university start-ups is now recognized as a distinct sector of technology transfer, one that largely complements and amplifies university patenting and licensing. At the same time, it poses a more difficult challenge to TTOs. Start-ups require more work than a straightforward patent license. Then, TTOs prefer up-front payments and royalties that could be detrimental to the survival and success of a start-up. Accepting equity in a fledgling company links the financial interest of the TTO and the university to the fate of these enterprises—a situation critics have deplored for possibly encouraging favoritism. Instead, universities have adapted to the logic of this situation by offering greater institutional assistance to see them succeed.

Universities have increasingly organized formal help for launching a company or ensuring effective management; they have also provided economical incubators and sometimes invested research funds to cover the "gap." As TTOs have added units for these purposes, they have become technology transfer complexes rather than simply intellectual property offices. At the University of Arizona, for example, the Center for Innovation works with inventors to guide them from the laboratory to the spin-off stage. Once launched, start-ups graduate to the Center for Technology Commercialization, where they receive assistance with marketing and the transition to commercial operation. Providing help with management and business plans may be the most crucial intervention, especially for faculty inventors. In the words of one experienced entrepreneur, "novel technology . . . is usually not the most important element of the venture (even though founding scientists, like myself, would like to think otherwise). The management team is the most critical element for a new start-up, and we academic scientists typically do not have the skills, experience, time, or focus to serve in such a capacity." The University of Florida well represents this strategy, explicitly encouraging scientists to "stay in the lab" while their companies are confided to experienced management teams.[52] Of course, finding experienced management teams is yet another challenge for tech transfer complexes.

Where and how inventors perform the research needed to fill the "gap" is now recognized as a critical issue. This stage has been described as moving "discoveries from 'we think it will do this' to 'it isn't pretty, and it isn't optimized, but it works.'"[53] Some private universities and medical schools assist start-ups by allowing professors to operate out of their laboratories. This practice is rare at most public universities, which usually sponsor business incubators or, like Arizona, prebusiness incubators, where new companies can take advantage of low rents and shared services. Some private universities have established special funds or arm's-length organizations to invest in their start-ups, providing gap funding in exchange for equity. Some public universities, such as the University of Washington, have cobbled together such funds, but generally they are more apt to tap into state programs to sustain spin-offs or to help get them started. Georgia's VentureLab was designed just for this purpose, and the Massachusetts Technology Transfer Center was created in 2004 to provide seed grants and other assistance to bridge the gap. All together, these multiple developments promise to bolster the viability of university start-ups.

Over time, the operating procedures of TTOs have tended to converge. The AUTM no doubt deserves much of the credit. With annual meetings in late winter, regional meetings in the summer, and periodic "how-to" courses, it provides recurrent gatherings for technology licensing officers, and it produces the data that every office uses for benchmarking. However, even with these open lines for information sharing TTOs have adopted divergent strategies.

Two alternative strategies are focused versus extensive patenting. Many TTOs prefer to patent as many competent disclosures as possible. They reason that the market, rather than the fallible judgment of licensing officers, should be the ultimate determinant of commercial success. Putting more "balls in the air" or "hooks in the water" will therefore maximize the amount and value of technology transferred. Since an idea has a chance for commercialization only when it achieves a license, this approach provides better service to faculty inventors who wish to see their disclosures have that chance. A more focused approach is sometimes dictated by inadequate resources, but not always. The TTO at UC Berkeley is known for being choosy, giving it a low rate of patenting disclosures, but a very high rate of licensing patents. When TTOs cannot afford to patent large numbers of disclosures, or when staffing is too limited to pursue numerous licensees, they may of necessity concentrate on inventions likely to have the greatest commercial success, which often means favoring the life sciences.[54]

The technology licensing office at Stanford was long the undisputed leader. In the early years, when most TTOs assumed defensive and legalistic approaches, Stanford distinguished itself by aggressively marketing its technologies. This strategy was greatly abetted by Stanford's close ties with industry in and around Silicon Valley, but the service mission adopted by the office enhanced its effectiveness. Until the mid-1990s, Stanford did not require faculty inventors to assign the rights to the university, relying instead on the value of its services to ensure their cooperation. Other universities have sought to imitate this marketing emphasis with mixed results. Undoubtedly most successful was MIT, which temporarily hired Stanford's director, Niels Reimers, to restructure its own operations.[55] Stanford has multiple advantages in its entrepreneurial faculty and history of successful technology transfer. This past success also produces an ample income that supports the large staff needed to maintain close ties with faculty and industry.

The transformation of Yale into an entrepreneurial university illustrates the advantages of academic leaders, even with a late start, as well as the key role of TTOs. Entering the 1990s Yale had top-ten departments in all the key areas of the new biology, as well as number one rankings in physiology and pharmacy. However, the university was notoriously traditional toward technology transfer. Faculty leadership frowned upon anything associated with application, and the TTO, established in 1982, did little more than administer patents. Yale embarked on a new path toward economic relevance when Richard Levin became president in 1993. As an economics professor, Levin had written on the economic returns to R&D, and from the outset he pledged to reorient Yale to become an active force in boosting the economy of New Haven and the state of Connecticut. In 1996 he installed new leadership and reorganized the Yale TTO. According to Levin, within two years the office was transformed from a laggard to "a national example of best practice in the area of technology transfer":

> We sought out faculty with an interest in commercializing their results, used students at the School of Management to prepare business plans, drew upon Yale's extensive connections in the venture capital business to find financing, and helped to find real estate solutions in New Haven.

Yale had an immediate impact, largely in biotechnology and medicine. It established working relationships for the first time with Connecticut pharmaceutical firms, and it began to spawn start-up companies. This last result was aided by the creation of several business incubators. By 2007, some 40 Yale spin-offs were operating in New Haven alone.[56]

The state of Connecticut seems to have awakened to the possibilities of TBED only after Yale's reformation was largely accomplished. In 2000, the state passed the first of many widely supported measures to stimulate TBED and encourage universities to participate, including a stem cell initiative that supported Yale programs in stem cell biology. State initiatives have clearly assisted the biotechnology industry, but Yale's momentum in this area is impressive. Also in 2000, Yale announced that separate $500 million investments in science and technology would be made on the main campus and in the medical school. These commitments seeded a huge expansion of scientific facilities in and around New Haven, all now linked with technology transfer.[57] President Levin remains a spokesman for the university's role in enhancing economic development, and he now has the example of Yale's own community to prove his point. Indeed, the cultural transformation of stodgy Yale was an organizational feat, but its accomplishments in tech transfer had other factors working in their favor. The superior quality of Yale biosciences is one. The ability to attract talented individuals to leadership positions is another advantage of elite universities. Finally, wealth is an undoubted blessing.

Caltech adopted a distinctive strategy when it created its office of technology transfer in 1995. It chose to maximize the patenting of disclosures and the formation of start-up companies. An endowment was provided so that the office would not have to depend on cash flow, making it easier to accept equity in the firms it spawned. Marketing the inventions of start-ups may occur later in the technology cycle, when a product is more fully developed. In this sense, the approach is almost the opposite of Stanford's focus on marketing early-stage inventions, and it can apparently be implemented with a much smaller staff (5 licensing officers in 2004 versus Stanford's 13). The Caltech TTO also handles the intellectual property of the Jet Propulsion Laboratory, a national lab, giving it a huge R&D base. Soon after the reorganization, the institute became a national leader in disclosures, patents, and start-up companies launched. In 2006 it held equity in 60 start-up firms.[58]

Caltech's example stands out as a substantial up-front investment to raise the level of technology transfer. Most large and effective TTOs have followed the path of the Wisconsin Alumni Research Foundation (WARF): using the good fortune of windfall licensing revenues to expand staffing levels. Few universities have had the resources or the confidence in tech transfer as a university mission to make *ex ante* investments. MIT became a notable exception in 2002, when Jaishree and Desh Deshpande donated $20 million to establish an eponymous center in the MIT College of Engineering.[59]

The Deshpande Center for Technological Innovation focuses all of its resources on bridging the "innovation gap" between invention and commercial realization.[60] The Center is designed especially to foster start-ups. For MIT inventors it provides "Ignition Grants" of up to $50,000 for the earliest stage of developing ideas into inventions. "Innovation Grants" of up to $250,000 are targeted for the next stage in the technology cycle, where inventions (proof of concept with R&D and IP strategy) are advanced toward suitability for outside investors. The other focus of the center's activity is mobilizing the business acumen of entrepreneurs and investors to advise and guide inventors throughout the technology cycle. The centerpiece of these efforts is the "Catalyst Program," which recruits volunteers with expertise in commercializing early-stage technologies and strong network connections within a relevant industry sector. These individuals, who agree to stringent confidentiality and conflict of interest guidelines, work individually and collectively with inventors as they advance their projects. They also advise the center on grant reviews and programs and participate in center gatherings. In addition, the Deshpande Center sponsors an annual, invitation-only "IdeaStream Symposium," where entrepreneurs, venture capitalists, and

MIT researchers review the future prospects of cutting-edge research and innovation. Together, these networking activities largely solve the market-pull side of the commercial equation by introducing the expertise of experienced businesspeople at every stage of technology creation and transfer.[61]

The University of Southern California (USC) sought to transpose the Deshpande model with a gift of $22 million from alumnus and venture capitalist Mark Stevens and wife Mary Stevens. The Stevens Institute for Technology Commercialization was launched in March 2006 and recruited Deshpande director Krisztina Holly as its head. Despite being in the top 25 in research spending, concentrated in engineering and medicine, USC had been a laggard in technology transfer. Its average-size TTO was off campus and inconspicuous, and the faculty showed few entrepreneurial inclinations. The Stevens Institute, placed in the Viterbi School of Engineering, incorporated the old TTO and added the MIT-inspired functions of gap financing and networking. However, USC perceived a need for a broader mission. Much of its creative activity was located in its professional schools of cinematic arts, music, and communication, not to mention dentistry. And the administration recognized the importance of transforming faculty attitudes toward entrepreneurship. After just one year of operation, the institute was revamped to stress these last two goals.

Renamed the USC Stevens Institute for Innovation, it assumed the mission of spreading the gospel of innovation, or inventiveness, across the entire campus. Emphasis was shifted to inspiring innovators across the university's 17 professional schools, and USC Stevens (as it is called) assumed an educational role for students and faculty in addition to its technology transfer activities. With full university backing, it seeks to inspire USC students to become innovators who will improve society through creative contributions. The provost, for example, envisions an innovation component for all doctoral programs, so that innovation will become "the signature for the USC PhD diploma."[62] In keeping with its now-central role, Stevens was placed directly under the provost, and Holly was made a vice-provost. Plans call for a suite of offices on the main campus, as well as units at the medical school and the biomedical research park. With such steps, USC has elevated innovation to a prominent university mission, one that subsumes technology transfer and economic development. Instead of tech transfer, USC aims "to empower innovators"; instead of economic development, it aspires to "benefit society as a whole."[63] Although clichéd, this language transforms a potentially divisive mission into one intended to rally the entire institution.

Moreover, some substance or at least strategy lies behind these phrases: namely, removing the "tech" from tech transfer. USC's 17 professional schools already have multiple links with their respective industries. It is not far-fetched to see these linkages intensified and (to put it crassly) monetized through the same kind of developmental and networking assistance that facilitates high-tech start-ups. Innovators in both cases would provide the sparks that ignite the process.

## The Cons and Pros of TTOs

An observation often heard, only partly in jest, is that the greatest obstacle to university technology transfer is TTOs.[64] This sentiment reflects the negative reputations acquired by some TTOs for slowness, inept handling of faculty discoveries, and bureaucratic inflexibility. It also reflects perceptions by some stakeholders that they are not well served by the patenting and licensing process. TTOs themselves, after periodic reorganizations, admit to having had "a bad reputation" for having been "hard to work with" and boast of having become "less bureaucratic."[65] In part, these complaints and admissions are symptoms of weak performance; in part, they emanate from the nature of the task. The problems with the current system of technology transfer appear quite different when viewed from outside and from inside the system.

Current criticisms directed at the technology transfer process focus on inherent features of patenting and licensing: the conflict that can arise between technology transfer and revenue generation, the tensions between technology transfer in the life sciences and practices in engineering and physical science, and the proclivity to patent research tools and fundamental science. "To be successful [in tech transfer]," USC's Krisztina Holly observed regarding the first conflict, "you can't be greedy . . . by focusing only on the potential financial gains, you end up becoming difficult to work with."[66] More generally, a report from the Kauffman Foundation attacked what it called the "revenue maximization model of technology transfer." Instead of seeking to maximize patent licensing income, it advocated a "volume model" that emphasizes the number of university innovations and the speed with which they are moved into the marketplace.[67]

Holly's remark points up a difference between successful—and well-supported—TTOs that feel little pressure to generate immediate revenues and the large majority of more hard-pressed offices that do. Royalties are the chief source of TTO income, but they represent the yield from successful past transactions. The various levies imposed on technologies struggling to be born are more troublesome, yet they all have a rationale. Perhaps most crucial for TTOs with limited budgets is recovery of legal costs for patenting expenses. In many cases the number of patents that can be filed depends in part on how much of these costs are reimbursed by licensees. Beyond budgetary considerations, TTOs offer a different rationale: that payments equal commitment to a technology. According to this reasoning, inventors who wish to license back their inventions will be more diligent in developing, as opposed to sitting on, technologies when they have invested in the patenting costs. By this same logic, other licensees must also be motivated to do something with a technology by requiring annual or milestone fees. A third rationale for demanding payments pertains chiefly to the most prestigious universities, many of which have reputations for being the most inflexible in licensing terms. They have sufficient bargaining strength to adopt a "take it or leave it" position. Their focus is on technologies with such clear commercial value that licensees have little choice but to accept their standard terms. Their comparatively lower level of interest in more marginal technologies in which licensees are reluctant to commit up-front payments can inhibit technology transfer for riskier inventions.

Persistent allegations that TTO policies are detrimental to technology transfer via start-up firms would seem to contradict one of the dominant trends. Universities have altered policies to permit the acceptance of equity in new firms, TTOs have signaled their eagerness to launch and assist such firms, and leading universities, as just seen, have gone to great lengths to provide extensive advice and aid for these ventures. Nevertheless, standard operating procedures at most TTOs still tend to inhibit rather than encourage start-ups.[68] It is still common to insist that new firms pay patenting costs when they license back a technology, thus cutting into the working capital of a struggling enterprise. Detailed business plans are sometimes required to establish commercial potential, but can be far-fetched exercises for an embryonic technology facing lengthy development. Management plans and conflict of interest rules can be further impediments, although here the rationale is to protect the university rather than to raise revenues. In addition, most TTOs are reluctant to release a disclosed invention back to its author. In some cases, the finding is published and loses its patentability, but faculty inventors who wish to develop an abandoned disclosure on their own are often obstructed by their own TTO.

Research support is another area where the outlook of TTOs differs from that of those responsible for developing technologies. TTOs tend to be averse to trading licenses for research funds, since such arrangements divert income into a different account. However, additional research is usually included because it is vital to further develop a technology. TTO demands for IP provisions in sponsored research for industry have already been identified as a divisive issue. Both these situations are most pertinent to engineering technologies, and thus are part of the different outlooks of the physical and life sciences.

As seen in Chapter 2, patents play rather different roles in the life sciences than in most other manufacturing fields.[69] The bioscience-based industries deal with discrete products that can be effectively protected by patents. In many other areas of manufacture, patents provide only weak protection or can be "invented around," especially for complex products and systems. The life sciences industries, and most notably pharmaceuticals, depend heavily on patents to uphold the value of IP. For industries based on physical sciences, which encompass most fields of engineering, patents are only one of several IP strategies, including trade secrets and first-mover advantage. Firms in these industries nevertheless patent a great deal. Often collections of patents are used for defensive purposes, to ward off potential competitors. Individually, such patents tend to be much less valuable than those that define discrete products. They are frequently used as bargaining chips in negotiations among participants, leading to extensive cross-licensing without royalties. This dichotomy is rooted in the nature of the technologies, and hence carries over to academic patenting.

The explosion of academic patenting after 1980 coincided with the birth of the biotechnology industry. Before 1983, just 15 percent of academic patents were biological, but by 2003 that figure had jumped to 39 percent (Table 4.1). In comparison, just 6 percent of all U.S. patents were in these fields. University licensing revenues were even more skewed, with roughly 80 percent coming from the life sciences.[70] University TTOs not only rushed into the biotechnology industry, they largely adopted the strong-patenting paradigm associated with it. This approach emphasized patenting and licensing all university IP for fear of missing a possible blockbuster. It pushed the boundaries of patentable materials, claimed IP for universities in all research contracts, and demanded running royalties as a percentage of sales. The genesis of the revenue maximization model can be seen in these practices. This patenting paradigm has also largely been the culprit when TTOs are accused of being "inflexible." However, it suits the life sciences well. There patent protection is regarded as a necessity by scientists and entrepreneurs, and industry expects to pay for IP.

That commercial relations have permeated academic biotechnology is well known. Perhaps less appreciated is how the ethos of life scientists, determined to advance their field and their own stature within it, has been assimilated to the practice of academic patenting. Aside from the possibility of making a great deal of money, life scientists feel compelled to file patents for personal and professional reasons. Like inventors in all fields, life scientists often feel strong personal motivation to carry their unique contributions through to fruition, and such feelings are all the stronger for researchers dedicated to conquering disease. Patents may be necessary to preserve control over their own sphere of research by holding off possible blockage or encroachment by rival patents. Life sciences patents are also routinely used as leverage to acquire additional resources from the private sector. The dynamics of the field reinforce commercialization either through start-ups or collaborations with existing firms. In the rapidly advancing field of biotechnology, large advantages accrue to scale and centrality. Commercial units provide more hands, more lab space, and more specialized research tools with which to attack cutting-edge problems. Centrality is an inestimable advantage because innovation is linked so closely with organizational networks. With important scientific advances being made in the proprietary sector, participation in "networks of learning" has become a crucial factor for life scientists.[71] In sum, commercialization has become an almost inescapable complement to academic advancement for both the field and individual life scientists. The patenting regime of TTOs has been shaped to a large extent by the imperatives of this field.

This patenting regime is less congenial for engineering and physical science. The large numbers of patents issued in engineering fields tend to cover partial components of, or incremental improvements to, complex systems. Because the patents are weaker, or more easily invented around, companies protect their products with large numbers of them, creating patent "fences" or "thickets." In some years, for example, IBM has been issued more patents than all U.S. universities combined. The contributions of academic patents to this mix can be of strategic importance, but more commonly patents in these fields are of the partial or incremental type. Accordingly, engineers who work regularly with industry and occasionally patent take a different view of this process than life scientists. With little or no prospect for royalties, they prefer to trade IP to industry in return for research or lab support. Patents can be valuable to them and their students in building ongoing relationships with firms. TTOs sometimes oppose such arrangements as shortsighted—giving away the long-term potential value of IP for limited short-term rewards.[72] However, firms are adamantly against conceding royalties to the type of invention that makes only a small contribution to their own proprietary technology.

Most complaints about the inefficiency and inflexibility of TTOs emanate from the engineering and physical science side of campuses. Engineers and chemists, in particular, often develop long-standing relationships with industrial firms. These relationships are especially valuable for supporting, training, and placing students—one of the most effective means of technology transfer. Professors gain not only resources for their labs, but also problems and inputs that guide their research. When TTOs intrude into these relationships to uphold what they define as the interests of the university, they become adversaries rather than facilitators. From the point of view of affected faculty, the actions of TTOs serve to inhibit rather than promote technology transfer.[73]

The third set of concerns over academic patenting can be described as "overreach." In their zeal to patent, universities have engaged in practices that can scarcely be regarded as compatible with the public interest. These include claiming ownership over fundamental scientific knowledge or research tools and engaging in extended campaigns to obtain multimillion-dollar payoffs from often-tenuous invention claims.

Since the onset of the current patenting era, a persistent dialogue has juxtaposed public and private science, generally to express worry that private ownership was jeopardizing the public character of the scientific enterprise. In 1998, two legal scholars gave these concerns a cogent formulation as the "tragedy of the anticommons in biomedical research."[74] Unlike the well-known tragedy of the commons, when individuals overuse shared resources, the tragedy of the anticommons refers to diminished public good caused by the underutilization of resources due to mechanisms of exclusion (namely, patents). In biomedical science, the potential for this situation has resulted from the increased patenting of upstream fundamental research. The aim of such patents is to profit from their incorporation into downstream innovations. However, the very existence of diffuse, overlapping ownership of essential scientific knowledge could obstruct the very conduct of research. The authors identify three sources of obstruction: transaction costs, heterogeneous interests, and overvaluing IP. Although not specifically mentioned, TTOs are implicated in all three. Transactions are what they do—and what they are commonly criticized for doing slowly and bureaucratically.[75] Heterogeneity of interests refers to the inherent differences between firms and universities: firms resolve patent conflicts (when not suing one another) by negotiating cross-licensing or royalty agreements because their overriding common interest is in producing goods; the overriding interest of TTOs, however, is to produce licenses and revenues, leaving little basis for bargaining. Finally, TTOs, along with faculty inventors, have an inherent tendency to overvalue their IP. This natural tendency is exaggerated by a dread of being accused of undervaluing the university's property. Thus, the natural proclivities of TTOs serve to enhance the possibilities for an anticommons in research.

The sole empirical study to test this diagnosis found little evidence that upstream patent thickets were impeding either research or innovation. The authors found instead that industrial and university researchers devised "working solutions" to circumvent potential patent blockages, although these were not without social costs.[76] The findings for research tools were more complicated, including cases where research tools were controlled to inhibit rival research. The authors cautioned that future developments ought to be monitored carefully. Indeed, in 2003 a group of land-grant university presidents published a statement deploring the existence of an anticommons situation in agricultural research and urging academic cooperation to counteract it.[77]

Economist Richard Nelson, long a scholar in this area, has concluded that the establishment of property rights over "ideas, materials, and techniques that themselves represent important inputs into the scientific research process" may well impede the progress of research. Moreover, Nelson implicates TTOs in this development. One corrective measure he urges is better management by universities of the complex trade-offs in technology transfer.[78] However, much of the blame for this situation lies outside academe in the patenting system itself. One scathing indictment has shown how the scope of patenting has expanded since 1980 at the same time that the quality of work by patent examiners has declined.[79] This disastrous combination provides the backdrop to the current controversy. Nelson and others offer sensible ways to reduce the current excesses of the patent system by strengthening the public safeguards in the Bayh-Dole legislation, restricting the patenting of natural phenomena, and insisting on the presence of usefulness (as opposed to scientific findings) in utility patents.[80] However, for years a battle has been raging in the courts over expanding versus constricting patent protection. Universities have generally entered the lists with entrepreneurial firms in advocating broader protection, and hence greater value for their own IP.[81] When money is on the table, it seems, universities take a narrow view of the public interest.

Most universities define the mission of technology transfer in language that highlights benefits to society, and these alleged benefits figure prominently in public pronouncements about this role. According to the 2000 president of AUTM, university patenting seeks "the best means to protect and disseminate . . . information for the public good."[82] However, social benefits or the public good can be slippery terms, subject to many interpretations. Universities could easily argue (although they seldom do) that the income they receive from patenting and licensing contributes to the social good. One portion rewards inventors, clearly a value in American society; another part supports directly or indirectly the operations of TTOs, thereby furthering innovation; and the remainder largely supports research-related activities. But who pays for these benefits? Ultimately, economists would say, the costs of innovation are passed through to consumers in the form of higher prices. In the case of new and improved goods and services, these costs are justified by the value added. For patents on fundamental knowledge or research tools, the situation is murkier. When patents are issued on processes that might otherwise be in the public domain, the resulting royalties amount to a tax. Universities have proved quite willing to impose such taxes, which scarcely benefit society. The story of the Axel cotransformation patent held by Columbia University is one case in point.

Between 1977 and 1979, Richard Axel of the Columbia College of Physicians and Surgeons published a series of papers describing how genetic material could be transferred into mammalian cells (cotransformation). This technique proved enormously valuable for understanding gene expression and ultimately for developing a number of new and effective biotechnology drugs. The university filed a patent in 1980, before passage of Bayh-Dole. It originally asked the National Institutes of Health (NIH) for permission to license the invention exclusively, but this was denied. Instead, it was licensed widely as a research tool, much like the Cohen-Boyer patents. And like them the license included "reach-through" provisions, granting a small royalty on all products developed with this tool. By the time the patent was granted in 1983, cotransformation had already been used in universities and industry for years, and one scientist's feeling that patenting "just doesn't seem right" was probably widely shared. The Columbia TTO never-theless began to systematically identify companies it suspected of using the process and force them to sign licensing agreements. The success of this tactic—and the success of the products developed using cotransformation—brought Columbia some $400 million in revenues by 2000—for a discovery that was originally considered to be in the domain of public science.[83] How-ever, the financial story did not end with the expiration of the patent in that year. Columbia lobbied Congress to get a patent extension written into an agriculture bill, but when this gambit was exposed, the resulting uproar caused the measure to be dropped. As an alternate strategy, Columbia filed a second patent on the process in 1995, which for reasons known only to the patent office was eventually issued in 2002. However, before the uni-versity could collect any more royalty checks, a barrage of lawsuits chal-lenged, and ultimately invalidated, the second patent. Regardless of how one views the original cotransformation "tax," Columbia's schemes to ex-tend this bonanza were hardly consistent with the public interest.

A more egregious overreach by the University of Rochester illustrates why universities favor the broadest possible interpretation of patent law. University scientists in 1992 succeeded in isolating the COX-2 enzyme, which causes inflammation, from the closely linked COX-1 enzyme, which protects stomach lining. Their discovery suggested, but did not specify, how a drug to suppress only COX-2 might be developed to relieve arthritis pain without causing the stomach problems of existing pain relievers. When the Rochester patent was issued in 2000, Celebrex, the first of sev-eral COX-2 inhibitors, had already been on the market for a year and had annual sales of $3 billion. The university immediately filed an infringe-ment suit, asking for royalties that would have ultimately totaled billions of dollars. Explained Rochester's combative president, Thomas H. Jackson, who had taught business law at Stanford, "universities aren't looked upon as groups that can fight, [but] it's the right thing to do." Rightness for Jackson meant defending higher education's ability to patent fundamental discoveries—"the kind of work that higher education institutions do."[84] With trustee approval he assembled an eight-figure war chest to battle the giants of the drug industry, in this case Pharmacia-Pfizer. However, in 2003 a U.S. District Court judge threw out the university's claims. The Rochester patent, he explained, constituted a plan or first step toward developing a drug, but did not specify or test any specific compounds. President Jackson soldiered on, claiming to uphold the rights of research universities to have basic research discoveries protected by patent law. But the usually sympathetic Court of Appeals of the Federal Circuit agreed with the district court, and the Supreme Court refused to consider the case.[85] In retrospect, the university was seeking an enormous payoff for a legitimate scientific discovery, but one quite anterior to the actual development of COX-2–inhibiting compounds. As for principle, the rights the university ostensibly championed would have moved academic patenting further in the direction of an anticommons gridlock.

Possibly the most interesting case of overreach may not be resolved for years. The Wisconsin Alumni Research Foundation has been issued patents giving it the "legal right to exclude everyone else in the United States from making, using, selling, offering for sale, or importing any [human or primate embryonic stem] cells." The patents themselves seem to confirm accusations of shoddy work by the patent office. The "discovery" of reproducible stem cell lines paralleled widespread work in this field and, if not "obvious" as some contend, was certainly no breakthrough. WARF submitted four applications for essentially the same discovery: two were rejected and one was erroneously issued, while the fourth sailed through. On this basis, WARF has sought to control (and profit from) the entire technology platform for human embryonic stem cells. To justify its management of this field, it invokes the future benefits of scientific breakthroughs and cures for debilitating diseases. However, others have charged that WARF's terms for using stem cells have actually retarded research, discouraging small companies with high fees and pushing other companies to do research offshore (the patents are only recognized in the United States). Besides the high fees charged to industry, the most controversial feature was the requirement that other universities sign licensing agreements in order to conduct stem cell research. The issue in both cases is reach-through rights: WARF apparently sought royalties on any product developed with the use of human or primate embryonic stem cells. Since 2006, under pressure from NIH and widespread criticism, WARF has scaled back its demands. This apparent moderation seems intended to preserve, above all, the validity of its patents and future claims to reach-through royalties. Once again, a university attempt to garner huge payoffs runs counter to the public interest (which WARF, ironically, has always claimed to uphold). In April 2007, the patent office issued a preliminary ruling invalidating the patents, but a subsequent court decision restored them. Litigation seems destined to continue.[86]

The revenue model that dominates TTOs cannot be blamed for all embarrassing, unacademic actions. However, it is clearly implicated in the dysfunctional aspects of the current patenting regime—namely, obstructing some forms of technology transfer, threatening to impede scientific progress, and encouraging university greed. But these symptoms are not easily altered precisely because current practice works so well in other respects. Hence, one must look within TTOs to grasp the inner logic of what they do.

## The Spirit of Bayh-Dole

According to one licensing officer, the mission of TTOs is defined by "the spirit of Bayh-Dole."[87] By that he meant the effort to move technology created in university laboratories out into practical application in the world of industry. Most TTOs explicitly embrace this mission, even though it represents the ultimate result of their work rather than their daily activities: TTOs basically advance a technology to the point of licensing, but only the licensee can develop and market real products. Still, this definition of mission conditions the outlook of TTOs.

The spirit of Bayh-Dole in fact represents the ideology of TTOs—a transcendent set of ideas that link their work with the public good. This spirit is consciously cultivated by the AUTM, which has allocated a section of its Web site to Bayh-Dole and frequently invokes it in publications. According to one offering, the Bayh-Dole Act transformed university-industry relations "into a Congressionally-mandated partnership, intended to advance technology and benefit the public," and thus created for universities "an implied duty to commercialize."[88] The imperative may be exaggerated here, but it is not inaccurate. The Bayh-Dole University and Small Business Patent Protection Act of 1980 was an important adjustment of patenting law and the foundation for a uniform policy governing federally financed research. It was also another chapter in the perpetual jockeying over patent rights. Enacted at the height of concern over lagging U.S. economic competitiveness, it was explicitly intended to mobilize the fruits of university research for economic development and to make these fruits more accessible to small businesses. The act required, among other things, that universities file U.S. patent applications on discoveries made with federal research funds and actively seek to commercialize them. Universities also had to share resulting income with inventors and devote the balance to research and educational purposes.[89] These obligations became the implicit charter of TTOs, their institutional raison d'être and their social mission. TTO directors and licensing officers do not regard their work as part of an alien world of commerce; transferring technology is a mandated mission of the university.

When the goal of tech transfer is thus defined as getting technology out the door and into the economy, it conditions how licensing officers approach their various tasks. Although many licenses may be negotiated, relatively few result in a developed product. Only those few produce royalties on their sales, or in the case of start-ups, create value in their equity. From this perspective, revenue generation is not the end purpose for a licensing officer, it is the validation that she is contributing to the social good— fulfilling the spirit of Bayh-Dole. Of course, one of the duties of officers is to structure licensing deals so as to create the kind of incentives that will lead to royalties. The inflexibility that is often complained of partly reflects the dictates of this process.

When viewed in terms of downstream products, university TTOs do not appear very productive.[90] The average licensing officer at a major research university in 2004 would have handled 24 disclosures, 20 patent applications, and fewer than 7 licenses. The picture is even bleaker if one considers how few inventions eventually become revenue-producing products. These figures indicate that much of the effort of licensing officers goes into technologies that will never escape the laboratory and never fulfill the Bayh-Dole goal. TTOs in fact provide a variety of services by coaching and advising university inventors, actual or hopeful. One can see why TTOs might be hardheaded about demanding fees to recover some of the costs of this predominantly unfruitful activity.

Nonetheless, the general consensus in the profession is that the average university TTO is understaffed, underfunded, and underappreciated. Since the early 1990s, the number of TTO employees has increased steadily, both in absolute terms and relative to real research expenditures (see Table 4.4). This growth suggests a persistent effort to bridge the gap between staffing and workload. The root of the problem is that only a minority of TTOs are financially self-supporting. The expectation that they should be is more often implicit than budgetary. Most TTOs are supported from several revenue sources, which are not always consistently reported, making it difficult to determine whether or not they are "profitable."

A number of universities have established research foundations that receive licensing revenues and serve as a kind of endowment for the TTO, as well as other purposes. The Wisconsin Alumni Research Foundation, founded in 1925, is the granddaddy of these and the envy of other universities. With an endowment of $1.6 billion, it serves as the university's TTO and provides millions of dollars to the university each year not only for research-related purposes but also for special initiatives.[91] The presence of a research foundation as intermediary obscures the economics of TTOs.[92] Some universities have also been able to tap into state economic development funds to subsidize their TTOs.[93] As for licensing income, a major portion usually goes to the university, generally for research-related purposes. Thus, a TTO might not cover its costs through its direct share of revenues, but could still be a net asset to the university.

For 2003–2005, about 27 universities averaged more than $10 million per year from licensing income, and with such revenues should have been able to finance a fully staffed TTO. Another 17 universities averaged between $5 million and $10 million, and they too should have been net earners.[94] By way of comparison, almost all of these institutions were among the 80 universities that performed at least $200 million of research in 2005—roughly half of the 158 universities that responded to the 2005 AUTM survey.

No doubt every university would like to be earning $5 million or $10 million or more from technology transfer, but relatively few universities seem willing to increase their investment in TTOs. Nor is it clear that more personnel would produce more income. Technology transfer and economic development are only one component of the mission of most universities, and placing undue emphasis on them would be divisive on many campuses. Nevertheless, as just seen, Caltech and the University of Southern California have taken this step, both rhetorically and financially. Harvard started a process of increased investment in 2005. In the public sector, the University of Florida revamped its TTO in 2000, hiring a new director and tripling its licensing staff. The University of Washington took similar (though smaller) steps beginning in 2003. Both are close to the top earners among public universities, with licensing incomes of $40 million and $29 million, respectively, in 2005. Besides enlarging staff, they have concentrated greater attention on working with industry and launching start-ups.

When TTO directors are asked where they would deploy additional resources, they generally indicate downstream marketing, improving connections with industry. This emphasis is consistent with the spirit of Bayh-Dole, and mirrors the organizational shifts that have actually taken place. The most dynamic TTOs have become increasingly proactive in this area. Setting aside the limited number of exceptional technologies that corporations will readily recognize and license, a great many university inventions must struggle to develop real products, viable business strategies, and market niches if they are to enter the economy at all. In this process, networking with entrepreneurs and venture capitalists provides invaluable guidance. Hence the practices of the Deshpande Center, replicated in USC Stevens and VentureLab. Other universities, including the University of Washington, have sought these kinds of links by establishing advisory boards. The increased emphasis on providing additional services for university start-ups is part of this general trend, although these new units belong to the "technology transfer complex" rather than the licensing office per se. However, university start-ups embody the spirit of Bayh-Dole in its purest form—they represent technologies that would be unlikely to ever reach the economy without determined university efforts to promote commercialization.

The prevailing model of university technology transfer, whether called the revenue model or the spirit of Bayh-Dole, performs well for the life sciences, where patents are strong and royalties the norm; and it appears to be perfecting tactics for launching successful start-up firms. On the other hand, forms of technology transfer that are less readily monetized may suffer from relative neglect and underperformance. The need, or lure, of revenue would seem to determine decisions rather than broader considerations of technology utilization. However, behind this dichotomy or trade-off lies a larger question: does the current organization and structure of TTOs optimize the contribution of research universities to economic activity?

Numerous studies have addressed aspects of this question, largely through quantitative analysis of AUTM and other data. The generality of such findings across institutions and over time is often unclear, particularly since few studies document developments after 2000.[95] A consistent picture nevertheless emerges for several features of TTOs' roles. The rapid growth in patenting and licensing by universities during the period 1991–1996 was characterized by increased productivity from all types of universities, rather than only "catching up" by relatively inefficient institutions. One of the factors invoked to explain this development was "increasingly experienced, knowledgeable and demanding TTOs."[96] Indeed, during these years of rapid expansion and increasing AUTM influence, it would have been odd if TTOs had not become more effective across universities. Nevertheless, it is not clear how long this trend persisted. Other studies have shown that increasing the number of licensing officers produces more university spin-offs and more executed licenses. However, more licenses in these cases were not accompanied by more licensing revenue.[97] Perhaps more telling was the finding that additional disclosures yielded a declining percentage of licenses at the margin, and that those marginal licenses produced fewer royalties.[98] In other words, diminishing returns set in as additional disclosures consisted, on balance, of poorer-quality discoveries.

This conclusion raises the possibility that the activities of TTOs may have a muted impact on the amount of commercially valuable IP generated in a university. The importance of academic quality for all aspects of technology transfer is well established. Quality correlates with numbers and success of spin-offs, and also with revenues from royalties.[99] In the 1990s, academic quality was found to be more significant in engineering, a highly competitive buyer's market, than in the life sciences, where numerous manifestations of biotechnology flourished.[100] This would suggest that quality should have a growing impact over time as fields of commercialization become increasingly competitive, and indeed, this appears to have happened. In the early 1980s, the leaders in commercial activities were somewhat distinct from the academic leaders, but over time the two groups converged. Commercial leaders to some extent levered their resources toward greater academic strength, while noncommercial academic leaders, perhaps more easily, entered and succeeded in commercial activities.[101] Universities avidly pursue academic quality as a fundamental input for teaching and research, but often an incidental contributor to technology transfer. Yet its pervasive significance suggests possible limits to university generation of IP.

An updated and relatively simplified view of the evolution of technology transfer activities is provided in Table 4.4. Basically, from 1992 to 1998 (and certainly before 1992), the commercial output of universities was rising more rapidly than the principal input—research expenditures. Since 1998, however, in spite of the increase in TTO personnel, that has not been the case. Disclosures seem to track research expenditures most closely across this entire period, but they are essentially flat after rising 10 percent in 1992–1998 (all figures corrected for inflation). New patent applications are the one category that continued to rise, perhaps reflecting the output of additional TTO employees. However, the number of patents issued has not kept pace. The most important measures for innovations reaching the economy all reflect relative stagnation. The 2004 rate of licensing is only 20 percent above 1992. Relative licensing revenues are flat with 1998.[102] And, despite the recent efforts to augment university spin-offs, their numbers seem to have peaked.

**Table 4.4** Indicators of University Technology Transfer per $100 Million of Research Expenditures (in 2000 dollars), 1992–2004

| Indicator | 2004 | 2001 | 1998 | 1995 | 1992 |
|---|---|---|---|---|---|
| Research expenditures, millions of 2000 dollars | 33,867 | 26,843 | 22,140 | 18,563 | 14,692 |
| TTO FTEs | 4.87 | 4.69 | 4.2 | 2.76 | 2.82 |
| Licenses | 12 | 12 | 14 | 11 | 10 |
| Licensing revenues, millions of 2000 dollars | 2.9 | 3.15 | 2.9 | 1.7 | 1.4 |
| Disclosures | 44 | 42 | 43 | 39 | 39 |
| New patents filed | 28 | 22 | 19 | 12 | 11 |
| Patents issued | 10 | 12 | 12 | 8 | NA |
| Start-ups | 1.36 | 1.59 | 1.38 | 1.03 | NA |

*Source:* Calculated by authors from Association of University Technology Managers (AUTM) data.

The output of university-generated innovations is affected by the actions of TTOs, the state of the economy, and the supply of university discoveries. Regarding TTOs, the rising number of employees, their increasing knowledge and experience, the convergence on best practices under the aegis of the AUTM, and the reorganizations and revitalizations noted above all should have served to increase, rather than decrease, the output of technology transfer.

Economic factors may have played some role. The lackluster economic environment from 2001 to 2004 could have had a dampening effect on spin-offs, for example, and might also have inhibited the small technology companies that license most university IP. More generally, industry seemed to have an increasing appetite for university IP in the 1990s and especially through the dot-com boom. Those expansive horizons definitely narrowed after 2000, as indicated by declining corporate spending on university research and restrained R&D budgets in most industries.

Since the supply of university discoveries with commercial potential depends importantly on the amount of research supported in critical areas and the quality of academic researchers, these represent limiting factors. Growth in quality (if it could be measured) is undoubtedly a slow process, probably lagging the increase in research expenditures. The apparent stagnation seen in Table 4.4 may well indicate that university TTOs as a whole are relatively efficient in identifying and processing the most promising discoveries. The rising number of patent filings, coupled with the flat levels of important outputs, suggests that TTOs have reached the point of diminishing returns—expending more effort on less promising technologies.

This picture is quite different from the conventional view of TTOs, which sees them as a growth field, capable of conveying an ever-rising stream of innovations to the nation's economy. The scenario suggested by our evidence is not incompatible with a moderate growth story. However, growth would depend on the gradual expansion of active licenses and start-up companies stemming from the continuing rise in real academic research expenditures, especially for science-based technologies; a slow augmentation of talent and expertise (quality) in those critical fields; and possibly the adoption by relatively inefficient TTOs of more effective techniques for facilitating the licensing of IP.

Several implications follow from this scenario. First, TTOs will continue to fulfill and deepen the role they have come to play under the strong-patent, life sciences paradigm. Continuity here is due to a process known in the social sciences as "path dependency," meaning that the organizational features created at the beginning of a development serve to shape its future path. Path dependency is particularly powerful when organizations achieve early success. For TTOs, the original features of university patenting were confirmed first by the mandate of Bayh-Dole and then set in concrete by biotechnology and the subsequent success of the patenting leaders. But this endeavor has now become a "mature industry"—one that can expect to grow with its sector of the economy, not outpace it. Hence, the second implication: universities should probably not harbor grandiose expectations for their TTOs to bring new riches to the institution or revitalize tired economies. They most likely will continue to transfer technologies effectively in strong-patent fields, and may yet achieve the occasional windfall. Their continued focus on these tasks points to the third implication: university efforts to improve patenting and licensing are not likely to address the weaknesses of university technology transfer identified above. For universities to optimize their contribution to economic activity, to increase the volume of technology transfer rather than the income, they will have to find ways to circumvent the path now dominated by TTOs and enhance other channels for cooperating with industry, especially with large, technology-based corporations.

CHAPTER **5**

# Economic Relevance and the Academic Core

The incentives for universities to embrace economic relevance are substantial. Relationships with industry are a source of funds and ideas, as described in Chapter 2. Connections with state and local economic development agendas bring financial and political support, as shown in Chapter 3. Commercializing intellectual property contributes to industrial innovation and carries the seductive hope of financial payoffs, as discussed in Chapter 4. This chapter examines implications of the rise of economic relevance for the academic core of the university.

The combined pursuit of prestige and resources drives university strategies to exploit economic relevance. From the perspective of universities, intellectual leadership in the science-based technologies allows them to claim tangible contributions to the economy through scientific breakthroughs and discoveries, without the intellectual trade-offs historically associated with applied research and technical assistance to industry. Instead, achieving prominence in those fields brings both resources and prestige to the university. Still, university organizational structures were created around the traditional model of discipline-based, small-scale investigation. Universities have therefore pursued several strategies to unleash scientific collaborations across the traditional academic structure, to partner with industry, and to contribute to their regions' economies while strengthening their knowledge assets. In particular, they have devised new organizations to accommodate the interdisciplinary nature of science-based technologies; they have sought to create large research organizations in fields with significant external support; and they have developed novel strategies for the appointment of new faculty in order to build strength in strategic subjects. To appreciate the significance of these changes, one needs to understand the underlying tensions between the departments—

156

the basic academic units of universities—and the new interdisciplinary research organizations.

## Universities and the Organization of Research

The academic department is the basic organizational unit in the American university, responsible for organizing and instructing courses and certifying grades and credits. Departments operate quite autonomously, and their members are closely connected to their respective national and international disciplinary communities. Departments exert primary control over faculty recruitment and evaluation, degree programs and curricula, and graduate student admissions. They place highest value on faculty and students who are accomplished or promising in terms of research. Scholarly publication and research funding are the standard measures of competence and promise, and both are subjected to the rigors of peer review. Once in the department, promotion and tenure also depend on research productivity, and thus indirectly on external peer assessments. Evaluation processes for promotion and tenure entail additional consultation with experts in the field, who judge the value of an academic's intellectual contributions. Departments thus sanction and reward faculty productivity that relates to research expectations in the field, and academic scientists have strong incentives to remain attuned to their disciplines. The reputation of departments depends on the collective eminence of their faculty. The opinions of disciplinary experts about the quality of departments are frequently surveyed in assessments ranging from the respected National Research Council's ratings of doctoral programs to the often disparaged but widely noticed rankings of *U.S. News & World Report.* Insofar as those assessments influence perceptions of quality, departments may criticize but still publicize their standing, as do universities. Thus, through their control of faculty recruitment and evaluation, departments shape the nature of the research performed on university campuses. Because departments are oriented toward the academic disciplines, important personnel decisions are made according to the norms and standards of these external scholarly communities.

Besides employing similar kinds of scientists and scholars, departments come to look alike in the education they give to students. Faculty members with roughly the same kind of training, who share assumptions about how students ought to be educated, ensure some homogenization in departmental practices. There are shared understandings among chemists, for instance, regarding the fundamentals of chemistry research, its important subfields, and the expectations for graduate training. Chemistry departments reflect those disciplinary understandings. The success of PhD graduates in the academic labor market is also important. Novice researchers are trained and socialized into the norms of the discipline, and they carry those forward as they move to academic employment.[1] Thus, departments come to embody the norms of their disciplines by designing the curriculum to match standard expectations for the training of students, by focusing on research areas of recognized importance, and by recruiting faculty accordingly.

This arrangement whereby university departments embody the intellectual orientation of academic disciplines was institutionalized in the late nineteenth century. The implications of these early developments in American universities were profound and lasting. Ever since, departments have been the building blocks of university teaching and research. Each university clusters the same basic types of departments in the several disciplines within similar types of colleges and schools. The external components of this arrangement are the academic disciplines with their professional associations, conferences, and journals.

The close link between departments and disciplines early in the rise of the research university contributed to the strengthening of disciplines in American science. On university campuses, instructional revenues supported departments and generated employment for the growing number of trained academics. Moreover, the relatively large number of universities pursuing research in the United States assured the development of a critical mass of researchers in the various disciplines. A national academic labor market emerged. Departments recruited faculty on the basis of research achievements, as faculty communicated nationally with their peers in the same fields. This relationship between disciplines and departments was partly the product of the organizational features of American universities. Departments allowed for junior and senior faculty alike to pursue their research interests autonomously. In other major scientific powers such as Germany and France, chaired professors controlled the research agenda and the careers of their younger colleagues, and PhD training was not as standardized. Significantly, academic disciplines were not as strong in those countries well into the twentieth century.[2]

The strengths of this arrangement are well known. The number of recognized disciplines and fields of study has grown substantially over the past century, and the volume of academic research has increased at an accelerating pace.[3] The specialization of disciplines has allowed researchers to probe increasingly esoteric subjects in greater depth. The reliance on peer review in research funding and publication decisions upholds intellectual rigor and rewards the best science, a notion that is occasionally questioned but rarely attacked directly.[4] Disciplines evolve over time, new ones are created, and others merge to originate new hybrid fields. Biochemistry and bioengineering each emerged at a particular historical juncture, shaped by internal and external developments. They reflect a different type of specialization, as compared to their predecessors.

The apparent uniformity of departments does not obscure the underlying intellectual diversity and fragmentation within those units. Scientists and scholars specialize in subfields and find their particular niches in the ecology of knowledge. Colleagues in a department may seldom interact, attending different professional conferences and reading different journals. Each department brings together specialized researchers performing different kinds of work under the broad umbrella of the discipline. Hence, the basic intellectual units of the university are the research groups, labs, and networks that link faculty members with similar specialized interests.[5]

Some limitations of the discipline-department nexus are also well known. The specialization and disciplinary orientation of academic departments create separate communities of researchers and students that may barely communicate on campuses, even when this would be appropriate or desirable. This feature of university organization has long attracted the criticism that academic research is fragmented and excessively specialized. The emphasis on disciplinary standards to judge research quality and merit has historically created barriers for interdisciplinary work or other research activities not considered important and prestigious within disciplines. In addition, university policies, organizational structures, and administrative practices have reinforced the isolation of academic units and the preference for discipline-based research. Universities' operating budgets and other resources such as space and faculty positions normally flow through colleges and departments, and it is often hard to support research that cuts across or falls between academic units. Faculty seeking to collaborate with colleagues in other schools or outside academia may find no institutional support, or outright disincentives, to do so. Colleges and departments themselves typically have little incentive to support and reward such activities, since traditional forms of funding and recognition come from performing well within the respective fields of study. Moreover, as knowledge advances, schools and departments may not keep pace with developments in adjacent fields. Hence, the disciplinary basis of academic structures facilitates a fruitful specialization in the creation and dissemination of knowledge, but also has its drawbacks.[6]

Thus, a constant challenge in universities is to accommodate the evolutionary dynamics of the academic disciplines in organizational structures appropriate for the conduct of the underlying research. Large-scale organizational change in universities is rare, as it demands much effort and resources. Martin Trow documented the reorganization of biology at UC Berkeley in the 1980s, undertaken in reaction to the slipping competitiveness of the university in this field. Crucial to the effort was the realization that university divisions and departments reflected an outdated version of biology. Such was the complexity of Berkeley's reforms that Trow estimated they took two decades to complete.[7]

The rise of the innovation imperative in science policy has fostered debate on the place of interdisciplinarity and problem-oriented research in academia since at least the 1980s. Federal agencies, professional societies, scientific associations, and universities themselves have asserted the desirability of more research collaboration across fields. In this debate, schools and departments are often characterized as "silos," reflecting their isolation and inward disciplinary orientation. However, research areas such as stem cells, nanotechnology, and the environment all require expertise from multiple disciplines. Such a critique often arises when universities themselves find traditional practices and structures to be an obstacle to organizing research and education in emerging fields. Universities thus face the problem of reorienting research directions toward large problems with high potential impact. Industry too supports efforts to redirect academic research from the theoretical perspectives of disciplines to real-world problems.[8]

For decades universities have created research centers and institutes to address real-world problems and the interests of sponsors. Federal agencies, state governments, private foundations, and industry have contributed to this trend.[9] Besides meeting the needs of research sponsors, centers are created to accommodate faculty interests and to handle external funding. They have been a common solution to the problem of organizing research across departments and schools. Despite their proliferation since World War II, centers are often regarded as auxiliary or peripheral units. Because they do not normally control faculty appointments and degree programs, they depend on schools and departments for those crucial tasks. Centers typically rely on departmental faculty and their graduate students to carry out research. In some fields, centers may be able to support a full-time staff of nonfaculty investigators to help conduct research projects and operate facilities and equipment.[10] Analysts have long expected that the university response to external demands for innovation would elevate the importance of interdisciplinary centers,[11] but there are wide variations across fields. For example, centers have a huge organizational and financial imprint in the biomedical sciences, where research is increasingly interdisciplinary and the National Institutes of Health (NIH) provides substantial funding for center-based infrastructure and research.[12] There are also differences among universities in the relative importance of centers on campus.

University-industry centers are an important element in the relationship between universities and corporate R&D.[13] Units such as the Center for Integrated Systems at Stanford University were established to make university-industry connections "more intimate and more effective."[14] This center, like many of its kind, allows firms to join an advisory board and participate in the discussion of the unit's overall research agenda. While academic research informs corporate R&D in many formal and informal ways, centers create a structure for a range of interactions. MIT's entrepreneurialism, for example, has been attributed in part to the tradition of organizing large interdisciplinary labs.[15]

The overlaying of centers on top of academic units forms a matrix structure. Matrix structures were popularized in industry in the 1970s as firms sought to create flexible work teams to focus on the development of a project or product by drawing on professionals from multiple functional departments (e.g., marketing, engineering, R&D). Matrix structures were viewed as a way to redress the separation among traditional departments that slowed the reaction of firms to changing circumstances as their competitive environments became more complex. Problem-oriented teams were formed, cutting across the traditional divisions to focus on large and complex tasks and respond more quickly to the needs of customers. This approach enjoyed a period of popularity and then fell into obscurity, as accounts of problems and complexities of organizational matrices overshadowed the initial promise. Confusing reporting relationships and turf battles between units in the matrix were frequent, and top management had to deal with power conflicts resulting from overlapping authority and the different priorities of functional and project units.[16]

Universities know those difficulties as well: centers and institutes often find it hard to develop long-term research programs when they depend on the voluntary cooperation of academic departments, and when institutional policies and reward systems reinforce the centrality of departments and discipline-based research. Scientists whose activities in centers are not well known and esteemed by colleagues in their departments find prestige and promotion at risk. Center directors usually count on the resources they control to entice department-based faculty to participate in their units. However, as major decisions regarding the evaluation, promotion, and tenure of academic scientists take place in departments, centers have little power over their collaborators. That situation is well described by one center director as "having some carrots and no sticks."[17]

Thus, universities balance the disciplinary orientation of academic departments with the problem-oriented, boundary-crossing emphasis of centers. Nonetheless, academic disciplines continue to be the reference points for scientific careers and institutional reputations. Professional journals and funding agencies traditionally rely on discipline-based peer review to evaluate research, despite the ongoing attempts of the latter to create interdisciplinary panels. Universities, always thirsty for greater eminence, rely on the judgments of external disciplinary experts about the excellence of their PhD-granting departments to gain national and international recognition. On the other hand, universities pursue funding and meet the needs of research sponsors through a wide array of centers. Centers also allow for some experimentation in emerging research fields, as resources can be aggregated temporarily and redistributed across the campus if expectations do not materialize.

The evolution of science-based technologies has challenged the organizational capacity of universities. Universities want to move quickly and adaptively into these booming scientific fields. Federal agencies have emphasized large-scale research programs and interdisciplinary collaboration, and traditional schools and departments have served them poorly. Hence, a common thread has connected university initiatives in fields such as biotechnology, genomics, proteomics, information technology, and nanotechnology, not to mention the fledgling area of bioenergy. They all have required universities to tinker with existing academic structures and create new ones that can facilitate the multidisciplinary collaborations regarded as crucial for knowledge advancement. Even where a department is identified with these fields, the total campus efforts in these areas transcend the confines of a single unit. For example, Cornell has long had a computer science department, but it recently created the new Faculty of Computing and Information Science involving other departments and programs in related areas. Likewise, Penn State has a department of materials science and engineering, but its Materials Research Institute involves 15 departments in five colleges. Structures such as these add density to the university matrix, by creating new nodes of scientific activity that cut across academic divisions, schools, and departments.

These developments are paramount for the future of innovation. Science-based technologies draw on theories and methods from more traditional basic disciplines, which are also more removed from potential applications. Whether particular innovations start with or cause fundamental investigation, future technologies depend on deepening the knowledge base. "Generic research" performed by universities, as discussed in Chapter 2, is a key input for corporate innovation. Moreover, by enabling long-range research and graduate training in emerging areas of expertise, universities promise a steady flow of highly skilled scientists who excel in those fields. The next section examines how leading universities have advanced initiatives involving science-based technologies. Elite (and wealthy) universities can make major commitments in science-based technologies both to retain their intellectual leadership and to further economic relevance.

## Initiatives in Science-Based Technologies

In 2004 Harvard University conducted an extended inquiry into future trends in science and technology and Harvard's ability to retain intellectual leadership. A task force of faculty from the schools of arts and sciences, medicine, and public health concluded that a substantial increase in facilities and programs was essential and could be addressed by devoting the new campus at Allston to collaborative science. The task force consulted with faculty and visited research institutions in the United States and abroad. When asked about conditions necessary for future success in science, members of the Harvard faculty stressed "multi-disciplinary research, the value of the educational aspect of the mission, and the relationship between commercial activities and scientific research."[18]

Interestingly, the task force did not suggest the creation of new academic units, or the development of new steeples of excellence within the Harvard schools. Instead, it identified 13 "multidisciplinary initiatives" to be developed on the new campus, mostly in or involving science-based technologies.[19] When these initiatives will flourish is still uncertain, but Harvard has determined the need for and direction of change. In 2006, Harvard's planning committee for science and engineering assessed the university's ability to organize collaborative research and education programs in key scientific areas. The committee's report condemned the decentralized organizational model of the university. It highlighted the weakness of an academic structure built around departments:

> Many faculty members find it difficult to conduct interdisciplinary research or establish new educational programs, especially across school and departmental boundaries. Support for cross-departmental initiatives is ad hoc, joint appointments are challenging and time-consuming, and cross-school grant administration and protocols are not standardized. . . . [Moreover,] science and engineering resource and space planning is largely done within the departmental and school structures, hindering the University's ability to make overall decisions about investments in its research portfolio. . . . [T]here are no clear processes for launching or supporting interdepartmental initiatives. . . . [W]e would benefit from a structure where faculty could propose new activities in response to emerging opportunities and have their proposals evaluated in a predictable way.

The report also pointed out that the problems affected education as well as research; professors outside the faculty of arts and science were not encouraged to teach undergraduates, "despite the strong interest some have in doing so."[20]

The committee's report included recommendations for new programs, structures, and governance mechanisms. Following one of the recommendations, Harvard established a university-wide standing committee on science and engineering early in 2007, involving administrators and faculty from several schools. With an initial $50 million, the committee will plan investments in collaborative and interdisciplinary programs and shared research infrastructure, and work on policy changes to facilitate the governance of new crosscutting organizations emerging from these efforts. Other proposed changes involve the creation of cross-school departments, new processes to elicit and fund faculty initiatives, and the recognition in university policies of several different organizational models for interdisciplinary programs.[21]

The funding required to meet the identified needs for faculty, infrastructure, and programs is substantial, and will involve the commitment of central university resources and external support from philanthropy and industry. The report suggests that Harvard "will have to do better in the generation of subsidiary income from the commercialization of technology and intellectual property, from co-development and real estate activities undertaken with the private sector, from grants, gifts, contracts and other forms of partnership with the private sector, and from . . . sponsored funding." The usual disclaimers apply: "All of these avenues have challenges; all can be misused to the detriment of the scholarly University mission," but the potential rewards are great, since "all have the potential to support innovation and speed the transition of new scientific knowledge into public good, new therapeutics, and economic development for this region."[22]

If anything, Harvard's analytical exercise is recognition that the traditional organizational model of single-investigator science within established disciplines creates disincentives for the kinds of research now deemed essential. Moreover, the old model cannot accommodate the prompt exploitation of emerging areas of science that involve collaborations across academic units. Such activities usually depend on faculty working across organizational boundaries, on sponsors encouraging new forms of research organization, and on support from the university administration for centers, institutes, and other crosscutting structures. Harvard has also recognized the relationship among academic research, intellectual property (IP), and innovation in the current era.

Harvard is by no means exceptional in these ambitions. This chapter discusses how universities have sought to combine these ingredients through campus efforts to boost research in science-based technologies. Some university initiatives involve direct linkages with firms, the expectation that IP will be generated, and provisions for commercialization. Others are more removed from these outcomes, but still anticipate that innovation will flow from scientific discoveries in relevant areas. The universities' efforts discussed here have attempted to correct the lack of institutional channels for allocating resources to areas of research that span conventional disciplinary and departmental boundaries. They have also aimed to avoid the creation of the isolated, self-contained research institutes so common in previous missions of technology transfer discussed in Chapter 1. Fostering interdepartmental collaboration is key in these efforts to pull together various academic and research units to exploit hybrid research areas. Often coupled to the idea of fostering innovative research approaches and interdisciplinarity, they are not exclusive to science and technology, though financial commitments to the social sciences and the humanities are relatively minor in comparison.

Universities naturally vary in the scope of initiatives involved, organizational approaches taken, and level of resources invested in addressing these priorities. Duke and Stanford illustrate the trends among elite private universities, both having the wherewithal to make major financial commitments. While each university followed a distinctive trajectory, they shared similar underlying objectives. Their efforts reflect the pursuit of excellence above and beyond the established academic disciplines, an attempt to organize ambitious scientific programs dependent on cross-disciplinary collaborations, and large investments in science-based technologies.

In the late 1990s, Duke's administration realized that organizational obstacles and structural disincentives remained for interschool collaboration, despite the university's long tradition of innovative programs and identification with interdisciplinarity. Provost Peter Lange, appointed in 1999, made interdisciplinary collaboration a top priority. In 2000, Duke engaged in a major strategic planning exercise. In the words of a senior administrator, the university had previously had strategic documents, "but there'd never been an exercise, a big exercise" like the one leading to the 2001 plan, *Building on Excellence.*[23] Presenting detailed analysis, explicit goals, and implementation strategies, the plan unveiled 13 new initiatives that received over $90 million to cover programmatic costs alone.[24] Six of the initiatives clearly involved science-based technologies—and commanded the largest investments.[25] The senior leadership of the university viewed these initiatives as a way of facilitating the flow of faculty between traditional units and innovative research programs, building an "interconnected matrix structure of intellectual life."[26]

Genomics was a major target of Duke's strategic exercise. At the turn of the century, Duke feared it was falling behind in this mushrooming field. The university decided to carve its own niche by creating the Institute for Genome Sciences and Policy with $55 million in start-up funds. A director was hired in 2002 with carte blanche to shape the organization. The institute was devised as a "school without walls," to tap the expertise of several Duke schools. Previously existing research centers were reorganized under the institute's umbrella, and seven new ones were created.[27] The institute has helped to recruit about 25 faculty members, who have a departmental tenure home. Twenty other faculty members also participate in its activities. Building partnerships with departments is thus crucial for the institute's development. It aspires to leadership in "both genome discovery and the translation of those discoveries into useful advances for society."[28]

Ventures such as the Institute for Genome Sciences and Policy enable scientific research of a scope and kind that could hardly emerge spontaneously. The institute's research program in genomic medicine, for example, involves scientists from several units with expertise in biomedicine, engineering, health economics and policy, statistics, and information science. The commercial potential of discoveries in research areas such as cancer and cardiovascular genomics is unmistakable. Recognizing this potential, an "entrepreneur-in-residence" program was created to encourage scientists to consider the commercial potential of discoveries and the appropriate innovation track to pursue.

The unit adds also to the provision of interdisciplinary education for Duke students. Courses, summer fellowships, and research opportunities in institute labs have been offered to undergraduates, and an undergraduate program in genome sciences and policy is planned. The existing Duke PhD program in genetics and genomics is associated with the institute, as is a new program in computational biology. The engagement with undergraduate education is viewed as a comparative advantage of the institute over comparable units at other campuses, which focus exclusively on the graduate and postdoctoral levels.[29]

Duke envisions a periodic renewal of these initiatives. Central funds are to provide the basis for the development of new programs and units, but they are expected to find other sources of sustaining revenue inside and outside the university. The notion is to free up resources in the institutional budget to allow for new initiatives at each strategic planning cycle. Of the 13 initiatives created in *Building on Excellence*, only the Institute for Genome Sciences and Policy and the John Hope Franklin Humanities Institute were reendorsed as centrally supported initiatives in Duke's 2006 strategic plan, *Making a Difference*. The university introduced two new "signature initiatives": the Global Health Institute and the Institute for Brain, Mind, Genes, and Behavior.[30]

Enabling and sustaining crosscutting activities requires continual exertion. Resources are a concern, even at this relatively wealthy institution. Fundraising was envisioned to play a part in the sustainability of the Institute for Genome Sciences and Policy, but there are many competing priorities and fundraising strategies have traditionally been school-based. In addition, the centrality of departments and disciplines to academic life also surfaces, despite Duke's reputation for interdisciplinarity. The institute's strategic plan notes that "one often has to rely on creativity, good will and generosity within the academy to address issues such as course approval by disciplinary committees, balanced teaching loads between disciplinary and interdisciplinary units, credit for obtaining research funding, annual salary increases, promotion and tenure decisions, and assignment of space."[31]

Duke has sought to foster organizational and scientific innovation through systematic planning and funding mechanisms. By creating incentives for new units to emerge, evolve, and seek integration with schools and departments, Duke can cyclically redirect institutional resources into new and emergent areas. These efforts are portrayed as crucial elements in Duke's institutional aspirations, which it describes as "targeted not towards rankings but rather towards achieving a place of real leadership based on substantive contributions to society."[32] This is markedly different from the traditional path of university growth by accretion, slowly adding new academic units that reflect the expansion of scientific fields. The emphasis of the new Duke units is not on creating narrowly defined research and instructional programs within new academic silos, but on sparking transformations in how research is conducted and students are taught.

At Stanford, strategic initiatives evolved gradually from the bottom up. Four major "multidisciplinary initiatives"—in human health, environment and sustainability, international studies, and the arts and humanities—have emerged organically since the 1990s, each at a different time and for a different reason. After faculty formed interschool collaborations, they were endorsed and supported by the administration. President John L. Hennessy alerted the university community that "a comprehensive effort to increase the resources we devote to multidisciplinary research and teaching creates several challenges and pitfalls. Some of the most significant challenges arise from a disconnect between interdisciplinary initiatives and the existing structure of schools and departments." He then stated emphatically, "the Provost, the Deans, and I . . . are determined that institutional barriers will not become stumbling blocks to these initiatives."[33]

The human health initiative, incidentally the initiative with the most salient economic relevance, is by far the most developed of the four. Its roots are in longstanding research collaborations among Stanford faculty members. In the late 1990s, a faculty group approached the central administration and obtained support for a project dubbed Bio-X, intended to foster interdisciplinary interactions involving biology and diverse science and engineering fields. Part of the plan was to build a new facility to foster the linkages among the various academic units and the medical center, thus sparking broader interactions. Thanks to a $90 million gift from former Stanford professor and Silicon Valley entrepreneur James Clark and an anonymous $60 million donation, the university erected the Clark Center in 2003. Located between the main campus and the hospital, the building is designed for collaborative science: 38 faculty members from various disciplines are clustered together in large, open work spaces that accommodate between five and eight labs. Shared equipment and common areas facilitate social interactions among researchers working in the building and elsewhere, and some work spaces were provided for temporary visitors. Bio-X organizes seminars, events, and courses and sponsors graduate fellowships. Around 100 faculty are affiliated with Bio-X.[34] Bio-X and the Clark Center embody the movement of biological and medical science toward greater interdisciplinarity.

Besides fostering research, Bio-X has pursued links with industry in typical Stanford fashion. The Bio-X corporate forum provides a number of benefits to affiliated firms, with the overarching goals of developing relationships and attracting funding for research programs. Member companies participate in annual meetings with the faculty, may participate in Bio-X seminars and events, and enjoy opportunities to interact with scientists, postdocs, and students. They are also kept informed about relevant technologies managed by the Stanford Office of Technology Licensing. Each member firm is assigned a faculty liaison as contact and host on campus visits. Firms that wish to develop close working relations with Bio-X faculty may have researchers spend up to six months in the faculty member's lab, as part of the visiting scholar program. So far, there are 10 corporate affiliates, all large firms in the biotechnology, health care, and medical device industries.[35]

The visibility and philanthropic support that have allowed Bio-X to flourish set the standards for the other multidisciplinary initiatives. Some internal seed support has been provided, but they all rely on external funding to build facilities and programs. The three initiatives are a key element of Stanford's $4.3 billion fundraising campaign launched in late 2006. Of that total amount, $1 billion is targeted to the health, environment, and international initiatives and another $400 million to support multidisciplinary research at large.[36]

Duke and Stanford created formal structures to institutionalize research and educational programs across traditional academic divisions. Both institutions defer to the faculty for intellectual leadership in their research directions, but acknowledge that faculty efforts alone are not sufficient to bring about significant organizational change or to assemble the resources such change requires. Duke in particular has tied the development of new initiatives to its strategic planning cycle, bringing a periodic appraisal of ongoing commitments and new opportunities for major institutional investments. Stanford has designated its multidisciplinary initiatives as campus priorities by making them central components of its capital campaign.

Public universities have created initiatives with similar ambitions but more modest financial commitments. UC Berkeley and Penn State, for example, have taken different approaches to building expertise across departmental lines.

In 2001 UC Berkeley requested ideas from the faculty for new boundary-crossing programs, as part of its strategic planning process. These were clustered into themes, and full proposals were solicited. Berkeley's approach was heavily collegial, with participative decision-making processes: 10 campus meetings provided faculty input between the first call for ideas and the last review of proposed initiatives.[37]

As a result of this effort, 21 full-time-equivalent faculty positions were allocated to new programs in computational biology (7), nanosciences (7), new media (2), and regional and metropolitan studies (5). Investments in computational biology involved creating new undergraduate and graduate specializations, because "individual departments are unwilling to make a significant change in faculty hiring to develop the critical mass necessary for a graduate program and to change the focus of undergraduate education in the biological sciences." Faculty members are recruited into the new Center for Computational Biology, with teaching duties and tenure homes in appropriate academic departments. The nanosciences initiative has unmistakably followed the path of economic relevance. The new Berkeley Nanosciences and Nanoengineering Institute links researchers and students in physics, chemistry, biology, and engineering, as well as the Lawrence Berkeley National Laboratory. As in computational biology, students from several PhD programs can join the institute's specialization in nanotechnology. Commercialization of nanotechnologies is also an explicit goal. In addition to working with start-up and large nanotechnology companies, the institute sponsors a certificate program in technology management with the engineering and business schools, where students learn the technical and managerial skills to design high-tech products and bring them to market.[38]

At Penn State, the central administration has used internal cost savings since the late 1990s to fund interdisciplinary institutes in the life sciences, environmental research, and materials research. The institutes help academic departments hire faculty in strategic interdisciplinary areas, and provide infrastructure and seed grants for collaborative research. The largest of these units, the Huck Institute of the Life Sciences, also coordinates interdisciplinary degree programs that operate across colleges, in fields such as ecology, genetics, bioinformatics and genomics, molecular medicine, and neuroscience. Students benefit from the mentorship of faculty in different disciplines, and take courses in multiple departments.

The paths taken by Berkeley and Penn State are not uncommon. During the decade, several universities have relied on redeployment of internal resources to build interdisciplinary centers and programs.[39]

Whether large or small, university pledges to strategic initiatives signify deliberate attempts to harness expertise from multiple disciplines into larger research endeavors. These efforts change the organizational conditions on campus for basic research in key scientific areas. Federal agencies are powerful drivers as they adopt modes of research support that emphasize large-scale research, collaboration, and relevant impacts. Moreover, the new units and programs make sophisticated training opportunities available to graduate students and postdocs. As they experience multidisciplinary approaches to research during their training, these students acquire a richer knowledge base and skill set. Courses, summer fellowships, and research-experience programs for undergraduates have also proliferated. A bonus of sorts, these programs give students the experience of operating in the team-based and inherently multidisciplinary environment of industrial R&D.

Economically relevant discoveries are inherent possibilities in the science-based technologies that are the focus of these university initiatives. Harvard's somewhat tardy embrace of economic relevance is perhaps the ultimate sign of a general acceptance of these trends. As described above, small steps to facilitate technology transfer have been part of these internal efforts. But universities, particularly public and land-grant institutions, have also sought to compete in cutting-edge fields of research by garnering support from states and industry. The results of these partnerships are more outwardly oriented and closely linked to economic development rationales than the initiatives described above.

## Building Research Capacity

Universities seek to improve their relative position in the national competition for prestige and resources by gaining support for a greater economic role. This section examines some of the major academic structures emerging from these efforts. How were such structures built and organized, and how did they change their campuses? Arizona State University and the University at Albany, both considered in relation to state policy in Chapter 3, are returned to here as exemplars of aggressive strategies for economic relevance.

Riding the wave of recent TBED initiatives in Arizona, Arizona State envisions the formation of a "new American university" that connects academic research more closely to regional needs and economic development. Interdisciplinary and boundary-crossing units are components of that vision. The university has benefited from significant state investments for new programs and infrastructure to elevate its stature as a research-intensive institution. The Biodesign Institute is one of Arizona State's biggest bets for the realization of its aspirations. Biodesign links all the threads of the new institutional vision; its mission is to advance innovations "to improve human health and quality of life through use-inspired biosystems research and effective multidisciplinary partnerships."[40]

Lacking a medical school, Arizona State was handicapped in biomedical science. The university started receiving state funds from Proposition 301 in 2000, and a portion was used to support bioscience research. In 2002, the university made a more ambitious commitment. A new institute would build existing strengths in engineering and computer science to exploit strategic areas in the life sciences, with an overall emphasis on "biodesign." The Biodesign Institute involved the construction of a four-building complex totaling over 800,000 square feet of new research space. The university invested $69 million in the first building, inaugurated in 2004. Benefiting from the state research infrastructure bill, Arizona State invested $78.5 million in the second building, opened in early 2006. These facilities not only expanded research space, but have become an asset in the recruitment and retention of scientists.

The institute aims at quickly expanding Arizona State's sponsored research by tapping the huge biomedical research market. The high expectations of returns are reflected in the institute's entrepreneurial management style. Biodesign has aggressive goals for increasing sponsored research: 25

percent annual increases in research funding, 20 percent annual increases in industrial partnerships, and a doubling of its research capacity in five years. The institute has actively helped hire tenure-track faculty by providing start-up funding and salaries. It has a tightly managed infrastructure and a clear focus on areas leading to industrial and clinical applications. An administrative staff of almost 50 manages Biodesign's complex operations. The institute's research takes place in 10 centers, distributed in contiguous laboratory spaces to facilitate interdisciplinary interactions.[41] Space is allocated through a "real estate" model, whereby faculty must attract external funding in proportion to the laboratory space requested. The key requirement for faculty participation and residence in the institute facilities is productivity.

Biodesign concentrated university resources in a field with high prospects of economically relevant research. Consistent with its mission to advance innovation, the institute actively pursues technology transfer. Given its sheer size—about 500 people work at the institute, which has an operating budget of around $60 million—Biodesign can hardly be regarded as a peripheral enterprise at Arizona State. Not surprisingly, Biodesign is presented in Arizona State strategic documents along with colleges and schools as a major unit on the Tempe campus and praised as an "exemplar project."[42]

Such major research centers tend to emerge in the life sciences, given the size of the research market, the high cost for research, and the interdisciplinary modes of work that characterize the field. Universities have had to significantly upgrade facilities and infrastructure to compete in this area.[43] Like Arizona State, Rensselaer Polytechnic Institute (RPI) has erected the Center for Biotechnology and Interdisciplinary Studies with state support, and expects that the center will boost research productivity and economic relevance. The RPI center builds upon a similar triad of engineering, information sciences, and the life sciences to seek biomedical discoveries.[44] The Life Sciences Institute of the University of Michigan, initiated after the state committed tobacco settlement funds to creating a life sciences corridor in 1999, was inaugurated in 2003 and is already regarded as "a centerpiece of [the] campus." It has cohired 25 jointly appointed faculty to occupy the facility.[45]

Cornell refers to its Life Sciences Technology Building as "the most ambitious scientific research facility ever undertaken" by the university, which will help bring about the "21st century vision of Cornell." State support also contributed to this facility. Interestingly, the building will house the

Innovation Development and Economic Application Center (IDEA Center), a unit dedicated to supporting start-up companies and the commercialization of technologies. These academic structures are internalizing the logic of the life sciences paradigm of innovation. Given the importance of discoveries arising from basic science for both large firms and start-up activity, the close association of research-oriented units to technology transfer reflects the dominant patterns of innovation in the field.[46]

A different pattern is illustrated in the efforts of the University at Albany to build a nanotechnology research and industrial base. Counting on substantial state and corporate support, the university established the nation's first College of Nanoscale Science and Engineering (CNSE) in 2004. In a rather unusual development, the college emerged out of the Albany Nanotech complex. The college is far from a conventional academic unit. It does not have academic departments but rather faculty "constellations" in nanoscience, nanoengineering, nanobioscience, and even "nanoeconomics." It has about 30 faculty members in all.[47] The strategic place of the college within the university is denoted by the vice-presidential appointment held by professor Alain Kaloyeros, the college's "chief administrative officer." Kaloyeros has been the driving force behind the development of nanotechnology in Albany since the early 1990s, and his entrepreneurship has been heftily rewarded. An increase in his salary in 2007 has been described in the media as the biggest salary raise in state history, and his $667,000 remuneration makes him better compensated than most university presidents. The university's acting president seemed unfazed by the unwelcome publicity, and defended Kaloyeros as "one of the main economic drivers for the development of upstate New York." The raise was linked with an increase in economic development duties for Kaloyeros; indeed, his role in attracting SEMATECH International North to Albany has been touted in local publications.[48]

The college's self-styled leadership in the field is predicated upon an infrastructure intended to attract and retain industrial R&D facilities in the region, thanks to $3 billion in state ($500 million) and corporate ($2.5 billion) investment.[49] That infrastructure comprehends a sprawling 450,000-square-foot complex that offers an array of resources to lure industrial partners. Albany Nanotech has four nanofabrication facilities for the design and pilot manufacturing of computer chips, in addition to several research centers, tools, and specialized laboratories. The college and the complex claim to have more than 250 corporate partners, in keeping with their strategy of transcending single relationships with firms. The goal is to pursue partnerships with companies throughout a product's value chain. To this end, corporate labs are located side by side in spaces dedicated to developing the different components that feed into a larger technology platform. The dynamics of cooperation envisioned at the complex are symbolized in a recent $330 million agreement between IBM and Applied Materials to conduct collaborative R&D at Albany Nanotech, including multi-million dollar investments in equipment and 100 researchers.[50]

In sheer numbers, CNSE and Albany Nanotech have a much greater industrial than academic presence. Albany Nanotech houses over 1,350 R&D personnel from multiple multinational electronics corporations. With about 80 percent of total revenues accruing from industry, the college depends on close working relationships with corporate partners and looks to New York State for the relentless upgrading of infrastructure. Expansion programmed for 2008 will enlarge the facilities by 250,000 square feet, allowing another 2,000 industrial scientists and engineers to work there. Identifying and meeting the needs of industry are central to the operations of the complex.[51] However, an extreme orientation to industry may not be conducive to upholding academic standing. The trade magazine *Small Times* noted, "while CNSE stands out in its work with industry, it has been less successful with pure research. As a young institution, the college appears to be still ramping up its faculty and research output."[52]

CNSE clearly defies the traditional academic models, although it is unclear whether this is a temporary strategy or a permanent ethos. Without the commitment to supporting the development of industrial technology, the university would not have gathered the resources it did to build the college. Kaloyeros offered his answer a few years ago, buoyed by the success in recruiting SEMATECH: "students here are going to be able to do their research in some of the most exciting research areas using toys no one else in the world can afford . . . You think at an Ivy League school you're going to get a better education with everything that's going on here?"[53] But to date, the top nanoscale scientists and students appear to favor academic reputation over Albany's toys.

Albany's endeavor to build a nanotechnology cluster epitomizes the policy rationales in vogue at the state level. Furthermore, the extensive partnerships with large corporations represent a different paradigm of innovation, rooted in the materials and electronics industries (see Chapter 2). Albany Nanotech has developed long-range partnerships with large firms in mature industries who are interested in and capable of engaging in R&D efforts that will shape the industry's future. Their internal R&D operations have been attracted to the region by the crucial importance of infrastructure. Attracting these corporate labs pleases the state government for the jobs they create, and they assure Albany of long-standing research relations. Albany's foray into industrial recruitment demonstrates why at many institutions the phrase "and economic development" has been added to the title of vice presidents for research. This was not the case at Albany, but its chief of nanotechnology has entrepreneurially embraced the role.

Another example of wedding a university and an industry is Clemson University's commitment to strengthening the automotive industry in South Carolina. The core structure in Clemson's strategy is the International Center for Automotive Research (ICAR), envisioned as a "true research campus" involving academic and industrial R&D labs. Clemson has established partnerships with BMW, Michelin, and Sun Microsystems for building the center. The relationship with the German auto firm is particularly close, reflecting the state's successful recruitment of extensive manufacturing facilities. BMW will have input into instructional programs, faculty recruitment, and construction projects. A $10 million gift by the automaker has endowed two professorships at the new graduate engineering center, which will offer master's and doctoral programs in automotive engineering. At Clemson's invitation the company provided input into the curriculum of those interdisciplinary programs, which will allow students to learn from a variety of fields that feed into corporate "systems integration."[54] By financing about 85 percent of the projects performed at the center, BMW has ensured that the lion's share of the research will be oriented toward its needs. The state of South Carolina also subsidized the BMW Center for Information Technology Research, which opened in 2005 as the company's dedicated facility for performing systems integration research. The center director has endorsed this relationship, remarking that it is "a new model to invite private interests to partner so aggressively with you."[55]

The extension of industry partnerships into the academic realm of curriculum and education seems to be a growing phenomenon. IBM has developed an instructional program in "service sciences, management, and engineering," which involves fields such as computer science, engineering, operations research, management science, and business. The firm's interest obviously lies in workers whose training is multidisciplinary and oriented toward innovative problem solving. IBM calls service sciences a "new academic discipline," but one that fits quite closely with the company's evolving emphasis on business services. Accordingly, the firm sponsors conferences and agreements with universities that involve the teaching of service sciences. At North Carolina State, IBM employees have codeveloped the curriculum in a services management major and even teach some courses. University administrators have justified these arrangements as a response to the needs of a major employer of NC State graduates. UC Berkeley has also offered a certificate program in IBM's service science, and Arizona State's Carey School of Business has embraced the concept through its Center for Services Leadership, which has launched a Services Science Initiative. Indeed, for IBM, creating an "academic discipline" may be a viable strategy to create the workforce it needs. This initiative seems to have dovetailed with faculty interests in business services and management. This is also the case with Intel's low-key approach to disseminating specialized curricula. The company seeks to collaborate with academic experts to develop curriculum in key technological areas. Intel will disseminate these materials, but seeks no association with a packaged set of courses and programs. Intel's approach is consistent with its "open collaborative research model" for R&D, described in Chapter 2.

Clemson's model resembles NC State's Centennial Campus, where academic and industry buildings are commingled and interaction is the objective. Initially greeted with some skepticism, the Centennial Campus is now regarded so favorably that the university is replicating the model in a second such campus for the life sciences. These long-term partnerships with large firms represent the corporate track for innovation. They also illustrate how large corporations have conveyed their instructional interests to universities, following research relations.

Universities have gone beyond the creation of individual centers and institutes to complement the research roles of colleges and departments. These new academic structures create the organizational conditions for discovery-oriented research and direct links with industry. They are not isolated at the border of the campus, recruiting their own research staff, as were the older generation of applications-oriented research institutes. Rather, these units are interwoven in the academic fabric of their respective universities, drawing on the expertise of faculty from a cross section of schools and departments. Educational programs are also prominent, most notably at the graduate level.

### Targeted Faculty Recruitment

Universities, through the operations of academic departments, are self-replicating machines. Their knowledge and learning outputs are highly conditioned by the system of academic disciplines, their traditions, norms, and preferences. Universities face the challenge of transforming the faculty when radically different fields gain importance in the intellectual and sponsored research markets. Universities' contributions to innovation depend on assembling expertise in critical areas, sometimes spanning conventional organizational units. Outside support can be helpful to build endowed chairs and infrastructure to please talented scientists. But internal commitments are necessary to produce consequential change. Targeted faculty recruitment strategies all invoke interdisciplinarity, and both of these are broader than economic relevance. Different university strategies have achieved different degrees of change in university practices and organization.

Traditional faculty hiring is controlled by colleges and departments, and reflects the priorities of those units. Colleges authorize positions to be filled, often specifying rank and specialty; departmental search committees evaluate candidates and recommend appointments. Their choices are usually ratified, so that the new appointees are selected by departments. Other forces counterbalance this traditional approach. The ongoing needs of academic units to replace departing faculty and expand their size are often in tension with the staffing needs of research units and new university priorities. State economic development programs and engagements in long-term industrial partnerships create the need for faculty with expertise in strategic research specialties. Senior university administrators are always mindful of the hiring and retention of faculty talent, but they are also responsible for formulating institutional priorities, including the personnel needs associated with new and emergent fields. Thus, universities can experience tension between the inertia of existing academic units and their staffing needs, the need to support emerging scientific fields of inquiry, and occasional external opportunities to obtain funding for new faculty lines.

Funding from state economic development programs has allowed universities to pursue targeted faculty recruitment. Such recruitment processes do not start from departmental requests, but stem from the shared interests of universities and partnering organizations. Sometimes, as was the case at Berkeley, interdepartmental committees are created to make decisions about recruitment priorities. Because research drives targeted recruitment, even more weight is placed on the academic's scientific prowess in the selection of candidates. A match with an academic department becomes one step in the recruitment process, as opposed to the primary criterion.

The University of Wisconsin at Madison has made one of the largest efforts of this kind. The university went through a prolonged fiscal drought in the 1990s and lost some 288 faculty positions.[56] Perceiving the receptivity of state officials to the rationale of TBED, UW Madison lobbied the state to support the hiring of additional scientists in biotechnology. This gambit succeeded, and 20 positions were funded in 1997. Subsequently, the university developed a strategy dubbed the "Madison Initiative," consisting of a four-year investment plan involving state and private revenues. UW Madison chancellor David Ward sought $57 million from the state between 1999 and 2003, with a promise to match it with $40 million in philanthropic support. The initiative had four thrusts: hire and retain faculty, enhance student learning through technology, improve financial assistance to needy students, and renovate buildings. Faculty recruitment would be pursued selectively, emphasizing campuswide priorities. Baptized the Cluster Hiring Initiative (CHI), it entailed the creation of 150 faculty lines for the campus, to be allocated competitively to interdisciplinary "clusters" proposed by the faculty.

With matching funds from the Wisconsin Alumni Research Foundation (WARF) and the University of Wisconsin Foundation, the university obtained $5 million from the state toward a total $15 million for cluster hiring. A report justified the initiative as a remedy for the perceived weaknesses of conventional faculty recruitment: "the prevailing academic cultures and structures tend to replicate existing areas of expertise, reward individual effort rather than collaborative work, limit hiring input to a single department within a single school/college, and limit incentives and rewards for interdisciplinary and collaborative work."[57] Four rounds of cluster competitions took place between 1998 and 2001, whereby 143 faculty positions were allocated to 49 clusters. Individual clusters were allowed to request between one and five faculty lines. The first two rounds involved the life sciences, followed by an emphasis on the humanities and social sciences in 1999, and various fields in 2000 and 2001. Cluster hires accounted for between 14 and 20 percent of all newly appointed academics at UW Madison between 1999 and 2004.[58] Recognizing that the clusters fall outside the budgetary structure, the provost's office instituted an annual grant competition in 2002 to provide clusters with modest funds for programmatic expenses.[59]

The UW Madison experiment demonstrates the complexities of recruiting faculty across traditional units. The process of defining clusters evolved over the years, but as it was last conducted in 2001, it started with a call from the provost's office for cluster preproposals. A broadly representative faculty advisory committee evaluated the preproposals. Full proposals were then invited. Approved proposals were assigned a number of faculty positions and a lead dean, who appointed a search committee to conduct recruitment. The committee involved faculty from fields of relevance to the cluster, not particular departments or schools. Search committees had the task of identifying promising candidates who could fulfill the requirements set for the cluster, and matching them with departments. Once a potential match was found, both the search committee and the possible home department had to agree for a job offer to be made. Start-up packages were also negotiated among the graduate school, the college, and the hiring department. Once hired, faculty members become for all academic purposes incorporated in the department, with full salary support from the provost's office. After they are formed, the clusters are completely autonomous. They do not report to anyone on campus, nor are they accountable for whether or not they meet their original goals. The clusters function as informal groupings, whose specific activities vary depending on the faculty involved, the nature of their work, and connections with other ongoing interdisciplinary programs. If a cluster faculty member leaves the university, the faculty position returns to the provost's office and may be allocated elsewhere.[60]

Other universities have adopted their own versions of cluster hiring. Florida State University started an initiative with the same name in 2005 to add 200 new members to its faculty over five years. Like UW Madison, Florida State funds these positions through a mix of state support and fundraising, and elicits new clusters from the faculty. After the first round in 2005–2006, six clusters were approved and 38 faculty hires, including 12 full professors, were authorized.[61] The university focused on STEM fields (science, technology, engineering, and math) in the second round, for recruitment in 2007–2008. Clusters have been created in nanoscience, neuroscience, genotype-phenotype research, and advanced materials, among others. Cluster hiring is viewed as a way to augment research funding and enhance institutional recognition, with a clear preference for fields of economic relevance.[62]

RPI has adopted a strategy to build faculty "constellations" in biotechnology and information technology as part of its ambition to advance as a research-intensive institution. The recruitment of constellations has taken place amid a hiring wave at the institute made possible by a $360 million unrestricted gift received in 2001. Overall, 73 new faculty positions have been added.[63] The notion of building faculty constellations is useful as a fundraising tool for RPI, and it featured prominently in the $1.9 billion 2004–2009 campaign.[64] RPI seeks to attract "stars" in seven focus areas. Interestingly, the areas arose from consultations with leading experts from *outside* RPI, and have clear connections with technological innovation: future chips, multiscale computation, tetherless world, tissue engineering, integrative systems biology, biocomputation and bioinformatics, and biocatalysis and metabolic engineering.[65] Part of the appeal is the economic relevance of the underlying research. RPI president Shirley Ann Jackson explained the aim of the future chips constellation, the recipient of two hires, as "nothing less than transforming many sectors of the economy, including communications, medicine, defense, entertainment, and the environment."[66] The RPI constellations are defined by the administration as interdisciplinary teams with a clear research focus, led by senior scientists together with junior faculty members, postdocs, and graduate students. As in the Wisconsin clusters, faculty hired into the same constellation can have appointments in different departments. By 2007, eight constellation faculty had been recruited.[67] Dependent on fundraising, RPI will likely create new positions slowly, but its approach is the most targeted. Some of the recruited faculty are prolific patent holders and have established relations with firms.

These processes raised both excitement and tensions on their respective campuses. At UW Madison there was dissatisfaction among some academic units with the cluster hiring strategy. Colleges and departments were hoping to replace lost faculty lines when the new model was proposed.[68] At RPI, when the new strategic plan was launched in 2000–2001 with priorities accorded to constellations in biotechnology and information technology, some resentment was felt that the faculty did not have sufficient input into the decision-making process.[69] At Florida State, the concern was raised that cluster hiring could affect the ability of the university to increase salaries of existing faculty.[70] These laments will no doubt recur among existing faculty as senior administrators steer the faculty recruitment process, because such recruitment strategies challenge long-standing notions of departmental sovereignty and breadth of coverage in the disciplines.

In a somewhat different pattern, the University of Southern California announced the "cluster hiring" of a multidisciplinary team of scientists from different institutions by the Wrigley Institute for Environmental Studies. As requested by the university, the scientists organized themselves as a group and applied for the positions together, with a collective research agenda. The selection process emphasized the complementarity in their expertise and their ability to function as a team. While not entirely original, hiring research teams is unique in the primacy accorded to research and to planned collaboration.[71]

Cluster hiring strategies all aim, in varying degrees, to foster interdisciplinary interaction and build concentrated research strength in areas of scientific opportunity. They are a weaker strategy for attaining those goals than the larger structural approaches seen at Duke, Stanford, and ASU, for example. Still, the different versions of cluster hiring represent different levels of commitment to these goals. Except for team hiring, they are essentially gradual approaches that will bring marginal increments of progress toward their goals, but the most telling factor is probably whether they express faculty proclivities or administrative choices. Thus, the Madison cluster hiring is likely to have the most diffuse impact, given its lack of structure, unfocused mandate, and limited degree of administrative oversight. Berkeley managed to achieve somewhat more focus with a similar bottom-up approach, but a much smaller initiative. The other strategies aimed to produce a more definite impact on research. RPI's version of constellations targeted the hiring of scientists with established records of productivity in carefully chosen areas of technological innovation. And when existing clusters of researchers are hired en masse, or in the case of the Georgia Research Alliance–sponsored Eminent Scholars (see Chapter 3), universities know exactly what they are getting.

Like older technology transfer missions, economic relevance has involved adaptations: new research institutes, cross-departmental programs, and outside relations that influence academic work. Part of these adaptations has involved organizing research across traditional disciplines in the science-based technologies. The abundance of federal funding in these areas makes a university presence almost mandatory. Universities do not commit to these areas to peddle intellectual property; rather, their academic standing is at stake if they should falter in keeping pace with these mushrooming fields of science. That anxiety is reflected in the efforts of the leading institutions to revise internal structures and practices that may inhibit the ability to address pressing scientific problems. The emphasis of those initiatives is on organizing research programs across traditional schools and departments. Some have an educational component, most often at the graduate level. These efforts are in part a response to the long-term trends in federal science and technology policy, which has supported science-based technologies through the research funding agencies.

University commitments to these fields are propelled by the quest for federal funding and prestige, and yet, they are important components of the larger ecology of innovation. For industry, these efforts are crucial not only for the research that they enable but also for their effects on the training of graduate students. Highly skilled professionals with state-of-the-art training in emerging areas of inquiry are key assets for corporate innovation. As seen above, some companies like IBM, BMW, and Intel have also sought to advance curriculum that relates to their areas of innovation. Universities are crucial agents in the institutionalization of areas of investigation that may constitute entire new industries through scientific breakthroughs.

The competition among universities for standing in the steep hierarchy of prestige pressures institutions outside the top tier to seek alternative strategies to advance, or at least not fall behind. State funding and industrial partnerships present opportunities for additional resources for this purpose. Universities such as NC State and Albany have committed to more or less permanent relationships with industry by recruiting firms to locate labs and scientists on their campuses, as has Clemson with its automotive campus. These strategies presumably have two advantages for these institutions. First, building prestigious departments the way Frederick Terman did at Stanford in the 1950s and 1960s is probably no longer possible.[72] He accumulated precious resources from foundations, the federal government, and alumni, but such funds are heavily claimed by the current academic leaders. Indeed, the inadequacy of federal research funds, or the fierce competition for them, is often invoked as a reason for seeking increased funding from industry. Close working relationships with industry represent a different playing field where these institutions have an opportunity to excel. Second, these engagements have been enmeshed with state policies and politics of economic development, with the respective universities as protagonists. Their efforts stem from entrepreneurial administrators and faculty who have forged links with state officials and industry leaders. Direct commitments to economic development have thus been aggressively pursued, and at least some states have rewarded such activities handsomely.

The magnitude of some recent university investments in entrepreneurial research institutes nonetheless raises questions about the place of these units in the university. Conventional wisdom contends that centers belong on the university "periphery" because they lack degree programs or control over faculty promotion and tenure. They depend upon the ability to attract resources to survive and gain legitimacy.[73] However, major centers in science-based technologies possess massive research infrastructures; they blend different disciplines and seek to foster the links between science and commercialization. Being central to the advancement of their institutions, such centers are pacesetters in research productivity on the campus. For example, the Biodesign Institute and Albany Nanotech are central to the development of the university's research enterprise. This role contrasts with that of other large mission-oriented centers that have long existed at the margin of university campuses to serve specific governmental patrons.[74] The new institutes create explicit links between research collaborations, innovation, and technology transfer. Moreover, knowledge spillovers are deliberately encouraged rather than expected to happen by chance. The idea of economic relevance is internalized in the design and operation of these structures and programs. As such, these research complexes transcend traditional academic disciplines and the departmental structure. The costs of these trade-offs have yet to be determined. But a "center versus department" perspective is likely to offer little insight. The experience of universities such as MIT, UC Berkeley, and Georgia Tech with interdisciplinary research centers shows that those units can coexist in a fruitful way and help raise the stature of schools and departments, while augmenting resources and enhancing economic contributions.

Targeted faculty recruitment illustrates the tension between opportunities in science-based technologies and the traditional academic structure. Rather than wait for departments to recruit faculty in fledgling fields, universities have sought the means to secure new appointments in strategic areas more quickly and efficiently. Such approaches emphasize the research roles of faculty even more than conventional hiring practices do, by making the choice of departmental affiliation just an incidental step in the recruitment process.

As most of these efforts stem from research, the impact on students is greatest in graduate education and training. At the most advanced levels, student interest drives new academic programs organized across schools and departments, such as the interdisciplinary specializations at Berkeley and Penn State. Students are ultimately important agents of collaborations in science, as they do much of the underlying work that links the research activities of the different labs. Graduate students at Berkeley had an active role in fostering campus networking around the computational biology program.[75] Recognizing the importance of graduate students for good science, and the latent opportunity, Arizona State's Biodesign Institute has started a collaborative doctoral program.

Thus, the combined pursuit of prestige and resources underlies the internal strategies of universities to enhance economic relevance. Science-based technologies are well-funded areas of inquiry, and universities compete for intellectual eminence in those areas. Some universities have made major institutional and financial pledges to better accommodate large-scale, collaborative research in such fields. The scale and scope of commitments to science-based technologies varies dramatically along with universities' ability to gather external support. Universities have also used partnerships with industry and states to build research capacity. But the competitive dynamics in those fields are clear among research universities: scientific as well as economic relevance positioned genomics, nanotechnology, information technology, and more recently bioenergy as central fields of academic inquiry. Ambitious universities will not forgo the opportunity to thrive in those areas and claim a stake in the prestige and funding they entail. These engagements are rather indirect in terms of the university contributions to overall innovative activity, but crucial nonetheless.

# CHAPTER 6

# Universities and the Promise
# of Economic Growth

This book began by noting that since the year 2000 American universities have felt increasing pressure to assume active roles related to the commercial economy. With Thomas Friedman, we see changes that had been building during previous years accelerating around that date and, perhaps more dramatically, interacting in ways that magnified their impact. As a consequence, the commercial links that universities had already developed over the previous two decades passed a tipping point in terms of number of interactions and significance of internal changes made to facilitate interactions. University rhetoric invoked economic development as the fourth mission of the American university, after teaching, research, and outreach. Only a few universities have taken the kinds of far-reaching steps to elevate such a mission to prominence, let alone parity, but virtually all universities have embraced a more general notion of economic relevance as an institutional imperative. Thus, American universities are in the midst of an extended transition toward an uncertain destination.

The preceding chapters have focused on the most salient features of these ongoing changes and sought to probe the underlying causes. We have avoided normative perspectives or policy prescriptions because these events had their own story to tell. Accordingly, this inquiry has sought to understand and interpret the direction of events and their possible consequences. These phenomena are above all decentralized—spread across a dispersed system of research universities, science-based industries, and government bodies. The independent actions of these multiple actors create market-like conditions, in which actions of individual universities that are supported by the prevailing environmental conditions tend to be reinforced, and behaviors that run counter to those conditions are discouraged. Universities react to developments in corporate research, government policy, and above all

186

advances in knowledge. They proactively implement strategies to gain advantage in these same markets for research funds, resources, and intellectual distinction. By describing the trends formed by such incremental dynamics and relating them to underlying conditions, this book has sought to explain the realities now shaping the American research university.

The forces favoring economic relevance show no sign of abating as the first decade of the twenty-first century draws to a close. On the contrary, they appear to be gaining strength and momentum. Basic trends in science-based technologies, corporate innovation, and government policies for technology-based economic development (TBED) continue to reinforce economic relevance. Within universities, external and internal stimuli spur an expansion of technology transfer and additional adaptation to objectives related to the economy.

Biotechnology, the paradigmatic science-based technology, continues to be a dynamic science. As the research frontier advances from genomics to proteomics, feasible or future technologies remain anchored in basic research. A complex division of labor continues to evolve, with university science providing one stable pole. The horizons are just as wide for the nanotechnologies. If this science follows the general path of biotechnology, breakthrough applications lie in the not-too-distant future.[1] Perhaps some of the science-based technologies identified in the early 1990s have matured. High-temperature superconductivity may now be a purely engineering field. But new fields are burgeoning. The emphasis on homeland security has placed a premium on sensor technologies, which draw upon such other fields as nanotechnology, optoelectronics, and robotics, and can demand massive computational power.

The innovation imperative is shared widely throughout the corporate world. Since 2000, technological industries have identified their greatest challenges as "growing the business through innovation" and "accelerating innovation."[2] The prolonged prosperity of the global economy seems to have increased pressure on knowledge-based economies. Sustained economic growth has been transformative for newly industrialized economies, allowing them to move up the value chain to more knowledge- and capital-intensive activities. This development induces firms in developed countries to emphasize those activities that most intensively employ human capital in order to retain a competitive advantage.[3] This process appears consistent with the challenges reported above as well as the trends identified in Chapter 2.

Following a hiatus after 2000, investments by U.S. corporations in research and innovation have resumed vigorous growth. The underlying scientific thrust has come from science-based technologies and, indeed, the difficulty of gaining access to new and relevant technologies. These needs are exacerbated in many cases by the orientation of industry R&D toward traditional problems and processes. Attitudes of firms toward external knowledge acquisition have been altered by the popularity of management doctrines of "open innovation," which argue that the most effective business models exploit external knowledge while focusing on core competencies.[4] Competition abounds among suppliers of such external knowledge. However, as profitability has risen, at least some corporations have lengthened and broadened their planning horizons, making partnerships with universities more attractive to both parties.

The intersection of these two trends is exemplified in the explosion of interest in science-based energy technologies.[5] The world's large petroleum companies had previously taken little interest in university expertise outside of geosciences and petroleum engineering. This suddenly changed with the diminishing supply of accessible hydrocarbons and public anxiety over global warming. Challenged by changing conditions of supply and demand for energy, these firms were saddled with superannuated research staffs attuned to the old technologies. Fortuitously, the energy crisis also brought them an abundance of cash. They responded by launching huge, long-range projects to identify new sources of energy and ways of coping with a changed energy environment. Universities appear to be indispensable partners, as in the Stanford Global Climate and Energy Project, the BP-Berkeley initiative, and Chevron's several university partnerships. All these endeavors involve science-based technologies. What BP-Berkeley called "the energy biosciences" will draw heavily upon biotechnology; hydrogen and fuel cell research forms part of materials science; and advances in solar power seek to harness features of nanotechnology. Much fundamental research will precede any biofuel or carbon-free revolution.

The promise of biofuels and the emergence of energy bioscience have kindled state efforts to bolster resident biotechnology research. This development underlines the fact that the biotech industry extends far beyond large-molecule pharmaceuticals. The University of Illinois, for example, focused its efforts on agricultural biotechnology and became partner to the BP-Berkeley project. In 2007, additionally, stem cell initiatives began to disburse research dollars in at least five states. For governors, legislators, and voters, TBED appears to be a popular cause. Moreover, in an increasing number of states, omnibus bills are being passed that provide significant targeted resources for academic research. North Carolina in 2007, for example, for the first time invested in university research capacity in order to promote TBED. Legislation provided $32 million for seven different "bio-" initiatives, with most of these funds directed to universities. The bill also favored upstream investments, appropriating substantial funds for cancer and interdisciplinary research, endowed professorships, and graduate students in science and technology.[6] States no less than firms feel the imperative to stimulate innovation within their domains, and for now, universities and TBED seem inextricably linked. On the national level, the American Competitiveness Initiative promises to give research in the physical sciences the kind of sustained impetus that the life sciences have received.

With this wind at their back, the involvement of universities with economic activity could scarcely help but grow. The twenty-first-century university is basically open to collaborations with industry and eager to commercialize the fruits of research. It pursues these ends with multiple motives. Enhancing capabilities in science-based technologies builds prestige and recognition, while aiding in the competition for research funds. Such expertise is valued by industry and may yield inventions to commercialize. And conspicuous contributions to the economy build local and statewide good will. However, universities are multiproduct and multipurpose institutions. They not only vary in the ways they have adapted to economic relevance roles, they also differ in the ways those roles combine with their other missions and constituencies. This book has documented that economic relevance is a fact of life for the American university of the twenty-first century. But the actual picture is complex and nuanced.

## Patterns and Possibilities

Krisztina Holly, czarina of innovation at the University of Southern California, fears that, through casual use and overexposure, " 'innovation' will end up in the cliché junkyard." To prevent this, she warns that the realities underlying innovation are too important to be trivialized.[7] Indeed, the capacity of the U.S. economy to spawn new firms that dominate emerging industries, and of U.S. corporations to renew product lines and enter new markets, has earned the envy of other developed countries. The long-running justification that university ties with industry contribute to these innovative achievements has assumed even greater cogency in the twenty-first century. This book has scrutinized the connections between university research and industry in order to elucidate the empirical basis for these assumptions. In the large universe of industrial innovation, we have shown, university research plays a small but vital role. More specifically, the university contribution can be viewed as three roles with distinct contributions, problems, and implications: the traditional role of enhancing industry research, and the special university contributions to the two tracks of industrial innovation.

The traditional university activities of education and public research remain, as they long have been, invaluable assets for industrial R&D. Industry draws heavily from public science, the chief output of academic research, and it has increasingly supported public investment in its growth. Interest in hiring graduates is another powerful motivation for maintaining university ties. The most effective vehicle for technology transfer is still the moving van. These vital roles depend on the continued focus by universities on cutting-edge, science-based technologies, and on the ability of universities to harbor a good proportion of the highest-quality research—conditions that are not presently in jeopardy.

Academic research that is directly sponsored by industry supplies a broad range of inputs more narrowly targeted to the needs of industrial R&D. Chapter 2 detailed the different forms of this support and its contributions to company R&D. Given the careful monitoring of limited R&D budgets, this substantial body of research by its very existence represents intrinsic value. The federal government, by providing ample subsidies through multiple programs, in effect affirms that the value to society of university-industry research exceeds the private value that firms are willing to invest. Corporate support for university research nevertheless experienced an unprecedented and unexplained drop after 2000. Weak economic conditions may have been partly to blame, but universities also faced growing competition from other external research performers, domestically and internationally. After 2005, however, industry apparently returned to form, expressing intentions to bolster investments in university research and consortia. But the same respondents expressed equal or greater enthusiasm for seeking technology from federal labs, acquisitions, or joint R&D ventures.[8] Moreover, the capabilities of foreign universities and research institutes will only grow stronger. Fiercer competition for industrial research support would seem to be a condition of the new era. To respond, U.S. universities will need to exploit their considerable competitive advantages to secure the most highly prized tasks.

The preferred tasks are those that optimize the mutual benefits of both parties. For universities, these would be long-term relationships that support at least a core of basic research and provide resources to advance particular fields. For industry, such commitments are predicated on long-term outlooks that seek to explore the scientific underpinnings of future products and processes. When these conditions are met, universities can make unique contributions to corporate research and future innovation. Such an ideal is the objective of the university-industry partnerships described in Chapter 2, and would epitomize university economic relevance for the corporate track of innovation.

Partnerships are scarcely a new phenomenon, but their increasing popularity since 2000 seems to recognize a growing need of industry to tap cutting-edge research in science-based technologies. For this purpose, the piecemeal, intermittent contacts of traditional research arrangements are quite inadequate. Participation in consortia or National Science Foundation (NSF) centers improves on this situation, but still represents arm's-length relationships, often shared with competing firms. Recent partnerships have sought to capture more benefit for the firm through monogamous relationships with universities, including intermingling of researchers and involvement with students. Two different approaches were described: erecting laboratories next to universities, thereby staking out a more or less permanent relationship, but with a large measure of company control; and negotiating long-term arrangements with existing or newly created campus laboratories.

Locating corporate laboratories near concentrations of research and innovation is scarcely novel, as their prevalence in Silicon Valley illustrates. More recently, major pharmaceutical firms have moved labs to Boston and San Diego to be present in those biotechnology hubs. In these cases, the desire to participate in the networks within these clusters is no doubt as great a lure as proximity to university research. The Seagate laboratory in Pittsburgh represents a more direct link with university science. An even closer form of partnership has been achieved at North Carolina State, with firms located on its Centennial Campus, although in this case the initiative came from the university. The "open collaborative research model" developed by Intel represents perhaps the latest refinement of this type of relationship.

Much the same purposes can be achieved with long-term agreements for on-campus research. The approaches of Boeing and IBM reflect a desire on the part of industry to establish deeper and more lasting relationships. The advantages of such arrangements for universities are considerable, since the underlying basis is a continuing interest in and desire to enhance existing areas of academic expertise. When unrestricted research funds are offered, as with the Boeing strategic partnerships, the benefit is all the greater. Additional impact is produced by megapartnerships, like BP-Berkeley and Albany's College of Nanoscale Science and Engineering, which support the expansion of entire areas of research. Significantly, both of those arrangements had to be facilitated with investments of state funds.

Universities generally have become more open to industrial partnerships as sources of both fresh funds and fresh ideas. Nevertheless, there are probably limits to the expansion of such arrangements. Only the largest corporations are capable of making such concentrated investments in long-range projects, and they tend to look toward the premier universities. Beyond this limitation, however, the real weakness of partnerships lies on the corporate side. As MIT found, and as the Novartis Agreement showed, it has sometimes proved difficult for corporations to sustain the kind of long-range outlook that justifies investment in fundamental research.

In the past, universities have been criticized for having close or exclusive relationships with a single firm. Fears included domination of the research agenda by the firm, preferential access to intellectual property (IP), and the effective exclusion of rival firms. However, little evidence exists to document the existence of such effects. In fact, when MIT surveyed its faculty for such evidence, it found none. Universities may sign partnership agreements, but individual researchers carry them out. The latter have little interest in pursuing investigations that only benefit companies and do not advance their own field. One large advantage of these agreements is that they settle conditions for IP ahead of time. Knowing who owns what clarifies the relationship and removes impediments to research. Few projects are of sufficient magnitude to shut out relationships with rival firms. In fact, it would be difficult to imagine how a firm could monopolize an area of inquiry in the U.S. research system. This was a prominent concern with the Novartis Agreement, and yet research funding for the Berkeley department from other companies increased during the contract. In cases where a close identification is established, the benefits for each partner can far outweigh any negative effects. Washington University and Monsanto have had a long partnership that has been called a model of university-industry collaboration. It has also been credited with helping to transform Monsanto from an

industrial chemicals firm into one specialized in agrobiosciences.[9] These
kinds of close relations are more readily formed when both parties are located in the same city and share a commitment to the health of the local
community.

The contributions of universities to the small-business track of innovation
are more tangible and publicized than those to corporate R&D. This track is
the realm of small science-based companies, including university spin-offs,
where patents and licenses protect the intellectual property that these firms
seek to develop into commercial products. They express the spirit of Bayh-
Dole, in which the patenting of university discoveries is the road to commercial innovations. In addition, they represent a distinctive university contribution to economic development—innovations and particularly new
companies that would not exist without these efforts to commercialize university discovery.

The quarter century after Bayh-Dole witnessed a revolution in the creation and commercialization of university IP. By 2005, the Association of
University Technology Managers (AUTM) could report that universities
were responsible for nearly 10,000 active licenses and almost 3,000 operating start-up firms—as well as $1 billion in licensing revenues.[10] These are
small numbers in a $12 trillion economy, but the incremental contribution
is significant, particularly in the regions surrounding research universities.
However, very few university inventions were ready to be put in the hands
of consumers. Rather, the majority faced the three-pronged challenge of
being embryonic technologies, having to cross the "valley of death," and relying on tacit inventor knowledge. More recently, universities and supporting agencies have grasped the logic of this situation: the volume of university innovations that "would not otherwise exist" may well depend on
the effort and investment devoted to bringing them into existence.

The situation is essentially the same for a technology that must be developed to the point of attracting a licensee as for one that is confided to a start-
up company. Capital and inventor engagement are required to cross the
valley of death between support for basic research and commercial financing. Venture capital is by all accounts now reserved largely for latter-
stage innovations; angel investors may commit at a somewhat earlier stage;
but what these inventors need is seed capital to support applied, proprietary
research. The more successful patenting universities have now cobbled together seed funds for this purpose. Sometimes they have also provided special laboratory space for these activities. Business incubators have long been

popular, but fledgling inventions require, and are now being provided with, prebusiness incubation. Consigning inventions to faculty start-ups has become increasingly attractive to universities for spawning innovation. Serious commitment to this path requires that universities accept equity in lieu of licensing revenues in order to help the fledglings fly. Additional capital is sometimes available from a university's own affiliated venture capital fund or through economic development agencies. Start-ups need a great deal of assistance, and universities have been finding their own ways to provide it. As a result, tech transfer complexes that provide these services have been growing even more rapidly than technology transfer offices (TTOs).

Behind these efforts lie some large questions about the volume and the value of university inventions. How much potential innovation is produced in university laboratories? To what extent would more resources produce a greater output of innovation? In the absence of definitive answers, two scenarios seem plausible.

First, to the extent that faculty culture plays a significant role in commercial involvement, the spread of entrepreneurial attitudes should affect the output of innovation. A detailed study of a high-patenting department in the Stanford medical school by Jeannette Colyvas and Walter W. Powell found this to be a surprisingly slow process. Even in a setting known for entrepreneurial behavior, almost two decades elapsed before such behavior became generalized throughout the department. Prior to 1980, commercial engagement was controversial and carried some perception of risk to one's career. From 1980 until the early 1990s, it became more widespread and acceptable among senior scientists, although still contested in some respects. Only after the mid-1990s did entrepreneurship become routinely practiced and a hallmark of success. The authors document the leadership of senior faculty inventors in conveying these norms to junior faculty and students: "entrepreneurship spread from two early 'explorers' to other senior faculty of comparable status and then trickled down the career ladder to become an accepted activity of many life scientists."[11]

The Stanford department may not be typical, being distinguished by the eminence of the faculty and the large volume of funded research. However, the process of cultural diffusion that occurred there seems likely to operate in any department with successful entrepreneurial models. The fact that the Stanford department was such an obvious leader suggests that average departments more closely resemble its middle stage than its final one. If so, the output of inventions from these departments has the potential to grow substantially, as it did at Stanford. The invention productivity of the Stanford department may or may not have been maximized by 2000, when the study ended, but there can be little doubt that any potential innovation it produced faced near certainty of being disclosed and evaluated. Most TTOs, in contrast, do not feel that is the case at their universities. The frequent reorganizations of technology transfer offices seen in Chapter 4 are testimony to the belief that a greater volume of potential innovations could be or should be forthcoming from university scientists. However, tech transfer data cast some doubt on this view.

An alternative scenario is suggested by the fact that the productivity of technology transfer appears to have leveled off in all measures of output. From the late 1990s to mid-decade, disclosures, patents, licenses, licensing income, and start-ups all rose proportionally with constant-dollar research expenditures (Table 4.4). At the same time, the inputs that universities controlled, namely TTO personnel and patent filings, increased. The economic principle seems clear: given a finite amount of material (potential innovations), increasing the resources for extraction will lead to diminishing relative returns. And given the measures taken to enhance the commercialization of university inventions, diminishing returns in this situation means expending greater effort on less valuable, lower-quality inventions. Fragmentary evidence for this was cited in Chapter 4. From this perspective, the technology transfer process appears to be reasonably efficient, and the limiting factor in university patenting and licensing is the finite quantity of valuable faculty inventions.

These two possibilities have quite different implications. If university laboratories harbor untapped potential innovations, then existing efforts to improve the translation process by reorganizing or enlarging TTOs and encouraging faculty entrepreneurship should be intensified. If the process of translating technology is reasonably efficient and diminishing returns have set in, the challenge would be not to decrease investments in tech transfer but to bolster the innovative productivity of academic science. While any number of universities might be able to improve the realization of their innovative potential, we suspect that most major research universities have become reasonably efficient. These two alternatives are also important for public policy and help to frame the future possibilities for university contributions to economic development.

## Policies for Technology-Based Economic Development

Since at least 1980, technology transfer has been an explicit goal of federal science policy. Although Congress naturally tilts toward favoring small business, the principal efforts to advance science-based technologies have inclined toward large corporations. These policies have sought, above all, to enlarge and invigorate those areas of academic science and engineering most likely to produce useful technology. To some extent, these areas will generate patentable inventions as well, but the two outputs are not coextensive. The federal formula that has been effective for more than two decades has been to organize and subsidize collaborative university-industry research. This formula meshes with the corporate model for R&D, since only companies with large internal labs can devote the resources and adopt the long-range perspective needed to benefit from this precompetitive type of research—although, as seen in Chapter 2, this can sometimes be difficult even for them. For universities, these policies aim to bolster their internal capacity to generate innovation. Commercialization proceeds through the involvement of corporations, not through disclosures to the TTO.

Congress has not been unmindful of the other track of innovation. As noted, the Bayh-Dole Act was explicitly aimed at small business, and it was followed by legislation creating the popular Small Business Innovation Research (SBIR) and later Small Business Technology Transfer (STTR) programs. Intended to stimulate innovation, these programs rather tend to reinforce it where it already exists. SBIR funding is more skewed than federal research dollars (Table 3.1), flowing disproportionately to regions already rich with the science-based firms that win these awards, namely California and Massachusetts.

Both kinds of federal policies aim to stimulate economic growth through innovation, wherever it may occur. In both cases federal agencies make awards largely on a best-science basis, with admitted concessions to congressional geography. However, as noted in Chapter 3, this federal largesse did not meet the needs of individual states for economic stimulation within their borders. For this purpose, virtually every state has devised its own policies to harness its universities for economic development.

The fixation of states on endogenous growth long caused them to favor downstream approaches to economic development. They generally assumed that the challenge lay in bridging the gap between university invention and commercial innovation, with emphasis on the latter. This approach was evident in the way states employed the tobacco settlement windfall: most states established bioscience incubators, and half established programs to make seed funds or venture capital available to start-up firms. But the latest boom in biotechnology seems to have awakened states to the other dimension of economic development—generating university inventions in the first place. Nearly half the states now devote some tobacco funds to bioscience research.[12] The attractiveness of bioscience investments undoubtedly encouraged similar approaches in other technologies, so that many state programs encompass them as well. With extensive programs now in place to nurture new science-based firms, states have turned their attention to upstream investments in university research.

States have not so much made choices among the alternatives presented here as tried to have it all. The state programs discussed in Chapter 3 are oriented toward large corporations, yet expect to generate spin-offs as well. Matching funds for the new faculty chairs supported by the Georgia Research Alliance (GRA) largely come from corporate sponsors, but another program of the GRA, VentureLab, enables the effective organization of spin-off businesses. The GRA has targeted three industries, but other states have been more focused. Arizona seeks to create a bioscience hub in Phoenix that will attract existing corporations and also spawn new ones. New York's large investment in the Albany Nanotech complex was centered on IBM and information technology. But, like Arizona, the objective was to establish an industry cluster where all types of synergies would operate. California, which already possessed a productive infrastructure supporting innovation, could take an omnibus approach to the Institutes for Science and Innovation, assured that the investment would enrich the mix even further.

These and other state programs have had an impact far larger than the substantial funds they conveyed. They have determined to a large extent how and where universities could expand their intellectual base. These resources have been particularly crucial to state universities, which have seen other forms of public support erode. By adopting the agenda of economic relevance, they have garnered aid to strengthen cutting-edge science in important science-based technologies. The quid pro quo? Bring corporate scientists into the laboratories at times; disclose and patent resulting inventions; and spin off new companies that will create local jobs. These tasks carry few risks and promise some rewards. Most important, however, the resources associated with economic relevance serve to strengthen the university's primary goal of advancing learning.

## University Approaches to Economic Relevance

This examination has found the internal factors most closely linked with economic relevance to be involvement with science-based technologies, academic quality, a receptive faculty culture, and the effectiveness of the TTO. The adaptations of universities described in Chapter 5 focused on the first two factors, which are largely considered to be mutually reinforcing. Enhancing research capacity in economically relevant fields, which requires encouraging interdisciplinary arrangements, can also be expected to build or reinforce academic quality.

The changes under way at Harvard exemplify this connection. Perhaps most noteworthy is that the recommendations of the Harvard task force came from the grass roots of science rather than from any a priori convictions about innovation. The task force sought to assess the revolution in science taking place across the globe, and found compelling precedents for multidisciplinary research and engagement with commercially relevant scientific research.[13] Moreover, it sought to have these qualities permeate the entire campus rather than being confined to one or more institutes. Such steps were necessary for Harvard to take advantage of the unfolding scientific opportunities, and thus to preserve its academic leadership. When looking to implement this vision, Harvard remained consistent with its traditions, emphasizing its commitment to learning and obtaining the best scientists and engineers.[14] Thus, interdisciplinarity, having the "best," and the imperative of seizing scientific opportunities are inextricably mixed.

Harvard has aggressively upgraded its tech transfer operations, and in 2007 announced the first interdisciplinary, university-wide department, but it is still a comparative laggard as an entrepreneurial university. By belatedly joining these ranks, it underlines the more significant point that economic relevance and academic quality are now firmly joined. If one looks, for example, at the five most highly rated faculties of the 1990s, joining Harvard are MIT, Berkeley, Caltech, and Stanford. MIT and Stanford have long been the entrepreneurial leaders among U.S. universities. Caltech made an institutional commitment to tech transfer in 1995 and is now a leader in both patenting and generating spin-offs. UC Berkeley relies more on separate institutes and centers, but now has extensive corporate connections, including participation in two Cal ISI labs and the giant project with BP. These four universities, in fact, top the Milken Institute's University Technology Transfer and Commercialization Index. Other, only slightly less brilliant academic stars show the same tendencies.[15] The conversion of Yale to economic relevance has been described. UC San Diego has led all campuses of the University of California in entrepreneurship. The University of Michigan is the centerpiece of the state's University Research Corridor, and the University of Texas has been the economic catalyst for the Austin region. Columbia is possibly the most aggressive licenser, a pattern Penn seeks to emulate. Both Duke and Northwestern have linked their academic identity and economic relevance to interdisciplinary initiatives. In addition, though further inspiration was scarcely needed, Northwestern was the beneficiary in 2007 of the largest IP bonanza to date, selling future drug royalties for $700 million.[16] Significantly, private universities stand out in this list (and one could easily add Cornell, Johns Hopkins, and Carnegie Mellon). They are presumably not influenced by the hot breath of governors pushing economic development policies. Rather, like Harvard, they have responded principally to "scientific opportunities."

Entrepreneurialism can develop in academic units, like the Stanford department described above. But universities have been especially eager to organize cross-school collaborations with the potential to make major scientific and technological contributions. However, new organizational structures are sometimes required if researchers from different departments or schools are to collaborate on interdisciplinary projects. Both internal and external initiatives have prompted change. The NSF, in particular, has sought to induce universities to be interdisciplinary with its materials and nanoscale research centers, as have foundations supporting units such as the Beckman and Kavli Institutes at several leading universities. More than buildings and centers, these efforts aim to change patterns for conducting research, fostering and sustaining interactions that would otherwise not occur. Fundamental change nevertheless usually requires academic leadership, as new centers and buildings can easily serve as a façade for old research. Senior administrators can accomplish some of these goals even without massive external resources. Penn State facilitated interdisciplinary collaboration by shifting resources to several overarching institutes that support research programs across colleges. Such tinkering with limited funds is the reality for most universities.

In several cases university presidents have played a decisive role in leading their institutions toward economic involvement. Certainly Richard Levin was responsible for integrating Yale research with the Connecticut pharmaceutical industry. Purdue's Martin Jischke succeeded in unleashing the considerable economic potential of that land-grant university. Other presidents have embraced agendas of innovation and economic relevance to alter the identity of their universities.

Perhaps the most ambitious agenda has been pursued by Michael Crow at Arizona State. Before assuming the ASU presidency, Crow had supervised tech transfer and commercial relations at Columbia, where he became recognized for combining aggressive commercial undertakings with respect for academic values.[17] In Phoenix he recognized the extraordinary opportunities for the only research university in the nation's fifth largest city. He is dedicated to building the "new American university," and building it quickly, by combining academic and enrollment growth with economic contributions. In the Biodesign Institute, ASU hopes to consolidate existing research strengths and forge into new territories in the life sciences.

Shirley Ann Jackson has adopted a similar strategy of academic enhancement and economic relevance under almost inverse circumstances—small, private Rensselaer Polytechnic Institute in the academically crowded Northeast. To transcend RPI's reputation as a "hands-on" engineering school, her "Rensselaer Plan" was predicated on substantially upgrading research, because "education and research are inextricably linked in a world-class university."[18] With funding from New York State and a huge private gift, RPI has invested in the Center for Biotechnology and Interdisciplinary Studies, as well as participating in the Albany Nanotech complex. A vice-provost for entrepreneurship was added in 2006 to foster a culture of entrepreneurialism across the campus—all with a view to develop high-tech entrepreneurship and commercialization.

The University of Southern California under president Steven Sample made remarkable progress on traditional academic measures of undergraduate selectivity and faculty prestige. However, it has now chosen to emphasize economic and social relevance. Its faculty strategy has focused on hiring clusters of scientists in science-based technologies. And it has shaped USC Stevens to promote an institution-wide mission of innovation. Rather than simply focus on enhancing the economic relevance of medicine and engineering—strong units but not noted for tech transfer—the university opted for a more comprehensive formula that would encompass its thriving professional schools. Their contributions to their respective communities cannot be measured in patents or licenses. The stress on creativity and involvement instead invoke a different form of engagement with the Southern California economy that is more in keeping with USC traditions.

A handful of universities have introduced new models for working with industry by integrating industry partners on campus in more or less permanent arrangements. North Carolina State was the pioneer in mixing industry and academic buildings on its developing Centennial Campus. Rather than relying on propinquity alone, special steps were taken to assure that interaction would be natural and continuous. This widely watched experiment demonstrated that colocation could work and undoubtedly encouraged initiatives at other institutions. The Georgia Electronic Design Center at Georgia Tech originated as a focused effort to develop broadband technologies in the region. Inspired by a private initiative, it was launched with state job creation funds and now draws support from federal agencies and industry partners as well as the GRA. Located in Georgia Tech's new Technology Square complex, the center includes corporate laboratories within and adjacent to it. The Albany Nanotech complex is a much larger state-university-industry initiative. Successful in industrial recruitment, the College of Nanoscale Science and Engineering is actually overshadowed in scale by its industry partners. Finally, Clemson's inchoate International Center for Automotive Research (ICAR), like Albany's nanotechnology college, contributes to a larger state economic development program. Notably, it aspires to focus academic research on technologies hitherto largely confined to industry R&D.

These models can be judged by their respective contributions to universities, corporate sponsors, and economic development.[19] The Georgia Electronic Design Center has achieved academic distinction, establishing a plausible claim to be "the leading academic center in mixed-signal technology." The center has grown to 250 researchers, and 45 mostly large corporations are members or research partners. It aims at both innovation tracks, providing cutting-edge technology to microelectronics corporations and spawning start-up firms in the local economy. In both respects, the center has had an appreciable impact in bringing firms and jobs to Atlanta. The Albany College of Nanoscale Science and Engineering was the catalyst for an even larger influx of industrial investment, richly subsidized by the state. That situation, together with the state's investment, positioned it to become an important center for electronic nanotechnology—a valuable complement to industry if not yet an academic leader in this field. Much the same might be said of the Centennial Campus. A huge success in Raleigh, both for the university and the region, it has inspired a second campus devoted to the life sciences. The intangible attractions of university settings, linked by Richard Florida with gratifying the creative class, no doubt help to secure industrial tenants.[20] This model has served to strengthen the university academically and financially, but probably will not allow it to surpass its Research Triangle rivals in academic distinction. Clemson's ICAR has a relatively open track to excel in automotive technology. However, its close ties to BMW, which are subsidized by the state, have raised some concern. This would seem to be a case of the state, which has a huge stake in the German automaker's Spartanburg complex, tilting the table. BMW's favored position puts the onus on Clemson to construct a balanced academic program.

The novel models adopted by these four universities explicitly commit them to the mission of economic development. Georgia Tech has always embraced this mission, but for the others these close collaborations with industry represent some shift in identity. More universities, however, have sought greater economic relevance by directly addressing tech transfer.

Yale and Caltech in the 1990s, and Harvard more recently, first looked to their TTOs in order to enhance their economic relevance. The lure of licensing income was surely a motive, but each of these initiatives required substantial up-front investments. For these wealthy universities, academic reputation far overshadows all other considerations. Their predominant inspiration seemed to be to translate university discovery into the productive economy. This required adjustment of the attitudes of faculty researchers and considerable improvement in the process of translation. The subsequent outpouring of IP and spin-off companies showed that Yale and Caltech were correct in anticipating the existence of potential innovations, and this will likely hold true for Harvard too. For universities as a whole, however, we have already seen that the pool of potential discoveries may be a limiting factor.

A significant number of TTOs at major universities have undergone recent reorganization. Florida and Washington were mentioned in Chapter 4; Georgia Tech, UCLA, Minnesota, Boston University, and Penn could be added. A common goal seems to be to improve the efficiency of the tech transfer process. For that purpose, attention has increasingly focused on better communication with the entrepreneurial community to help nurture and market the embryonic technologies that typically arise from academic research. Such nurturing and marketing, however, require more resources to expand the technology transfer complex and to improve the chances of success for what are by nature high-risk endeavors.

The continued underlying turmoil in TTOs reflects the inherent contradictions identified in Chapter 4. Aside from the patent leaders, TTOs are generally under-resourced, but still not self-supporting. Efforts to maximize income are often inimical to maximizing technology transfer. And the strong-patenting regime shaped by the life sciences poorly serves tech transfer in engineering and information sciences. At bottom, universities intermittently demand that their TTOs generate more licenses, income, and start-ups. Yet the total picture of technology transfer painted here suggests that such expectations will be difficult to meet.

## Universities in the Twenty-First Century

Critics who fear that American universities have become dominated and exploited by capitalist corporations have interpreted this relationship backwards. The universities of the twenty-first century have essentially exploited the opportunities inherent in economic relevance to garner increased resources from both industry and government. The economic relevance of advanced research has allowed universities to claim a larger and more sophisticated role in regional development. State governors and legislatures have willingly funded university research and infrastructure, even if these investments show little evidence of results in the short run, and few can gauge their longer-term impacts. Universities have actively and willingly engaged in relationships with industry. Universities need not depend on industrial contracts and TBED funding for their survival or sustenance. Those relationships and resources are pursued as part of universities' perpetual aspirations for institutional advancement. Economic relevance has been accretive to learning, irrespective of the latent hopes that the next blockbuster patent or Google will emerge on one's campus.

In this respect, universities have behaved no differently than in the past. The commitment to agricultural research by land-grant colleges after the 1887 Hatch Act, defense research after 1945, and the huge expansion of activities in the health sciences paralleling the growth of the National Institutes of Health have all required the extension of university roles, as well as the formation of new organizational units. These additional missions also stirred debate on the consequences and appropriateness of the new commitments, and provoked soul-searching about the nature of the university. But these commitments were the university responses to social needs linked with national interests, and they represented the extension, if not the hypertrophy,

204 Tapping the Riches of Science

of academic research. Unlike agriculture, defense, and health research, the current economically relevant fields of science and engineering are only partially encapsulated within separate academic units or research centers. The conduits of the new mission are research networks that cut across the campus and beyond it, modern facilities that house interdisciplinary research teams, contiguous labs for academic and industrial scientists, and intermediary organizations inside and outside the university that connect agents in the innovation system. As in agriculture, defense, and health, research activity is purposefully directed toward addressing relevant problems and the needs of external constituents. Also like those missions, economic relevance finds a solid base of support among dedicated interest groups.

Thus, economic relevance appears to have indeed become an institutionalized role of the twenty-first-century university. However, to fathom what that actually means requires some model of the somewhat anarchic operation of the modern university and a perception of what is truly new about the current situation.

Universities are highly compartmentalized in their structure, and the compartments have a high degree of autonomy. While fiscal control is exerted from the center, operational authority in these knowledge-based institutions resides with the knowledge-based units. Many of those units achieve an additional degree of autonomy by obtaining funding from external sources. The relative growth and prosperity of units results from a reciprocal relationship between the center (administration) and the units. Enrollment pressures do not automatically bring growth, since departments or schools are likely to respond by increasing selectivity. Even when numbers do increase, administrations are usually conservative in creating new faculty lines. Sometimes, unit growth is more readily achieved by obtaining resources from outside the institution, but in these cases too faculty lines are awarded only grudgingly. The most significant and lasting changes are generally sponsored by the center, reacting to and shaping developments at the unit level with new investments and commitments.[21] In twenty-first-century universities such new commitments have been heavily weighted toward expanding research in economically relevant fields.

For economic relevance, the defining development of the current era that began around 1980 was the establishment by every university of a technology transfer office to handle intellectual property. Both patents and IP were an afterthought at all but a handful of universities prior to 1975–1980; subsequently, tech transfer became an institutionalized function. The other transformative development was the expanding role of science-based technologies in both advancing science and generating technology to transfer. This expansion has been driven for the most part by federal agencies by means of research funding, but universities, states, and donors have enthusiastically built up campus capacity to ingest these federal research dollars. Until well into the 1990s, these two processes were assumed to work in a complementary fashion—more research of the right sort would yield discoveries, IP, and innovation for industry. And so it did. But it eventually became apparent that greater output might be had by improving these processes—by utilizing more resources and better design for the actual translation of research findings to innovations. Since 2000, economic relevance has been advanced through these kinds of adjustments.

The weaknesses of TTOs were never entirely obscured behind the AUTM façade of unrelenting progress. Outside of the handful of successful offices, productivity was poor. Greater effort might generate more disclosures and patent applications, but the bottom line—licenses for real products—showed a trickle of results. In imitation of the successful exemplars, efforts have been made to improve both the technology push and the market pull. For the former, provision was needed for more applied research that would advance embryonic inventions into working prototypes. For this purpose universities have established seed funds and special laboratory space—in effect, prebusiness incubators—for research on patented discoveries. To better meet the market, arrangements with entrepreneurs and venture capitalists have been developed to produce market-oriented business plans. TTOs have expanded into technology transfer complexes, able to offer assistance at every stage of the translation of a laboratory invention into a commercial product. In some cases universities have developed these strategies on their own, but for the Deshpande Center, USC Stevens, and VentureLab, among others, the initiative and the money came from closely associated outsiders.

For science-based technologies, the next step was the creation of special spaces where research and translation could coexist—could meld together in a more or less seamless fashion. This was accomplished by establishing large laboratories focused on technologies that were especially close to the R&D frontiers of high-tech industries. States were especially intrigued by this approach and provided most of the resources to establish the Cal ISI, Georgia Electronic Design Center, Biodesign Institute, and Albany Nanotech complex. Philanthropy has funded this model at private universities in such creations as the Clark Center at Stanford and the Broad Institute at

Harvard and MIT. Single corporations have also realized the possibilities inherent in this model, creating the dedicated institutes mentioned above. Each of these creations has its own version of interdisciplinarity, provisions for tech transfer, or relations with industry; in this respect they reflect the organizational genius of American universities for incorporating any arrangement that enhances learning. But they are all versions of a matrix model, where faculty appointments are with academic units and participants self-select research units on the basis of scientific interests and entrepreneurial inclinations.[22]

From this perspective, the university role of economic relevance is permanently embodied in bricks and mortar. It is the raison d'être of the tech transfer complex, often subsumed in an office of economic development led by a vice-presidential officer; and it resides with varying degrees of explicitness in the recent interdisciplinary units devoted to science-based technologies. In sum, it has become another compartment of the American university. As such, it has had surprisingly little impact on the academic core of the university. It occasionally influences the kinds of people hired to the faculty, favoring the specialties cultivated in the new institutes and sometimes ties with industry. However, such individuals are frequently hired with the additional resources that the economic relevance mission brings. Left to their own preferences, academic departments invariably place academic accomplishments uppermost in their appointment decisions. But this kind of trade-off seldom needs to be made. As illustrated above, the drive toward economic relevance has been led by the nation's most prestigious universities. Interdisciplinary research in science-based technologies is rewarded by academic prestige as well as federal grants and ties with industry. This is the high road to economic relevance, and universities are certain to ride it as far as it will take them.

But how far will this be? The short answer would be, not as far as the current boosters imagine. Rather, we foresee the economic relevance of American universities constrained by four sets of conditions.

First, the contributions that universities can make to innovation in the economy, and the resources that society will provide for that mission, are inherently limited. We have already discussed the relative stagnation of the outputs of TTOs in this decade. While a few universities undoubtedly have room for improvement, we doubt the existence of the kind of low-hanging fruit that was gathered by Yale and Caltech in the mid-nineties. Rather, the future output of potential innovations will likely depend on the expansion of expertise and research in science-based technologies. This seems likely to occur, but probably at a measured pace. Training high-quality future researchers is only part of the equation; finding places at the bench for them to utilize their expertise has been more daunting. In the life sciences the predicament of young researchers, immured in postdoctoral appointments, continues to worsen. Universities are innately conservative in creating new units for teaching or research. The beginning of the twenty-first century has been extraordinarily propitious for developing a kind of penumbra of research institutes around the academic core. Aside from a few endowments, these entities depend on external support to fulfill their mission. They are well founded, generally, and should prosper; but at the same time they make large claims upon available funds. With the academic R&D machine operating at full throttle, only incremental increases in the pace of innovation seem likely.

Corporations have been enthusiastic backers of public spending for economically relevant research, but they remain parsimonious with their own funds for this purpose. Although research partnerships between high-tech corporations and select universities have been prominent recently, there is no reason to expect industry to spend a larger portion of R&D budgets on universities. Firms appear to be seeking emerging technologies increasingly among the research boutiques, many of which were founded as university spin-offs. By helping to launch these research firms, universities have contributed significantly to a dynamic component of the innovation system, but have derived few benefits themselves. Ironically, the area that seems to have the greatest potential for growth is traditional university-industry research projects. Here universities have simply lost share to a growing roster of competitors. University competitiveness seems to have been compromised by the very ascendancy of economic relevance. The greater bureaucratization of research and particularly the fixation with IP has apparently undermined, at least in some fields, the tacit relationships that formerly characterized these transactions. But this is a problem that could be addressed if universities felt it worthwhile to regain their former share of industry research spending. Hence, a second general conclusion: the current emphasis on patenting and spin-offs has directed excessive energy and resources toward the small-business track of innovation while inhibiting to some degree university involvement with the corporate track of innovation. The greatest potential for enhanced technology transfer may consequently lie in expanding and diversifying partnership arrangements between academic research and corporate R&D.

Third, the growing economic relevance of U.S. universities has been impelled to a greater extent by government than by industry. Government expectations of university contributions to economic development have created a climate supporting university commitments, rhetorical and actual. More important, public investments have provided some of the resources for many of the university units in which this mission is now ensconced. These policies have been shaped by an unusual combination of substantial economic prosperity coupled with widespread economic insecurity. Globalization has been an important factor underlying both these conditions; together they gave plausibility to the innovation narrative. Stimulating greater and faster innovation seemed the best path for maintaining competitive advantage in a globalized economy. However, even if the innovation narrative retains its cogency, government policies will not necessarily continue to favor investments in enhancing university research. Technology-based economic development can have many outlets. Universities—and high-tech industries—have benefited from the upstream investments of the opening years of the twenty-first century, but looking forward, the issue may well be how long universities will be key beneficiaries of this process.

Finally, the involvement of universities with industry and the commercial economy raises larger philosophical and ideological issues that have deliberately been sidestepped in this empirical study. Nevertheless, an ongoing controversy exists over the definition of the public good and normative conceptions of the nature of the university. These issues may never be resolved. Nor should they be, since they invoke matters that need to be continually revisited. However, the perspective and the findings of this examination strongly support a definite view of the American university.

Arguments that invoke the public good to support or oppose economic relevance talk past one another. Critics assert that patenting, exclusive licenses, or partnerships with single corporations convert public, university science into private goods for the enrichment of their owners. The tech transfer and TBED communities insist that the private development of university inventions produces public benefits in the form of new and improved goods and services, increased economic activity, and jobs. Conversely, the record of university patenting, as seen in Chapter 4, provides examples of the disposition of IP that was probably not optimal for public science or the public good. And state policies for economic development tread a wobbly, thin line between subsidizing economic activity or private profit. But in the final analysis, government policies have far overshadowed the research demands of industry and the inherent proclivities of universities themselves in driving the economic relevance of universities. For their part, universities have readily responded, as usual, to a pressing social need, defined and supported by government.

Universities are based upon ideals, but the inhabitants of their multiple compartments tend to uphold rather different lists of them. Even those who wish to see universities as ivory towers, aloof from matters mundane and profane, often pursue their own social agendas. Supporters of economic relevance as the fourth mission of the university advocate an ideal that is viewed skeptically outside of their own precincts. If anything, the multiple ideals that universities invoke, at times ostensibly as needed, easily breed cynicism and accusations of hypocrisy.

There are nevertheless bedrock norms to which all academic institutions and their faculty members implicitly subscribe: truth seeking and truth telling in research, scholarship, and teaching; fair judging in the evaluation of the work of students, faculty, and other scholars; and fair dealing in the treatment of students and other professionals.[23] Universities have no need to transgress these norms in their contributions to economic relevance; in fact, as discussed in Chapter 1, any hint of doing so threatens great peril and embarrassment.[24]

The multifarious activities of the modern university are built for the most part on these bedrock norms. Universities tend to behave in ways that maximize learning—the learning of faculty, the learning of students, and the sharing of learning with other groups in society in ways that enhance the learning of all.[25] It has been noted repeatedly in this book that the additional units created to further economic relevance were "accretive to learning." That is, these undertakings enhanced the research opportunities of certain groups of university scientists, scholars, and students. Each group may be only a handful of individuals in the multiversity, but that is how compartmentalized universities operate. Exploiting discrete opportunities when they arise incrementally expands the total learning of the institution. By the same token, this disposition guards against the inclusion of routine or uninteresting work for industry, which critics have long feared. Activities that are not accretive to learning simply do not earn the attention of academic researchers.

Similarly, because economic relevance enhances learning, it has also benefited education. Critics who consider research, and especially research for industry, to be antithetical to student learning ignore the centrality of research for graduate education and the increasing involvement of under-graduates in research. Repeatedly in this volume, we have found the educational benefits for students portrayed prominently as fruits of university-industry collaboration. The opportunity to work on real-world problems, the career advantages that contacts with industry bring, and the additional student support all enhance education in their respective units.

In sum, although it has often been a contested mission for research universities, economic relevance should instead be seen as a complementary mission. The promise of generating innovations for the U.S. economy has brought universities the resources to augment their expertise in crucially important fields of science. And for that reason, virtually all research universities have pursued at least some portion of the economic relevance agenda. But it has essentially been an addition, like previous external missions, rather than a displacement of any other university commitments. In fact, dedication to economic relevance falls unevenly across the field of research universities and within individual universities. Only a few institutions, like Georgia Tech or North Carolina State, boast of being wholly committed to this mission. Others place their initiatives, major or modest, in compartments, quite separate from what they may consider more vital institutional priorities. The great strength of American higher education lies in the diversity within institutions as well as across institutional types. America's capacious universities, above all, are able to serve undergraduates in majors ranging from performing arts to practical branches of engineering, graduate students in even more varied fields, and research patrons in esoteric scientific specialties. It is precisely the responsiveness of the American university to a multiplicity of social needs in diverse fields of learning that has assured its continued usefulness—and its promise to contribute to economic growth.

# Notes

## Chapter 1: Technology Transfer as University Mission

1. Adam R. Nelson, "Nationalist Science and International Academic Travel in the Early Nineteenth Century: Geological Surveys and Global Economics, 1800–1840," *Perspectives on the History of Higher Education* 25 (2006): 43–88; Julius A. Stratton and Loretta H. Mannix, *Mind and Hand: The Birth of MIT* (Cambridge: MIT Press, 2005).

2. Roger L. Geiger, "The Rise and Fall of Useful Knowledge: Higher Education for Science, Agriculture, and the Mechanic Arts, 1850–1875" in Geiger, ed., *The American College in the Nineteenth Century* (Nashville: Vanderbilt University Press, 2000), 183–195; Roger L. Williams, *The Origins of Federal Support for Higher Education: George W. Atherton and the Land-Grant Movement* (University Park: Pennsylvania State University Press, 1991).

3. Roger L. Geiger, *To Advance Knowledge: The Growth of American Research Universities, 1900–1940* (New Brunswick, NJ: Transaction, 2004 [1986]); J. P. Swann, *Academic Scientists and the Pharmaceutical Industry* (Baltimore: Johns Hopkins University Press, 1988).

4. Jane Robbins, "Shaping Patent Policy: The National Research Council and the Universities from World War I to the 1960s," *Perspectives on the History of Higher Education* 25 (2006): 89–122; David C. Mowery et al., *Ivory Tower and Industrial Innovation: University-Industry Technology Transfer before and after the Bayh-Dole Act* (Stanford: Stanford University Press, 2004), 58–84.

5. Roger L. Geiger, "Science, Universities, and National Defense, 1945–1970," *Osiris* 7 (1992): 26–48; Stuart W. Leslie, *Cold War and American Science: The Military-Industrial-Academic Complex at MIT and Stanford* (New York: Columbia University Press, 1993).

6. Roger L. Geiger, *Research and Relevant Knowledge: American Research Universities since World War II* (New Brunswick, NJ: Transaction, 2004 [1993]), 230–269.

7. Recently, NIH alone supported about 27 percent of all academic research (2003). Source: National Science Foundation.

8. Kenneth M. Ludmerer, *Time to Heal: American Medical Education from the Turn of the Century to the Era of Managed Care* (New York: Oxford University Press, 1993).

9. Mowery et al., *Ivory Tower*, 85–98; David C. Mowery and Nathan Rosenberg, *Technology and the Pursuit of Economic Growth* (New York: Cambridge University Press, 1989), 205–296; Sheila Slaughter and Gary Rhoades, "The Emergence of a Competitiveness Research and Development Policy Coalition and the Commercialization of Academic Science and Technology," *Science, Technology and Human Values* 21 (1996): 303–339.

10. Geiger, *Research and Relevant Knowledge*, 296–309.

11. Mowery et al., *Ivory Tower*, 85–128; Roger L. Geiger, *Knowledge and Money: Research Universities and the Paradox of the Marketplace* (Stanford: Stanford University Press, 2004), 194–207.

12. Geiger, *Knowledge and Money*.

13. Richard Lugar and Michael Goldstein, *Technology in the Garden: Research Parks and Regional Economic Development* (Chapel Hill, NC: The University of North Carolina Press, 1991).

14. Philip Morowski and Robert Van Horn have labeled these camps the "Mertonian Tories" and the "Economic Whigs," respectively, and a third position of their own the "Trigs": "The Contract Research Organization and the Commercialization of Scientific Research," *Social Studies of Science* 35, no. 4 (August 2005): 503–548, quotes pp. 503–504.

15. David Dickson, *The New Politics of Science* (New York: Pantheon, 1984), 79–81; Geiger, *Research and Relevant Knowledge,* 318–319. Harvard had already taken a series of steps in the 1970s toward closer relations with industry, including abandoning its long-standing policy of dedicating medical patents to the public (1975) and establishing a university patent office (1977); Daniel J. Kevles, *"Diamond v. Chakrabarty* and Beyond: The Political Economy of Patenting Life," in Arnold Thackray, ed., *Private Science: Biotechnology and the Rise of Molecular Science* (Philadelphia: University of Pennsylvania Press, 1998), 65–79.

16. Derek Bok, *Universities in the Marketplace: The Commercialization of Higher Education* (Princeton: Princeton University Press, 2003); Sheldon Krimsky, *Science in the Private Interest: Has the Lure of Profits Corrupted Biomedical Research?* (New York: Rowman & Littlefield, 2003); Sheila Slaughter and Gary Rhoades, *Academic Capitalism and the New Economy: Markets, State, and Higher Education* (Baltimore: Johns Hopkins University Press, 2004); Jennifer Washburn, *University, Inc.: The Corporate Corruption of Higher Education* (New York: Basic Books, 2005).

17. Discussed more fully in Roger L. Geiger, "Real Crisis or Unpleasant Realities?" Symposium: Is the University in Crisis? *Society* 43, no. 4 (May-June 2006): 35–40.

18. Discussed most thoroughly in Krimsky, *Science in the Private Interest,* 73–90.

19. Ibid., 14–17; Bok, *Universities in the Marketplace,* 72–74; Washburn, *University, Inc.,* 19–20.

20. Discussed further in Chapter Four.

21. Quoted in Washburn, *University, Inc.;* also see Slaughter and Rhoades, *Academic Capitalism,* 335–338.

22. Discussed in Chapter Four.

23. Washburn, *University, Inc.,* 227.

24. Bok, *Universities in the Marketplace,* 78, 156; Mowery et al. express similar misgivings: *Ivory Tower,* p. 191.

25. Daniel S. Greenberg, *Science for Sale: The Perils, Rewards, and Delusions of Campus Capitalism* (Chicago: University of Chicago Press, 2007), quote p. 48.

26. Ibid., 272–273.

27. Bok, *Universities in the Marketplace,* 150.

28. Morowski and Van Horn, "Contract Research Organization."

29. Nathan Rosenberg and Richard R. Nelson, "American Universities and Technical Advance in Industry," *Research Policy* 23 (1994): 323–348; Nathan Rosenberg, "Why Do Firms Do Basic Research (with Their Own Money)?" *Research Policy* 19 (1990): 165–174; Mowery et al., *Ivory Tower.*

30. Geiger, *Knowledge and Money,* 194–196.

31. Partha Dasgupta and Paul A. David, "Toward a New Economics of Science," *Research Policy* 23 (1994): 487–521, quote p. 513.

32. Geiger, *Knowledge and Money,* 224–230.

33. Mowery et al., *Ivory Tower,* 179–192.

34. Ibid. Washburn too concludes with recommendations for tightening the patent system: *University, Inc.,* 231–233. See Chapter 4 in this volume.

35. Thomas L. Friedman, *The World Is Flat: A Brief History of the Twenty-first Century* (New York: Farrar, Straus and Giroux, 2005), 243–244.

36. Christopher Freeman and Luc Soete, *The Economics of Industrial Innovation* (Cambridge: MIT Press, 1997); see chap. 1.

37. J. Schumpeter, *Capitalism, Socialism, and Democracy* (London: Unwin University Books, 1952), 54–55.

38. See, e.g., Henry Chesbrough, *Open Business Models: How to Thrive in the New Innovation Landscape* (Boston: Harvard Business School Press, 2006); Richard K. Lester and Michael J. Piore, *Innovation: The Missing Dimension* (Cambridge: Harvard University Press, 2004); Edward Kahn, ed., *Innovate or Perish: Managing the Enduring Technology Company in the Global Market* (Hoboken, NJ: Wiley, 2007).

39. David C. Mowery and Nathan Rosenberg, *Paths of Innovation: Technological Change in 20th-Century America* (Cambridge: Cambridge University Press, 1998).

40. Ibid.

41. Keith Pavitt, "Public Policies to Support Basic Research: What Can the Rest of the World Learn from US Theory and Practice? (And What They Should Not Learn)," *Industrial and Corporate Change* 10, no. 3 (2001): 761–779. An identical conclusion, from different cases, is reached by Robert Buderi, "The Once and Future Industrial Research," in Albert Teich, ed., *AAAS Science and Technology Policy Yearbook* (Washington, DC: AAAS, 2002), 245–251.

42. Henry Chesbrough, *Open Innovation: The New Imperative for Creating and Profiting from Technology* (Boston: Harvard Business School Press, 2003); John Hagel and John Seely Brown, *The Only Sustainable Edge: Why Business Strategy Depends on Productive Friction and Dynamic Specialization* (Boston: Harvard Business School Press, 2005).

43. Such encouragement is often led by nonprofit organizations. The Council on Competitiveness has since 1996 published a succession of reports advocating measures to enhance innovation and competitiveness: for example, *Endless Frontier, Limited Resources: U.S. R&D Policy for Competitiveness* (April 1996), http://www.compete.org/publications/competitiveness_reports.asp (accessed July 25, 2006).

44. See http://www.nano.gov.

45. Steven Brint, "Professionals and the 'Knowledge Economy': Rethinking the Theory of Postindustrual Society," *Current Sociology* 49, no. 4 (July 2001): 101–132; Benoît Godin, "The Knowledge-based Economy: Conceptual Framework or Buzzword?" *Journal of Technology Transfer* 31 (2006): 17–30.

46. Jan Fagerberg, David C. Mowery, and Richard R. Nelson, eds., *The Oxford Handbook of Innovation* (New York: Oxford University Press, 2005).

47. Bruce Kogut, "Conclusion: From Regions and Firms to Multinational Highways; Knowledge and Its Diffusion as a Factor in the Globalization of Industries," in Martin Kenney with Richard Florida, eds., *Locating Global Advantage: Industry Dynamics in the International Economy* (Stanford: Stanford University Press, 2004), 261–282.

48. Friedman, *The World Is Flat,* 176. Friedman identifies the 10 forces driving change ("flattening the world") as the fall of the Berlin Wall, personal digitial devices, Netscape, work flow, outsourcing, offshoring, open-sourcing, insourcing, supply-chaining, and in-forming.

## Chapter 2: Universities and the Two Paths to Innovation

1. William J. Baumol, *The Free-market Innovation Machine: Analyzing the Growth Miracle of Capitalism* (Princeton: Princeton University Press, 2002), 13. As the title indicates, Baumol invokes the institutionalization of innovation under conditions of free-market capitalism to explain the miracle of economic growth, particularly because of the cumulative nature of innovative knowledge, the public-good property of improved technology, and the acceleration of innovation given steady investment (ibid., 51).

2. Jan Fagerberg, "Innovation: A Guide to the Literature," in Jan Fagerberg, David C. Mowery, and Richard R. Nelson, eds., *Oxford Handbook of Innovation* (New York: Oxford University Press, 2005), 1–26, quote p. 4.

3. William J. Baumol, "Education and Innovation: Entrepreneurial Breakthroughs vs. Corporate Incremental Improvements," NBER Working Paper 10578 (June 2004).

4. Baumol, *Free-Market Innovation,* 4 and passim. Additional factors include the "rule of law" and "productive entrepreneurship," meaning competition through productive innovation rather than rent seeking (through monopoly, lawsuits, or criminal activities).

5. Ibid., 35–36.

6. Robert Buderi, *Engines of Tomorrow* (New York: Simon & Schuster, 2000); Mark B. Myers, "Research and Change Management in Xerox," in Richard S. Rosen-

bloom and William J. Spencer, eds., *Engines of Innovation: U.S. Industrial Research at the End of an Era* (Boston: Harvard Business School Press, 1996), 133–150; Douglas K. Smith and Robert C. Alexander, *Fumbling the Future: How Xerox Invented, Then Ignored, the First Personal Computer* (New York: Morrow, 1988).

7. Buderi, *Engines of Tomorrow,* passim.

8. Ibid., 129, 242, 283.

9. Rosenbloom and Spencer, eds., *Engines of Innovation,* esp. Richard R. Nelson, Richard S. Rosenbloom, and William J. Spencer, "Shaping a New Era," 229–240.

10. David C. Mowery et al., *Ivory Tower and Industrial Innovation: University-Industry Technology Transfer before and after the Bayh-Dole Act* (Stanford: Stanford University Press, 2004), 35–84; Gary W. Matkin, *Technology Transfer and the University* (New York: ACE Macmillan, 1990), 16–38.

11. John P. Walsh, Ashish Arora, and Wesley M. Cohen, "Effects of Research Tool Patents and Licensing on Biomedical Innovation," in Wesley M. Cohen and Stephen A. Merrill, eds., *Patents in the Knowledge-based Economy* (Washington, DC: National Academies Press, 2003), 285–340.

12. Martin Kenney, "Biotechnology and the Creation of a New Economic Space," in Arnold Thackray, ed., *Private Science: Biotechnology and the Rise of Molecular Science* (Philadelphia: University of Pennsylvania Press, 1998), 131–143.

13. Roger L. Geiger, *Knowledge and Money: Research Universities and the Paradox of the Marketplace* (Stanford: Stanford University Press, 2004), 138. Previously, the Defense Advanced Research Projects Agency, or DARPA, had promoted research in what amounted to science-based technologies.

14. The central argument in Mowery et al., *Ivory Tower.*

15. Jerry G. Thursby and Marie C. Thursby, "Buyer and Seller Views of University-Industry Licensing," in Donald G. Stein, ed., *Buying In or Selling Out?* (New Brunswick, NJ: Rutgers University Press, 2004), 103–116.

16. Gregory Tassey, *The Economics of R&D Policy* (Westport, CT: Quorum, 1997).

17. This model by no means implies the much-criticized "linear model" of technological innovation, but rather tracks the path of a given invention from theory to application: David C. Mowery and Bhaven N. Sampat, "Universities in National Innovation Systems," in Fagerberg et al., eds., *Oxford Handbook of Innovation,* 209–239.

18. For example, Daniel S. Greenberg, *Science for Sale: The Perils, Rewards, and Delusions of Campus Capitalism* (Chicago: University of Chicago Press, 2007), 205–219.

19. Mowery et al., *Ivory Tower.*

20. James D. Adams, "Industrial R&D Laboratories: Windows on Black Boxes?" *Journal of Technology Transfer* 30, nos. 1–2 (2004): 129–137.

21. Similarly, Robert A. Lowe and Arvids A. Ziedonis conclude that "university inventors license inventions which are on average more tacit and require greater inventor effort (and presumably time) to develop": "Start-ups, Established Firms, and the Commercialization of University Inventions," unpub. ms., University of Pittsburgh (February 2, 2004), quote p. 18.

22. David B. Audretsch, Max C. Keilbach, and Erik L. Lehmann, *Entrepreneurship and Economic Growth* (New York: Oxford University Press, 2006), 29.

23. Raymond M. Wolfe, "U.S. Industrial R&D Performers Report Increased Expenditures for 2004," *InfoBrief,* NSF Science Resources Statistics, December 2006.

24. Audretsch et al., *Entrepreneurship,* 34–59; David B. Audretsch, *Innovation and Industry Evolution* (Cambridge: MIT Press, 1995), 178–180; Association of University Technology Managers, "AUTM U.S. Licensing Survey: FY 2004," p. 23. Includes start-ups and small companies (see below, Chapter 4).

25. Christophe Lécuyer, *Making Silicon Valley: Innovation and the Growth of High Tech, 1930–1970* (Cambridge: MIT Press, 2006), 169–210.

26. The following draws from Scott Shane, *Academic Entrepreneurship: University Spinoffs and Wealth Creation* (Northampton, MA: Edward Elgar, 2004). This discussion does not encompass nontechnical university spin-offs, which generally do not license university IP.

27. Lowe and Ziedonis, "Start-ups."

28. Robert A. Lowe, "Who Develops a University Invention? The Impact of Tacit Knowledge and Licensing Policies," *Journal of Technology Transfer* 31 (2006): 415–429.

29. Wesley M. Cohen, Richard R. Nelson, and John P. Walsh, "Links and Impacts: The Influence of Public Research on Industrial R&D," *Management Science* 48 (2002): 1–23.

30. Audretsch et al., *Entrepreneurship,* 41.

31. Shane, *Academic Entrepreneurship,* 23–25; Lynne G. Zucker and Michael R. Darby, "Movement of Star Scientists and Engineers and High-Tech Firm Entry," NBER Working Paper 12172 (April 2006).

32. Pontus Braunerhjelm and Maryann Feldman, eds., *Cluster Genesis: Technology-based Industrial* Development (Oxford: Oxford University Press, 2006); Joseph Cortright, *Making Sense of Clusters: Regional Competitiveness and Economic Development,* Discussion Paper, Brookings Institution Metropolitan Policy Program (March 2006); Kent Hill, "University Research and Local Economic Development," W. P. Carey School of Business, Arizona State University (August 2006).

33. David Audretsch and Paula Stephan, "Company-Scientist Locational Links: The Case of Biotechnology," *American Economic Review* 86 (1996): 641–652; Maryann Feldman and David Audretsch, "Innovation in Cities: Science-based Diversity, Specialization, and Localized Competition," *European Economic Review* 43 (1999): 409–429.

34. All R&D data from http://www.nsf.gov. This discussion omits a significant role of federally supported research performed by industry. Such research leverages the capabilities of industrial R&D and is sometimes performed in conjunction with universities.

35. Industry spending for basic research seems to have anticipated this pattern. Although it fluctuated somewhat, it did so on a level plateau, so that in constant dollars industry commitments for basic research in 2004 were little changed

from the early 1990s: National Science Board, *Science and Engineering Indicators 2006*, Appendix Tables 4–6, 4–10.

36. Calculated from *Science and Engineering Indicators 2006*, Appendix Table 4–6; scientific publications by industry scientists peaked in the first half of the 1990s, but fell thereafter (Figure 5–51).

37. Henry Chesbrough, *Open Innovation: The New Imperative for Creating and Profiting from Technology* (Boston: Harvard Business School Press, 2003); Walter W. Powell and Stine Grodal, "Networks of Innovators," in Fagerberg et al., eds., *Oxford Handbook of Innovation*, 56–85; Adams, "Industrial R&D Laboratories."

38. *Science and Engineering Indicators 2006*, chap. 4.

39. J. Scinta, "Industrial Research Institute's R&D Trends Forecast for 2007," *Research Technology Management* (January–February 2007): 17–20.

40. Richard C. Levin et al., "Appropriating the Returns from Industrial Research and Development," *Brookings Papers on Economic Activity* (1987), 783–831; Cohen et al., "Links and Impacts."

41. Wesley M. Cohen et al., "Industry and the Academy: Uneasy Partners in the Cause of Technological Advance," in Roger G. Noll, ed., *Challenges to Research Universities* (Washington, DC: Brookings, 1998), 171–200.

42. *Science and Engineering Indicators 2006*, chap. 4.

43. Data from Pharmaceutical Research and Manufacturers of America, *Pharmaceutical Industry Profile 2006*. For a critique of industry R&D claims, see Marcia Angell, *The Truth about Drug Companies* (New York: Random House, 2004), 37–51.

44. Marks & Clerk (patent and trademark attorneys), "Biotechnology Report 2007," reported in Cambridge Network; http://www.cambridgenetwork.co.uk/news/article/default.aspx?objid=35257. The other three patenters were Japan Science and Technology Agency (#1), NIH (#3), and the University of Tokyo (tie, #22). Patent families are multiple patents for the same invention.

45. Michael P. Gallaher, Albert N. Link, and Jeffrey E. Perusa, *Innovation in the U.S. Service Sector* (New York: Routledge, 2006), 90–92.

46. Arthur D. Levinson, quoted in *Wall Street Journal* (June 5, 2007), B2; see also Joseph Cortright and Heike Mayer, "Signs of Life: The Growth of Biotechnology Centers in the U.S.," Brookings Institution Center on Urban and Metropolitan Policy (2002).

47. Jason Owen-Smith and Walter W. Powell, "Accounting for Emergence and Novelty in Boston and Bay Area Biotechnology," in Pontus Braunerhjelm and Maryann Feldman, eds., *Cluster Genesis: Technology-based Industrial Development* (Oxford: Oxford University Press, 2006), 61–86.

48. Gordon E. Moore, "Some Personal Perspectives on Research in the Semiconductor Industry," in Rosenbloom and Spencer, eds., *Engines of Innovation*, 165–174, quotes pp. 168, 170; Buderi, *Engines of Tomorrow*, 325–342, quote p. 332. Intel now has programs to promote entrepreneurship in universities and recommendations for engineering curriculum: http://www.intel.com/education/highered/index.htm.

49. Buderi, *Engines of Tomorrow,* 310–311; *Guiding Principles for University-Industry Endeavors,* Report of a joint project of the National Council of University Research Administrators and the Industrial Research Institute (April 2006), p. 12; Roger L. Geiger and Paul Hallacher, "Nanotechnology and the States: Public Policy, University Research, and Economic Development in Pennsylvania," Report to the National Science Foundation (July 2005), 23.

50. Moore, "Some Personal Perspectives," 172.

51. David L. Kirp, *Shakespeare, Einstein, and the Bottom Line: The Marketing of Higher Education* (Cambridge: Harvard University Press, 2003), 207–220; www.gigascale.org.

52. The four units are Global Research Collaboration, Focus Center Research Program, Nanoelectronics Research Initiative, and Education Alliance: www.src.org.

53. Wayne C. Johnson, Testimony before the House Committee on Science and Technology, Subcommittee on Technology and Innovation, "Bayh-Dole—The Next 25 Years" (July 17, 2007), quote p. 4.

54. John Tao and Vincent Magnotta, "Open for Business: The Air Products and Chemicals Story," in Edward Kahn, ed., *Innovate or Perish: Managing the Enduring Technology Company in the Global Market* (Hoboken, NJ: Wiley, 2007), 189–222.

55. Susan B. Butts, Testimony before the House Committee on Science and Technology, Subcommittee on Technology and Innovation, "Bayh-Dole—The Next 25 Years" (July 17, 2007).

56. Johnson, Testimony, quote p. 9.

57. Rick Mullin, "Troubled Partnership," *Chemical and Engineering News* (March 19, 2007): 25–28; Tao and Magnotta, "Open for Business."

58. Mark A. Lemley, "Patenting Nanotechnology," *Stanford Law Review* 58 (2005): 601ff.

59. Radhika Prabhu, "Knowledge Creation and Technology Transfer in Nanotechnology at Research Universities," PhD thesis (Pennsylvania State University, 2007), 108, 120.

60. Michael R. Darby and Lynne G. Zucker, "Grilichesian Breakthroughs: Inventions of Methods of Inventing and Firm Entry in Nanotechnology," NBER Working Paper 9825 (Revised November 2003); Lynne G. Zucker and Michael R. Darby, "Socio-economic Impact of Nanoscale Science: Initial Results and Nanobank," NBER Working Paper 11181 (March 2005).

61. The PowerShares Lux Nanotech Portfolio ETF (PXN) has traded since November 2005.

62. Martha Collins, Director, New Applications Research, quoted by Henry W. Chesbrough, "Why Companies Should Have Open Business Models," *MIT Sloan Business Review* 48, no. 7 (Winter 2007): 22–28, quote p. 26.

63. Jerry Thursby and Marie Thursby, *Here or There? A Survey of Factors in Multinational R&D Location* (Washington, DC: National Academies Press, 2006) and "Where Is the New Science in Corporate R&D?" *Science* 314 (8 December 2006): 1547–48; Tao and Magnotta, "Open for Business," 204–208; interviews by the authors.

64. Thursby and Thursby *(Here or There?)* make an important distinction between research for new products and for familiar products: the latter is more like development, and the former is more likely to involve basic research. The story of Microsoft's basic research lab in Beijing illustrates the complexities and potential of conducting research in China; see Robert Buderi and Gregory T. Huang, *Guanxi (The Art of Relationships): Microsoft, China, and Bill Gates's Plan to Win the Road Ahead* (New York: Simon & Schuster, 2006).

65. Butts, Testimony.

66. Edwin Mansfield and Jeong-Yeon Lee, "The Modern University: Contributor to Industrial Innovation and Recipient of Industrial R&D Support," *Research Policy* 25 (1996): 1047–58; Lucien Paul Randazzese, "Profit and the Academic Ethos: The Activity and Performance of University-Industry Research Centers in the United States," PhD diss. (Carnegie Mellon University, 1996); Irwin Feller, Catherine P. Ailes, and J. David Roessner, "Impacts of Research Universities on Technological Innovation in Industry: Evidence from Engineering Research Centers," *Research Policy* 31 (2002): 457–474, see pp. 467–468; Geiger, *Knowledge and Money*, 182–186.

67. Roger L. Geiger, "Patterns of Industry Sponsored Research at Penn State: Implications for Economic Development," unpublished report to the Vice President for Research, Pennsylvania State University (August 2006).

68. Tao and Magnotta, "Open for Business," quotes pp. 195–196. Air Products has long analyzed university partnerships: John C. Tao, "Building Industry-University Research Partnerships: Corporate Perspective," in Chemical Sciences Roundtable, *Research Teams and Partnerships: Trends in the Chemical Sciences; Report of a Workshop* (Washington, DC: National Academy Press, 1999), 50–65.

69. Merrill S. Brenner and John C. Tao, "You Can Measure External Research Programs," *Research-Technology Management* (May–June 2001): 14–17.

70. Geiger, *Knowledge and Money*.

71. Feller et al., "Impacts of Research Universities."

72. Michael D. Santoro and Alok K. Chakrabarti, "Corporate Strategic Objectives for Establishing Relationships with University Research Centers," *IEEE Transactions on Engineering Management* 48, no. 2 (May 2001): 157–163. Gifts in kind (e.g. equipment) are frequently used for relationship building.

73. Cohen et al., "Links and Impacts," 16–17; Roger L. Geiger, "Corporate-sponsored Research at Penn State," unpublished report to the Vice President for Research, Pennsylvania State University (March 2008).

74. The 2007 solicitation of proposals for a third generation of ERCs explicitly added participation of small companies to the stipulated criteria.

75. The following draws on the evaluation of ERCs in 1995–1996 reported in Feller et al., "Impacts of Research Universities." See also D. Fennell Evans and Matthew V. Tirrell, "Research Teams at Universities: The Center for Interfacial Engineering," in Chemical Sciences Roundtable, *Research Teams*, 42–49.

76. Feller et al., "Impacts of Research Universities," p. 471.

77. Evans and Tirrell, "Research Teams," 49.

78. Santoro and Chakrabarti, "Corporate Strategic Objectives."
79. Charles Concannon, "University R&D Collaboration," presentation to SSTI Annual Conference, Oklahoma City, November 1, 2006.
80. See www.intel-research.net. Interview with David Westfall, Intel Research Pittsburgh (July 25, 2007). These labs also represent a significant shift in research strategy at the corporation toward more basic research and copublication with academic researchers. This strategy seems to have survived a corporate revamping in 2005.
81. Eric Brewer, quoted in "Intel Research Berkeley Collaborating to Change the World," http://www.intel.com/research/downloads/03-647_ir_insert_berk_r03 .pdf, accessed May 2, 2008.
82. Westfall interview.
83. Sachi Hatakenaka, *University-Industry Partnerships in MIT, Cambridge, and Tokyo: Storytelling across Boundaries* (New York: Routledge Falmer, 2004), 98–117; http://web.mit.edu/newsoffice/nr/2000/alliance.html. The corporate partners were Amgen, Merck, Ford, NTT, Merrill Lynch, DuPont, Microsoft, and Hewlett-Packard.
84. Charles M. Vest, *The American Research University from World War II to World Wide Web: Governments, the Private Sector, and the Emerging Meta-university* (Berkeley: University of California Press, 2007), 45–46.
85. Hatakenaka, *University-Industry Partnerships*, quote p. 108; Vest, *American Research University*, 45.
86. Alan P. Rudy et al., *Universities in the Age of Corporate Science: The UC Berkeley–Novartis Controversy* (Philadelphia: Temple University Press, 2007); Robert M. Price and Laurie Goldman, "The Novartis Agreement: An Appraisal," Administrative Review, University of California, Berkeley (October 4, 2002). Our thanks to Robert Price for providing this document.
87. For the circumstances that prompted the PMB solicitation and initial campus reactions to the agreement, see Todd R. La Porte, "Diluting Public Patrimony or Inventive Response to Increasing Knowledge Asymmetries: Watershed for Land Grant Universities? Reflections on the University of California, Berkeley–Novartis Agreement," in Chemical Sciences Roundtable, *Research Teams*, 66–84. The secrecy, which raised suspicions and criticism, resulted from the competition among firms for this contract.
88. For example, "the majority of people in PMB benefited only to the extent that a significant amount of money ($60,000–$200,000 per annum) was made more easily available to them. . . . It seems that graduate students also suffered no obvious harm. Whether their socialization to more permissive university-industry relations represents a decline in their moral and ethical standards we will leave for another discussion": Rudy et al., *Universities in the Age of Corporate Science*, p. 149.
89. Novartis merged its agricultural operations into Syngenta Corporation, which renamed the lab Torrey Mesa Research Institute. This institute was then closed at the end of 2002, with some operations moving to North Carolina and others sold to Diversa Corporation, a biotech start-up (ibid., 64–65).

90. "Academic" research here would have to include national laboratories and independent laboratories like The Scripps Research Institute.

## Chapter 3: Policies for Technology-Based Economic Development

1. National Governors Association and Pew Center on the States, *Investing in Innovation* (Washington, DC: NGA, 2007).
2. Specifically, science is still characterized by the "centralized federalism model," where the national government dominates policy making. In the 1970s a "functional federalism model" emerged in some areas where bureaucracies at various levels cooperated toward shared goals; and more recently an "intergovernmental management model" has appeared which includes networks of public and private organizations: Paul M. Hallacher, *Why Policy Issue Networks Matter: The Advanced Technology Program and the Manufacturing Extension Partnership* (Lanham, MD: Rowman & Littlefield, 2005), 22.
3. General Accounting Office, "Observations on the Small Business Innovation Research Program." Testimony before the House Subcommittee on Environment, Technology, and Standards, Committee on Science, June 28, 2005. The Small Business Administration oversees the SBIR and STTR programs: www.sba.gov/sbir/indexsbir-sttr.html.
4. David B. Audretsch, Juergen Weigand, and Claudia Weigand, "The Impact of SBIR on Creating Entrepreneurial Behavior," *Economic Development Quarterly* 16, no. 1 (February 2002): 32–38; Andrew A. Toole and Dirk Czarnitzki, "Biomedical Academic Entrepreneurship through the SBIR Program," NBER Working Paper 11450 (June 2005). In 2004 SBIR awards totaled around $2 billion and STTR awards around $200 million, both roughly triple the levels of 1997.
5. Barry Bozeman and P. Craig Boardman, *Managing the New Multipurpose, University Research Centers: Institutional Innovation in the Academic Community* (Washington, DC: IBM Endowment for the Business of Government, 2003).
6. For a review of evaluation studies, see Denis O. Gray and S. George Walters, eds., *Managing the Industry / University Cooperative Research Center: A Guide for Directors and Other Stakeholders* (Columbus, OH: Battelle Press, 1998); James D. Adams, Eric P. Chang, and Katara Starkey, "Industry-University Cooperative Research Centers," *Journal of Technology Transfer* 26, nos. 1–2 (2001): 73–86.
7. See David Roessner, "Outcomes and Impacts of The State / Industry-University Cooperative Research Centers (S/IUCRC) Program," final report to the National Science Foundation (Arlington, VA: SRI International, 2000).
8. Catherine P. Ailes, Irwin Feller, and H. Roberts Coward, "The Impact of Engineering Research Centers on Institutional and Cultural Change in Participating Universities," final report to the National Science Foundation (Arlington, VA: SRI International, 2001), esp. 106–125.
9. Irwin Feller, Catherine P. Ailes, and J. David Roessner, "Impacts of Research Universities on Technological Innovation in Industry: Evidence from Engineering Research Centers," *Research Policy* 31 (2002): 457–474; Catherine P. Ailes, David

Roessner, and H. Roberts Coward, "Documenting Center Graduation Paths: Second Year Report" to the National Science Foundation (Arlington, VA: SRI International, 2000).

10. Rutgers University, "National Science Foundation Awards $15 Million Grant to Rutgers-led Engineering Research Consortium; Collaborators Are New Jersey Institute of Technology, Purdue University, and the University of Puerto Rico," press release (May 17, 2006); http://ur.rutgers.edu/medrel/viewArticle.html ?ArticleID=5168.

11. Feller et al., "Impacts of Research Universities"; Ailes et al., "Documenting Center Graduation Paths"; D. Fennell Evans and Matthew V. Tirrell, "Research Teams at Universities: The Center for Interfacial Engineering," in Chemical Sciences Roundtable, *Research Teams and Partnerships: Trends in the Chemical Sciences; Report of a Workshop* (Washington, DC: National Academy Press, 1999). This ERC received continued core funding as a Materials Research Science and Engineering Center (see below).

12. National Science Foundation, *Engineering Research Centers Annual Report,* 2005–2006 (Arlington, VA: NSF, 2006).

13. Investment in such centers peaked in 2003 at around $363 million. Data from annual NSF budget requests to Congress, 1999–2007.

14. The effort to organize research in federally funded centers goes back to the Advanced Research Projects Agency (ARPA) and its Interdisciplinary Laboratory program in the 1950s. This program provided the financial basis for universities to initiate materials research in an organized fashion, drawing on expertise from several science and engineering fields. Arising out of the Sputnik crisis, ARPA looked at the R&D organizations of Bell Labs and GE in their heyday for inspiration. The departmentalization of disciplines is hardly a consideration for industry, and the traditional academic organization of colleges and departments was viewed as a structural obstacle. This program was later transferred to the NSF and partly inspired the creation of the ERCs.

15. National Research Council of the National Academies, *The National Science Foundation's Materials Research Science and Engineering Centers Program: Looking Back, Moving Forward* (Washington, DC: National Academies Press, 2007), 136–149. Of course, the NSF is not the only research agency to fund centers. NIH funds an estimated 1,400 centers of various kinds that take up around 9 percent of its massive budget; the Department of Defense also has its own center programs.

16. Ibid., 147–148.

17. Ibid., esp. 23–24.

18. Ibid., 136–149.

19. Roger L. Geiger, *Knowledge and Money: Research Universities and the Paradox of the Marketplace* (Stanford: Stanford University Press, 2004), 201–202.

20. Walter H. Plosila, "State Science- and Technology-based Economic Development Policy: History, Trends and Developments, and Future Directions," *Economic Development Quarterly* 18, no. 2 (May 2004): 113–126.

21. For example, the federal Manufacturing Extension Partnership Program, which required matching state funds, emphasized process improvement. See Plosila, "State Science- and Technology-based Policy," 120.

22. C. M. Coburn, *Partnerships: A Compendium of State and Federal Cooperative Technology Programs* (Columbus, OH: Battelle Press, 1995); Irwin Feller, "The Impacts of State Technology Programmes on American Research Universities," in Thomas G. Whiston and Roger L. Geiger, eds., *Research and Higher Education: The United Kingdom and the United States* (Buckingham, UK: Open University Press, 1992), 64–88; Plosila, "State Science- and Technology-based Policy."

23. David M. Hart, " 'Entrepreneurial' State Economic Development Policy: Advocates, Constituents, and Sustainability." Presented at the 2006 Fall Research Conference, Association for Public Policy and Management, Madison, WI, November 4, 2006. For an early account of the entrepreneurial state, see Peter K. Eisinger, *The Rise of the Entrepreneurial State: State and Local Economic Development Policy in the United States* (Madison: University of Wisconsin Press, 1988).

24. Roger L. Geiger and Creso Sá, "Beyond Technology Transfer: US State Policies to Harness University Research for Economic Development," *Minerva* 43 (2005): 1–21; Feller, "Impacts of State Technology Programmes."

25. For the continuity in S&T programs, see Plosila, "State Science- and Technology-based Policy," 119. For program and agency termination, see ibid., 121, and a more extended discussion in Geiger and Sá, "Beyond Technology Transfer," 10–12.

26. Feller, "Impacts of State Technology Programmes."

27. Ibid., 73.

28. The National Governors Association published the following reports: "Building State Economies by Promoting University-Industry Technology Transfer" (April 28, 2000); "Using Research and Development to Grow State Economies" (May 1, 2000); "A Governor's Guide to Building State Science and Technology Capacity" (July 15, 2002); and "Science, Technology and Economic Growth: A Practicum for States" (March 25, 2004).

29. Geiger and Sá, "Beyond Technology Transfer," 8–10.

30. By the terms of the agreement the states were supposed to spend 25 percent of their revenues on antismoking campaigns. However, this amount (around $1.5 billion in 2006) would produce an excessive and cloying volume of antismoking propaganda. Ironically, the states are now partners with cigarette companies in sharing the profits from smoking. See www.tobaccofreekids.org/reports/settlements/, accessed May 10, 2006.

31. John E. Jankowski, "What Is the State Government Role in the R&D Enterprise?" (NSF 99–348) (Arlington, VA: National Science Foundation, Division of Science Resources Studies, 1999).

32. Battelle Technology Partnership Practice and SSTI, *Growing the Nation's Bioscience Sector: State Bioscience Initiatives 2006*. Prepared for BIO—Biotechnology Industry Organization (April 2006); http://bio.org/local/battelle2006/.

33. Michael E. Porter, "Clusters and Competition: New Agendas for Companies, Governments, and Institutions," in Michael E. Porter, *On Competition* (Cambridge, MA: Harvard Business School Press, 1998), 197–288.

34. There are two operative definitions of clusters in the literature: one refers to special agglomerations that generate significant positive interactive effects (e.g., Pontus Braunerhjelm and Maryann Feldman, eds., *Cluster Genesis: Technology-based Industrial Development* [Oxford: Oxford University Press, 2006]); the other refers more generically to overrepresented firms in the same industry classifications that may or may not interact.

35. Bo Carlsson, "The Role of Public Policy in Emerging Clusters," in Braunerhjelm and Feldman, eds., *Cluster Genesis*, 264–278; BJK Associates, "The Influence of R&D Expenditures on New Firm Formation and Economic Growth" (Maplewood, NJ: BJK Associates for SBA Office of Advocacy, 2002); http://www.sba.gov/advo/research/technology.html.

36. Joseph Loscalzo, "The NIH Budget and the Future of Biomedical Research," *New England Journal of Medicine* 354, no. 16 (2006): 1665–67.

37. Battelle and SSTI, *Growing the Nation's Bioscience Sector*, 38, 41–43.

38. Jocelyn Kaiser, "Med Schools Add Labs despite Budget Crunch," *Science* 317 (September 7, 2007): 1309–10.

39. Ironically, New Jersey voters in 2007 rejected a bond initiative that would have provided continued funding for stem cell research: Constance Holden, "New Jersey Rejects Bonds for Stem Cell Institute," *Science* 318 (November 16, 2007): 1053.

40. Spitzer proposed a Stem Cell and Innovation Fund to "provide long-term investment, overseen by independent industry experts, for stem cell innovations and other types of applied research that will lead to direct commercial application." Eliot Spitzer, "One New York," New York State State of the State Address 2007 (Albany, NY: Office of the Governor, 2007), 12–13.

41. *SSTI Weekly Digest*, April 25, 2005; April 24, 2006. This issue remains contentious, and a number of states have passed legislation to limit or ban therapeutic cloning of or research on human embryonic stem cells (SSTI, April 25, 2005). John Aubrey Douglass, "Universities and the Entrepreneurial State: Politics and Policy and a New Wave of State-based Economic Initiatives," CSHE Research and Occasional Paper Series no. 14.06 (September 2006), 17–19. A discovery announced in November 2007 of a technique for creating stem cells from skin cells promises to revolutionize this "industry," and no doubt the policies predicated on the previous state of the art.

42. New York State Commission on Higher Education, "A Preliminary Report of Findings and Recommendations" (December 2007), www.hecommission.state.ny.us; quote p. 17.

43. National Governors Association and Pew Center on the States, *Investing in Innovation*.

44. Ibid., 23–24; these words are quoted from Battelle Technology Partnership Practice, whose basic approach is mirrored in this report. Battelle has shaped the TBED strategies of Arizona (discussed below) and Ohio, among others.

45. The compact for postsecondary education is presented as a framework to bring together states, industry, and universities to ensure that "postsecondary education policies, programs, curricula, and resources address current, emerging, and future economic realities." The task force asserts that "most research universities continue to focus on a simple 'pipeline' mode of innovation, whereby knowledge is created in university laboratories, licensed by companies through the technology transfer office, and then developed into successful products." It advocates an alternative approach, in which the strategies of universities relate more closely to local industrial circumstances: "in some states, the compact may be developmental in nature, seeking to build research capacity to attract federal and industry R&D. In states with thriving, knowledge-intensive industries, the compact may be more focused on the diffusion of knowledge created through high levels of federal research support and enhanced partnerships with industry." These differing circumstances are viewed as a progression from building research capacity to disseminating knowledge through various pathways, all to be monitored through the usual indicators of research quality—number of patents, licenses, start-ups, and relationships with industry. National Governors Association and Pew Center on the States, *Investing in Innovation*, quotes on pp. 1 and 13. See also National Governors Association, *A Compact for Postsecondary Education* (Washington, DC: NGA Center for Best Practices, 2007).
46. John W. Kingdon, *Agendas, Alternatives, and Public Policies*, 2nd ed. (New York: Longman, 2003), 122–124, 179–183, quote p. 179. For the political culture, see William Zumeta, "The Public Interest and State Policies Affecting Academic Research in California," presented at the conference "The Public Interest and Academic Research," Seville, Spain, November 2006, and Evans School Working Paper 2008–01.
47. Douglass, "Universities and the Entrepreneurial State."
48. For a history of the Master Plan, see John Aubrey Douglass, *The California Idea and American Higher Education* (Stanford: Stanford University Press, 2000).
49. Gary W. Matkin, *Technology Transfer and the University* (New York: American Council on Education and Oryx Press, 1990), 135–138.
50. Mary L. Walshok, *Knowledge without Boundaries* (San Francisco: Jossey-Bass, 1995), 175–191.
51. Mary L. Walshok et al., "Building Regional Innovation Capacity: The San Diego Experience," *Industry and Higher Education* (February 2002): 27–42. UC San Diego is complemented by The Scripps Research Institute, the Salk Institute, and four other biomedical institutes located in close proximity.
52. Zumeta, "Public Interest and State Policies," 18; University of California, Industry-University Cooperative Research Program, "Overview, 1996–2002," www.ucdiscoverygrant.org.
53. Douglass, "Universities and the Entrepreneurial State," 10–12, provides the fullest account of Cal ISI's origins.
54. Calit2, press release (December 27, 2006); www.calit2.net/newsroom/print_page.php?id=1015.

55. Rick DelVecchio and Mark Martin, "Cal to Be Hub for Study of Alternate Fuel," *San Francisco Chronicle* (February 1, 2007), A–1.

56. Other competitors were UC San Diego, MIT, Imperial College London, and the John Innes Centre. See Eli Kintisch, "Half-Billion-Dollar Bonanza for Plant Scientists," *ScienceNOW Daily News* (February 1, 2007); http://sciencenow.sciencemag.org/cgi/content/full/2007/201/1.

57. Erik Vance, "BP Awards $500-Million to California and Illinois Institutions for Alternative-Energy Research," *Chronicle of Higher Education* (February 2, 2007).

58. Zumeta, "Public Interest and State Policies," 17–18.

59. Ibid., 22–24; Douglass, "Universities and the Entrepreneurial State," 12–15; CIRM, press release (December 7, 2006): www.cirm.ca.gov/press/2006.asp.

60. Zumeta, "Public Interest and State Policies," 23–26.

61. John M. Bacheller, "Commentary on State-Level Economic Development in New York: A Strategy to Enhance Effectiveness," *Economic Development Quarterly* 14, no. 1 (2000): 5–10. Elizabeth Currid has argued, based on the occupational structure of New York City, that its true competitive advantage lies in the creative industries of the arts, design, media, and entertainment to a much greater extent than in financial and professional services; high-technology industries are considered unimportant for the city's economy in her analysis. See Elizabeth Currid, "New York as a Global Creative Hub: A Competitive Analysis of Four Theories on World Cities," *Economic Development Quarterly* 20 (2006): 330–350.

62. It was a central part of former governor Eliot Spitzer's platform: "We must adapt to the Innovation Economy. This is the knowledge-based economy of new businesses and new ideas that has become the driving force of job creation in the world today." Spitzer, "One New York," 9.

63. As quoted (p. 263) in Stuart W. Leslie, "Regional Disadvantage: Replicating Silicon Valley in New York's Capital Region," *Technology and Culture* 42, no. 2 (April 2001): 236–264.

64. RTDCs are designated centers of the federal Manufacturing Extension Partnership. Irwin Feller, "Rejoinder: Response to Coburn and Brown," *Economic Development Quarterly* 11 (1997): 310–312, quote p. 312. See also "New York Science & Technology Program Funding Restored," *SSTI Weekly Digest*, March 14, 1997.

65. NYSTAR, "Regional Technology Development Centers, Program Summary 2004–2005": www.nystar.state.ny.us/documents.htm, accessed May 30, 2007.

66. Ann Markusen, "Sticky Places in Slippery Space: A Typology of Industrial Districts," *Economic Geography* 72 (1996): 293–313.

67. Leslie asserts, "The Center for Industrial Innovation ended up supporting an outdated version of industrial innovation": "Regional Disadvantage," 261. RPI is also engaged in the struggle to revitalize the region. Since 2000—when Low's 1970s plan *Rensselaer 2000* would presumably make its achievements more visible—RPI has been once again aggressively pursuing institutional advancement anchored on economic relevance. President Shirley Ann Jackson's "Rensselaer Plan" hit some of the same buttons that Low did. One of the overarching goals is of course to strengthen the institute's research profile, and one of the

most salient strategies has been to focus on institute-wide priorities in information technology and biotechnology. Promoting scientific and technological entrepreneurialism is another key tenet of the plan. A $22.5 million grant from
the Gen*NY*sis program has helped the institute to build the Center for
Biotechnology and Interdisciplinary Studies, a massive research facility.

68. See Henry Etzkowitz, "From Zero Sum to Value-added Strategies: The Emergence of Knowledge-based Industrial Policy in the States of the United States,"
*Policy Studies Journal* 25, no. 3 (1997): 412–424, esp. 418.

69. Irwin Feller, "American State Governments as Models for National Science
Policy," *Journal of Policy Analysis and Management* 11, no. 2 (1992): 288–309.

70. The evaluation was conducted by SRI International. See Robert Bitting and
Richard M. Spriggs, "The Evaluation of New York State's Centers for Advanced
Technology Program: One Center's Perspective," *SRA Journal* 25, no. 2 (1994):
5–17.

71. Plosila, "State Science- and Technology-based Policy," 115–119.

72. As specified in the statutes of the CAT Program: "beginning in the sixth academic year . . . amounts provided by the foundation of up to seven hundred
fifty thousand dollars shall be matched equally by the center, amounts in excess
of seven hundred fifty thousand dollars shall be matched by the center in
amounts of at least the percentage set forth herein: in the sixth year, one hundred twenty percent; in the seventh year, one hundred forty percent; in the
eighth year, one hundred sixty percent; in the ninth year, one hundred eighty
percent; in the tenth year and each year thereafter, two hundred percent";
www.nystar.state.ny.us/cats/catsstatute.htm, accessed January 19, 2007.

73. Interviews by author (CMS) with three CAT directors, Albany, Troy, and New
York City (May 2006). See also Bitting, "Evaluation of New York State's Centers."

74. The $10 million state grant was complemented by $2 million from a federal
grant and $1.4 million from private sources.

75. State of New York, "Governor Pataki, Majority Leader, Speaker: State to Provide $15 Million for SUNY Albany's 300 mm Wafer Pilot Manufacturing Fa-
cility," press release (February 15, 2000).

76. State of New York, "Governor Pataki: New York Universities Win High-Tech Research Award; SUNY Albany and RPI Selected for Prestigious Multimillion
Dollar Research Program," press release (March 14, 2001).

77. One administrator at Albany humorously refers to the three politicians as
"competing among themselves to see who does more" for TBED. Interview by
author (CMS), May 2006, Albany.

78. Fifty million dollars for the first nanofabrication facility, completed in 2004;
$175 million for the second, finished in 2005.

79. George E. Pataki, New York State of the State Address 2004 (Albany, NY: Office
of the Governor, 2004).

80. College of Nanoscale Science and Engineering, University at Albany, "CNSE
Backgrounder," press release (August 2007), 2–9.

81. Steve Lohr, "New York Bets on High-Tech to Aid Upstate," *New York Times* (October 28, 2006).

82. New York State Commission on Higher Education, "Preliminary Report," (December 2007)14–19. http://www.hecommission.state.ny.us/report/CHE
_Preliminary_Report.pdf

83. *SSTI Weekly Digest* (October 24, 2007).

84. Philip Shapira, "Innovation Challenges and Strategies in Catch-up Regions: Developmental Growth and Disparities in Georgia, USA," paper prepared for International Symposium on Rethinking Regional Innovation and Change: Path Dependency or Regional Breakthrough? Stuttgart, Germany, February 28–March 1, 2002.

85. W. Henry Lambright, "Catalyzing Research Competitiveness: The Georgia Research Alliance," *Prometheus* 18, no. 4 (2000): 357–372.

86. Ibid., 367–370.

87. Paul Smaglik, "Georgia on the Mind," *Nature* 445 (February 2007): 790–791.

88. Georgia Research Alliance, Annual Report 2006 (Atlanta: GRA, 2007), 10.

89. For the impacts of the GRA, see Smaglik, "Georgia"; for its characteristics, see Shapira, "Innovation Challenges," 12–13.

90. For Yamacraw, see Geiger, *Knowledge and Money*, 210–212. See also Georgia Electronic Design Center, "October 2004 Status Report" (Atlanta: Georgia Institute of Technology, 2004), and "April 2007 Status Report" (Atlanta: Georgia Institute of Technology, 2007).

91. Louis G. Tornatzky, Paul G. Waugaman, and Denis O. Gray, *Innovation U.: New University Roles in a Knowledge Economy* (Research Triangle Park, NC: Southern Growth Policies Board, 2002), 27–41; Geiger, *Knowledge and Money*; Irwin Feller, "Who Competes with Whom, Who's Likely to Succeed, and Why." Paper presented at the symposium The Future of the American Public Research University, The Pennsylvania State University, University Park, PA. (February 25–26, 2005). *U.S. News and World Report* rated Georgia Tech fourth in engineering: "America's Best Graduate Schools, 2007 Edition," 30.

92. For a description of the centers, see http://georgiainnovation.org/.

93. Dennis Hoffman, "Jobs, Income, and Growth in Arizona: Individual versus Aggregate Measures of Economic Performance," Arizona State University W. P. Carey School of Business (March 2005).

94. The University of Arizona Office of Economic Development produced status reports on these clusters in 2001 and 2003. Although clusters have loomed ever larger in the economic development imagination, the second report in particular was quite critical of actual results. It found that participation by firms in the cluster organizations was quite low, and the organizations themselves seemed to have little to offer. As voluntary organizations they lacked resources, focus, or clarity of purpose. Most important, employment had declined in half of these cluster industries (and overall). See Industry Cluster Development Program, "Industry Clusters in Southern Arizona, 2001 Status Report" (Tucson: University of Arizona Office of Economic Development, March 2002).

95. Geiger, *Knowledge and Money*, 109–115; Goldie Blumenstyk, "University of Arizona Ends Program to Commercialize Research," *Chronicle of Higher Education* (July 21, 1995).

96. See www.tgen.org/about/index.cfm?pageid=2.

97. Battelle Technology Partnership Practice. *Arizona Bioscience Roadmap*. (Battelle Memorial Institute, December 2002).

98. See Arizona State University, "Annual Report of Sponsored Research Activity and TRIFF Supported Activity" (Tempe: Arizona State University, Office of Research and Economic Development, 2004), 37–40.

99. See www.biodesign.asu.edu/centers/.

100. Arizona House of Representatives, Forty-sixth Legislature, First Regular Session, 2003, House Bill 2529, esp. 1–2. See also Nancy J. Neff, "ASU Gains Needed Investment, Nod of Approval from Legislature," Arizona State University Office of Public Affairs, news release (June 30, 2003).

101. See "Prop. 102 Goes Down to Surprising Defeat," *USA Today* (March 11, 2004). For the views of Arizona voters on S&T, see *Arizonans' Attitudes toward Science, Technology, and Their Effects on the Economy* (Tempe: Arizona State University, Morrison Institute for Public Policy, 2006).

102. According to a Goldwater Institute policy paper, Proposition 102 "would have erased an important protection for taxpayers, opened the door to public corruption, and given select corporations an unfair business advantage." See Mark Brnovich and Vicki Murray, "How the Arizona Constitution Protects Taxpayers: The Importance of Safeguarding Article IX," Goldwater Institute Policy Report 196 (October 12, 2004), 1.

103. The groups are Flagstaff 40, Greater Phoenix Leadership, and the Southern Arizona Leadership Council.

104. Mary Jo Pitzl, "$150 Million Proposed for Biosciences," *Arizona Republic* (February 23, 2006).

105. Alberta Charney et al., "A Strategic Assessment of the Economic Benefits of Investments in Research in Arizona," Arizona State University W. P. Carey School of Business (June 2007). Harris served at the NSF from 1978 until 1996, where he headed the mathematical and physical sciences directorate.

106. The governor has proposed to renew the state commitment to SFAz in the 2008 budget. See Janet Napolitano, "The Executive Budget—Fiscal Years 2008 and 2009" (Phoenix: State of Arizona, Office of the Governor, 2007). See also Ken Alltucker, "Proposed Budget Boosts Sciences," *Arizona Republic* (January 14, 2007).

107. Walter H. Plosila and Mitchell Horowitz, "2006 Arizona's Bioscience Roadmap Progress Report," Battelle Technology Partnership Practice (December 2006).

108. Ronald J. Hanson, "Bioscience Report Is Upbeat," *AZCentral.com* (December 5, 2007); www.azcentral.com/business/articles/1205biz-biotech1205.html.

109. Robert D. Atkinson and Daniel K. Correa, *The 2007 State New Economy Index: Benchmarking Economic Transformation in the States* (Kansas City: Ewing Marion Kauffman Foundation and Information Technology and Innovation Foundation,

February 2007). The State New Economy Index is a composite of 26 measures, most of which are not related or only distantly related to university research.

110. Charney et al., "Strategic Assessment," chap. 2; A. Salter and B. Martin, "The Economic Benefits of Publicly Funded Basic Research: A Critical Review. *Research Policy* 30, no. 3 (March 1, 2001): 509–532.

111. Charney et al., "Strategic Assessment," 24.

112. GRA, 2006 Annual Report, 5, and 2006 Continuum Report, 8; Plosila and Horowitz, "Roadmap Progress Report."

113. GRA, 2006 Annual Report; Plosila and Horowitz, "Roadmap Progress Report."

114. Funded at $7.5 million, the faculty development program supported eight new midcareer appointments in 2006, four professors and four associate professors: www.nystar.state.ny.us.fdp.htm.

115. Florida invested $32 million to recruit the Torrey Pines Institute for Molecular Studies and $94 million in 2007 to bring a unit of Germany's Max Planck Society to the Scripps cluster. It also recruited the Burnham Institute for Medical Research to Orlando: *SSTI Weekly Digest* (October 31, 2003); Stephen Pound and Eve Samples, "Crist Revels in Biotech Boom," *Palm Beach Post* (November 28, 2007). Florida has also instituted university-based TBED initiatives similar to those described in this chapter.

## Chapter 4: Patenting and Licensing University Technologies

1. Jason Owen-Smith, "Public Science, Private Science: The Causes and Consequences of Patenting by Research One Universities," PhD diss. (University of Arizona, 2000), 121–226.

2. IP also includes material transfer agreements, copyrights, and software agreements, which are not discussed in this analysis.

3. For the process that shaped the standardized TTO, see Bhaven N. Sampat and Richard R. Nelson. 2002. "The Emergence and Standardization of University Technology Transfer Offices: A Case Study of Institutional Change," *Advances in Strategic Management*, 19 (2002) The New Institutionalism in Strategic Management Paul Ingram and Brian Silverman eds., JAI Press., 135–164.

4. Jane Robbins, "Shaping Patent Policy: The National Research Council and the Universities from World War I to the 1960s," *Perspectives on the History of Higher Education* 25 (2006): 89–122.

5. Farrell Center for Corporate Innovation and Entrepreneurship, Pennsylvania State University, "Technology Transfer Survey" (2004), retrieved at http://www.zoomerang.com/reports/public_report.zgi?ID=HTD2E54VVFAT. We would like to thank Anthony Warren for sharing this survey.

6. David B. Audretsch, Max C. Keilbach, and Erik E. Lehman, *Entrepreneurship and Economic Growth* (New York: Oxford University Press, 2006), 103–107; R. Henderson, A. B. Jaffe, and M. Trajtenberg, "Universities as a Source of Commercial Technology," *Review of Economics and Statistics* 80 (1998): 119–127; D. Hicks et

al., "The Changing Composition of Innovative Activity in the U.S.: A Portrait Based on Patent Analysis," *Research Policy* 30 (2001): 681–703.

7. David Blumenthal et al., "University-Industry Research Relationships in Biotechnology: Implications for the University," *Science* 232 (13 June 1986): 1361–65; Lynne G. Zucker and Michael R. Darby, "Star Scientists and Institutional Transformation: Patterns of Invention and Innovation in the Formation of the Biotechnology Industry," *Proceedings of the National Academy of Sciences, USA* 93 (November 1996): 12709–16.

8. Jason Owen-Smith, "Trends and Transitions in the Institutional Environment for Public and Private Science," *Higher Education* 49 (2005): 91–117.

9. Real expenditures for academic research were about two-thirds higher in 2000–2002 than in 1990–1992, so 45 patents in 1991–1993 is (very) roughly equivalent to 75 in 2001–2003.

10. One statistical study found that "commercial productivity" (not just patents) of universities rose steadily for 1991–1997, and that more of the increase was due to productivity gains of efficient (i.e. mature) producers than to late starters catching up: Jerry G. Thursby and Sukanya Kemp, "Growth and Productive Efficiency of University Intellectual Property Licensing," *Research Policy* 31 (2002): 109–124.

11. Jason Owen-Smith, "From Separate Systems to a Hybrid Order: Accumulative Advantage across Public and Private Science at Research One Universities," *Research Policy* 32 (2003): 1081–1104.

12. Martin Meyer, "Are Patenting Scientists the Better Scholars? An Exploratory Comparison of Inventor-Authors with their Non-inventing Peers in Nanoscience and Technology," *Research Policy* 35 (December 2006): 1646–62; Paula Stephan et al., "Who's Patenting in the University? Evidence from the Survey of Doctorate Recipients," *Economics of Innovation and New Technology* 16, no. 2 (2007): 71–99.

13. Deepak Hegde, "Public and Private Universities: Unequal Sources of Regional Innovation?" *Economic Development Quarterly* 19, no. 4 (November, 2005): 373–386.

14. Blumenthal et al., "University-Industry Research Relationships."

15. Zucker and Darby, "Star Scientists"; Lynne G. Zucker and Michael R. Darby, "Movement of Star Scientists and Engineers and High-Tech Firm Entry," NBER Working Paper 12172 (April 2006); Scott Shane, *Academic Entrepreneurship: University Spinoffs and Wealth Creation* (Northhampton, MA: Elgar, 2004), 84–86.

16. Stephan et al., "Who's Patenting in the University?".

17. Walter W. Powell and Jason Owen-Smith, "The New World of Knowledge Production in the Life Sciences," in Steven Brint, ed., *The Future of the City of Intellect: The Changing American University* (Stanford: Stanford University Press, 2002), 107–130; Owen-Smith, "Public Science, Private Science," 100–107.

18. Jason Owen-Smith and Walter W. Powell, "To Patent or Not: Faculty Decisions and Institutional Success at Technology Transfer," *Journal of Technology Transfer* 26, nos. 1–2 (2001): 99–114.

19. See the Administration's FY2008 budget request, which emphasizes federal support for research in the indicated areas and deemphasizes explicit federal programs for economic development, preferring to leave TBED to the states: "FY08 Budget Request: Research Up; Economic Development Down," *SSTI Weekly Digest,* Special Federal Budget Issue (February 5, 2007).

20. Creso M. Sá, *Interdisciplinary Strategies of Research Universities,* PhD diss. (Pennsylvania State University, 2006).

21. Donald S. Siegel, David Waldman, and Albert Link, "Assessing the Impact of Organizational Practices on the Relative Productivity of University Technology Transfer Offices: An Exploratory Study," *Research Policy* 32 (January 2003): 27–48.

22. Jeannette A. Colyvas and Walter W. Powell, "From Vulnerable to Venerated: The Institutionalization of Academic Entrepreneurship in the Life Sciences," *Research in the Sociology of Organizations* 25 (2007): 219–259; Irwin Feller et al., "A Disaggregated Examination of Patent and Licensing Behavior at Three Research Universities," paper presented to the Western Economic Association (July 3, 2000); Sheila Slaughter, Cynthia Joan Archerd, and Teresa I. D. Campbell, "Boundaries and Quandaries: How Professors Negotiate Market Relations," *Review of Higher Education* 28, no. 1 (2004): 129–165; Yong S. Lee, "University-Industry Collaboration on Technology Transfer: Views from the Ivory Tower," *Policy Studies Journal* 26, no. 1 (1998): 69–84.

23. Rory P. O'Shea et al., "Delineating the Anatomy of an Entrepreneurial University: The Massachusetts Institute of Technology Experience," *R&D Management* 37, no. 1 (2007): 1–16, quote p. 9.

24. Janet Bercovitz and Maryann Feldman, "Academic Entrepreneurs: Social Learning and Participation in University Technology Transfer," Working Paper (2004); Irwin Feller, "Technology Transfer from Universities," *Higher Education: Handbook of Theory and Research* 12 (1997): 1–42, esp. 26–29; Shane, *Academic Entrepreneurship,* 81–83.

25. Association of University Technology Managers, "AUTM U.S. Licensing Survey: FY 2004."

26. Richard A. Jensen, Jerry G. Thursby, and Marie C. Thursby, "Disclosure and Licensing of University Inventions: 'The Best We Can Do with the S**t We Get to Work With,'" *International Journal of Industrial Organization* 21 (2003): 1271–1300.

27. Owen-Smith and Powell, "To Patent or Not."

28. Gideon D. Markham, Peter T. Gianiodis, and Phillip H. Phan, "An Agency Theoretic Study on Knowledge Agents and University Technology Transfer Offices," unpub. ms.

29. Owen-Smith and Powell, "To Patent or Not"; W. Patrick McRay and Jennifer L. Croissant, "Entrepreneurship in Technology Transfer Offices: Making Work Visible," in Jennifer Croissant and Sal Restivo, eds., *Degrees of Compromise: Industrial Interests and Academic Values* (Albany: SUNY Press, 2001), 55–76.

30. Ibid.; Walter W. Powell and Jason Owen-Smith, "Universities and the Market for Intellectual Property in the Life Sciences," *Journal of Policy Analysis and Management* 17, no. 2 (1998): 253–277.
31. Owen-Smith and Powell, "To Patent or Not."
32. In May 2006, the board of Texas A&M took the initiative to add "patents or commercialization of research, where applicable" to the criteria considered in tenure reviews. Prior to this action, the executive committee of the faculty senate had nearly unanimously rejected this step. Texas A&M may have been the first to take this action on a university-wide basis, but individual units where tenure is granted, usually colleges, have certainly done so: Scott Jaschik, "Teaching, Research, Service . . . & Patents," *Inside Higher Ed*, http://www .insidehighered.com (May 30, 2006). Some academics object that patents bear little relation to the quality of research.
33. Colyvas and Powell, "From Vulnerable to Venerated."
34. Jason Owen-Smith, "Dockets, Deals, and Sagas: Commensuration and Rationalization of Experience in University Licensing," *Social Studies of Science* 35, no. 1 (2005): 69–97; McRay and Croissant, "Entrepreneurship in Technology Transfer Offices"; Corrinne McSherry, *Who Owns Academic Work? Battling for Control of Intellectual Property* (Cambridge: Harvard University Press, 2001), 154ff.
35. Jerry G. Thursby, Richard Jensen, and Marie C. Thursby, "Objectives, Characteristics and Outcomes of University Licensing: A Survey of Major U.S. Universities," *Journal of Technology Transfer* 26 (2001): 59–72; Richard Jensen and Marie Thursby, "Proofs and Prototypes for Sale: The Tale of University Licensing," NBER Working Paper 6698 (August 1998). The 12 percent figure found in this survey might be compared with the 2004 AUTM finding that "fewer than 20 percent" of start-ups had technology "at a stage where it could attract venture capital investment on its initial funding": "AUTM U.S. Licensing Survey: FY 2004," 29.
36. In 2004 the AUTM reported 6,191 provisional applications, followed in 2005 by 1,794 utility applications: AUTM U.S. Licensing Surveys, FY 2004, FY 2005.
37. Shane, *Academic Entrepreneurship*, 249–254.
38. Thursby et al., "Objectives, Characteristics and Outcomes."
39. Shane, *Academic Entrepreneurship*, 115–123.
40. Ibid.; AUTM, "AUTM U.S. Licensing Survey: FY 2004." The percentages cited in this paragraph vary from year to year, but are generally near these figures.
41. Thursby et al., "Objectives, Characteristics and Outcomes."
42. "Jewels in the Ivory Tower," *The Economist* (January 28, 1989): 82.
43. AUTM, "AUTM U.S. Licensing Survey: FY 2004," 26–27.
44. For FY2001–2004, on average, about 100 universities accepted equity in 250 start-ups and 100 other deals: ibid., 29; Shane, *Academic Entrepreneurship*, 63–64.
45. The argument of Jensen and Thursby, "Proofs and Prototypes for Sale."
46. Shane, *Academic Entrepreneurship*, 152–155.
47. Ibid., 152–162; Robert A. Lowe and Arvids A. Ziedonis, "Start-ups, Established Firms, and the Commercialization of University Inventions," unpub. ms., University of Pittsburgh (February 2, 2004).

48. Shane summarizes his own and other research findings in *Academic Entrepreneurship*, 17–36.
49. The AUTM survey asked for the source of initial funding; most start-ups would probably receive funding from multiple sources over time: AUTM, "AUTM U.S. Licensing Survey: FY 2004," 28–29.
50. Lowe and Ziedonis, "Start-ups."
51. The experience of the Utah Centers of Excellence program, inaugurated in 1986, illustrates the varying results for start-ups. In 20 years, these centers produced 180 spin-offs, of which 67 were active in 2006, employing between 1,500 and 1,800 people. The University of Utah start-ups had a survival rate of 52 percent (27 of 53), including two firms in its research park that accounted for at least half of all employees. The other universities had a survival rate of 30 percent (40 of 134) and on average employed about 20 people: Jan Crispin and Sapna Sinha, "Utah's Centers of Excellence Program: A 20-year Review," *Utah Economic and Business Review* 66 (July–August 2006): 1–11.
52. Jim Collins, "Want to Maximize University Tech Transfer? Here's a Little Advice," *Xconomy* (August 13, 2007), www.xconomy.com; Michael Arndt, "MIT, Caltech—And the Gators?" *Business Week* (May 21, 2007).
53. Abigail Barrow, "Building Better Bridges over the Valley of Death—An Optimist's View," *Xconomy* (December 3, 2007), www.xconomy.com.
54. Janet Bercovitz et al. argue on the basis of three case studies that the structure of TTOs also has important effects on strategy and outcomes: "Organizational Structure as a Determinant of Academic Patent and Licensing Behavior: an Exploratory Study of Duke, Johns Hopkins, and Pennsylvania State Universities," *Journal of Technology Transfer*, 26 (January 2001): 21–35.
55. Gary W. Matkin, *Technology Transfer and the University* (New York: Macmillan, 1990), 131–133.
56. Richard Levin, "Universities, Economic Growth, and Regional Development" (September 23, 2005), www.yale.edu/opa/president/speeches/; Shiri Breznitz, "From Ivory Tower to Industrial Promotion: The Case of Yale University and the Biotechnology Cluster in New Haven, Connecticut," Working Paper STE-WP-28-2005, Technion—Israel Institute of Technology (May 2005).
57. Yale University, Office of Public Affairs and Office of Cooperative Research.
58. www.ott.caltech.edu (May 28, 2007).
59. Large gifts that establish new units are negotiated with universities, and in that sense reflect university priorities.
60. http://web.mit.edu/deshpandecenter.html (May 27, 2007). In its first four years, the Deshpande Center supported 47 projects and yielded nine spin-offs that attracted $40 million in capital: Carl Marziali, "USC Stevens to Lead Tech Transfer," *USC News* (March 1, 2006).
61. The Deshpande Center also links MIT inventors with "a host of entrepreneurial and business resources inside and outside of MIT, including venture capitalists, local business resources, MIT Technology Licensing Office, MIT Venture Men-

toring Service, partnerships with MIT Sloan School of Management Courses, MIT Entrepreneurship Center, MIT $50K Entrepreneurship Competition, MIT Industrial Liaison Program, MIT Sloan School of Management, and MIT Enterprise Forum®": *SSTI Weekly Digest* (November 15, 2002).

62. "USC Innovation Institute Reinventing Itself," *Los Angeles Times* (May 28, 2007), http://stevens.usc.edu/press_news.php.

63. "USC's New Institute for Innovation," *Business Week* (March 29, 2007). President Steven Sample describes the mission as "nurturing ideas and inventions that would benefit society the most": "USC Innovation Institute" (see note 62).

64. Virtually a cliché for conference talks, this sentiment is echoed on campuses: Ed Silverman, "The Trouble with Tech Transfer," *The Scientist* 21, no. 1 (January 2007): 40ff; McCray and Croissant, "Entrepreneurship in Technology Transfer Offices," 64; Donald S. Siegel et al., "Toward a Model of the Effective Transfer of Scientific Knowledge from Academicians to Practitioners: Qualitative Evidence from the Commercialization of University Technologies," *Journal of Engineering and Technology Management* 21, nos. 1–2 (2004): 115–142, esp. 131–132; Owen-Smith and Powell, "To Patent or Not"; interviews by the authors.

65. Kirsten Orsini-Meinhard, "UW Tech-transfer Program Putting Discoveries to Work," *Seattle Times* (May 27, 2007); Siegel et al., "Assessing the Impact," 40, 43.

66. "USC's New Institute" (see note 63).

67. Robert E. Litan, Lesa Mitchell, and E. J. Reedy, "Commercializing University Innovations: A Better Way," Working Paper, National Bureau of Economic Research (April 2007), quotes pp. 7, 13.

68. G. Markman et al., "Entrepreneurship and University-based Technology Transfer," *Journal of Business Venturing* 20 (2005): 241–263.

69. Wesley M. Cohen, Richard R. Nelson, and John P. Walsh, "Protecting Their Intellectual Assets: Appropriability Conditions and Why U.S. Manufacturing Firms Patent (or Not)," NBER Working Paper 7552 (February 2000).

70. Biological patents are Classes 426 (drugs), 435 (molecular/microbiology), and 800 (organisms): USPTO, "U.S. Colleges and Universities—Utility Patent Grants, Calendar Years 1969–2003"; Roger L. Geiger, *Knowledge and Money: Research Universities and the Paradox of the Marketplace* (Stanford: Stanford University Press, 2004), 219.

71. Powell and Owen-Smith, "New World of Knowledge"; Walter W. Powell, Kenneth W. Koput, and Laurel Smith-Doerr, "Interorganizational Collaboration and the Locus of Innovation: Networks of Learning in Biotechnology," *Administrative Science Quarterly* 41 (1996): 116–145; Zucker and Darby, "Star Scientists."

72. McRay and Croissant, "Entrepreneurship in Technology Transfer Offices," 62–66.

73. David C. Mowery et al., *Ivory Tower and Industrial Innovation: University-Industry Technology Transfer before and after the Bayh-Dole Act* (Stanford: Stanford University Press, 2004), 190–191; interviews by the authors; Owen-Smith, "Public Science, Private Science."

74. Michael A. Heller and Rebecca S. Eisenberg, "Can Patents Deter Innovation? The Anticommons in Biomedical Research," *Science, 280* (1 May 1998): 698–701.

75. For example, Litan et al., "Commercializing University Innovations," 12–13.

76. John P. Walsh, Ashish Arora, and Wesley M. Cohen, "Effects of Research Tool Patents and Licensing on Biomedical Innovation," in Wesley M. Cohen and Stephen A. Merrill, eds., *Patents in the Knowledge-based Economy* (Washington, DC: National Academies Press, 2003), 285–340. Working solutions include licensing, inventing around patents, going offshore, using public databases and research tools, court challenges, infringement, and liberal use of the research exemption. Academic scientists also take advantage of the reluctance of firms to enforce patents against universities (p. 331).

77. Richard C. Atkinson et al., "Public Sector Collaboration for Agricultural IP Management," *Science, 301* (11 July 2003): 174–175. For examples of previous patent obstruction, see R. Merges and Richard R. Nelson, "On the Complex Economics cf Patent Scope," *Columbia Law Review* 90 (1990): 839–916.

78. Richard R. Nelson, "The Market Economy and the Scientific Commons," *Research Policy* 33 (April 2004): 455–471; Mowery et al., *Ivory Tower,* 179–192, quote p. 185.

79. Adam B. Jaffe and Josh Lerner, *Innovation and Its Discontents: How Our Patent System Is Endangering Innovation and Progress, and What to Do about It* (Princeton: Princeton University Press, 2004), esp. 64–68.

80. Nelson, "Market Economy."

81. The basic issues are critically examined by Roberto Mazzoleni and Richard R. Nelson, "The Benefits and Costs of Strong Patent Protection: A Contribution to the Current Debate," *Research Policy* 27, no. 3 (1998): 273–284. The authors argue that "the basic argument behind Bayh-Dole . . . is for the most part empirically wrong," that "transaction and litigation costs are considerable" for "the establishment of markets for information and techniques that were previously the domain of public science," and that "while the granting of patents on findings and techniques that still are a long way from practical application has helped spawn research specialist firms in biotechnology, and perhaps a few other areas, we are not sure that this phenomenon unambiguously represents a net benefit for society" (p. 280).

    In the summer of 2007, universities strongly opposed legislation before Congress that might weaken certain aspects of the strong-patent regime (S 1145 and HR 1908).

82. James A. Severson (2000 president of the AUTM), Testimony to the House Committee on the Judiciary, Subcommittee on Courts and Intellectual Property (July 13, 2000).

83. Robert A. Lowe et al., "What Happens in University-Industry Technology Transfer?" in Mowery et al., *Ivory Tower,* 152–178, quote p. 157.

84. Goldie Blumenstyk, "Taking on Goliath: U. of Rochester Risks Millions in Patent Fight with Pharmaceutical Giants," *Chronicle of Higher Education* (September 20, 2002), A27.

85. Goldie Blumenstyk, "Federal Court Dismisses U. of Rochester's Suit That Sought Billions for Patent Infringement," *Chronicle of Higher Education* (March 21, 2003), A31.

86. See Jeanne F. Loring and Cathryn Campbell, "Intellectual Property and Human Embryonic Stem Cell Research," *Science* 311 (24 March 2006): 1716–17, quote p. 1716; Goldie Blumenstyk, "A Tight Grip on Tech Transfer," *Chronicle of Higher Education* (September 15, 2006); Constance Holden, "U.S. Patent Office Casts Doubt on Wisconsin Stem Cell Patents," *Science* 316 (13 April 2007): 182.

87. Interview by authors.

88. Jennifer A. Henderson and John J. Smith, "Academia, Industry, and the Bayh-Dole Act: An Implied Duty to Commercialize," http://www.cimit.org/coi_part3.pdf.

89. For background, see ibid.; Mowery et al., *Ivory Tower*, 85–95. See also U.S. General Accounting Office, *Technology Transfer: Administration of the Bayh-Dole Act by Research Universities*, GAO/RCED-98-126 (May 1998).

90. AUTM database, U.S. Licensing Survey, FY2004.

91. WARF also serves as a national spokesperson for technology transfer and was instrumental in the developments leading up to Bayh-Dole. For background, see David Blumenthal, Sherrie Epstein, and James Maxwell, "Commercializing University Research: Lessons from the Experience of the Wisconsin Alumni Research Fund," *New England Journal of Medicine* 314, no. 25 (June 19, 1986): 1621–26.

92. One attempt to analyze the economics of TTOs relies chiefly on estimates: Joshua B. Powers, "Profits and Losses in University Technology Transfer: A National Investigation of Financials," Association for the Study of Higher Education, Annual Meeting (November 2005).

93. For example, the Ben Franklin Technology Partnership of Southeastern Pennsylvania supports technology licensing officers at the University of Pennsylvania and Drexel University through the Nanotechnology Institute; the University of Arizona supports its economic development office with Proposition 301 funds (see Chapter 3).

94. Authors' rough estimates based on interviews and TTO annual reports.

95. Frank T. Rothaermel, Shanti D. Agung, and Lin Jiang, "University Entrepreneurship: A Taxonomy of the Literature," *Industrial and Corporate Change* 16, no. 4 (2007): 691–791.

96. Thursby and Kemp, "Growth and Productive Efficiency," quote p. 120. Other factors named were greater demand from industry for university IP and internal reallocation of university resources toward commercial activity.

97. Rory P. O'Shea et al., "Entrepreneurial Orientation, Technology Transfer and Spinoff Performance of U.S. Universities," *Research Policy* 34 (2005): 994–1009; Siegel et al., "Assessing the Impact," 35.

98. Thursby et al., "Objectives, Characteristics and Outcomes," 69.

99. Ibid.; O'Shea et al., "Entrepreneurial Orientation," 1002–03.

100. Thursby and Kemp, "Growth and Productive Efficiency," 119.

101. Jason Owen-Smith, "From Separate Systems to a Hybrid Order."

102. Licensing revenue figures are distorted by the failure of some large earners to report: Stanford, Yale, Princeton, and Columbia did not report in the AUTM survey for FY2004.

## Chapter 5: Economic Relevance and the Academic Core

1. Andrew Abbott, *Chaos of Disciplines* (Chicago: University of Chicago Press, 2001), esp. 131–136.

2. For the early institutionalization of disciplines and departments in the university, see Laurence R. Veysey, *The Emergence of the American University* (Chicago: University of Chicago Press, 1965), 320–322. For the mutual reinforcement between disciplines and universities, see Roger L. Geiger, *To Advance Knowledge: The Growth of American Research Universities, 1900–1940* (New Brunswick, NJ: Transaction, 2004 [1986]), 37. For the strong disciplinary system, see Andrew Abbott, "The Disciplines and the Future," in Steven Brint, ed., *The Future of the City of Intellect: The Changing American University* (Stanford: Stanford University Press, 2002), 205–230, esp. 208–210.

3. See National Academies, *Facilitating Interdisciplinary Research* (Washington, DC: National Academies Press, 2004), 138. See also Burton Clark, "Substantive Growth and Innovative Organization: New Categories for Higher Education Research," *Higher Education* 32, no. 4 (1996): 417–430.

4. For a treatment of the topic, see Daryl E. Chubin and Edward J. Hackett, *Peerless Science: Peer Review and U.S. Science Policy* (Albany: State University of New York Press, 1990).

5. Burton Clark, *Places of Inquiry: Research and Advanced Education in Modern Universities* (Berkeley: University of California Press, 1995), 234–236.

6. For comprehensive treatments on the issue of interdisciplinary collaborations and the critique of disciplinary fragmentation, see Julie Thompson Klein, *Interdisciplinarity: History, Theory, and Practice* (Detroit: Wayne State University Press, 1990) and Lisa Lattuca, *Creating Interdisciplinarity: Interdisciplinary Research and Teaching among College and University Faculty* (Nashville: Vanderbilt University Press, 2001). For an analysis of faculty involvement with technology transfer activities, see Janet Bercovitz and Maryann Feldman, "Academic Entrepreneurs: Social Learning and Participation in University Technology Transfer," presented at the Knowledge Clusters and Entrepreneurship in Regional Economic Development Conference, University of Minnesota, September 13–14, 2004.

7. Martin Trow, "Biology at Berkeley: A Case Study of Reorganization and Its Costs and Benefits," Center for Studies in Higher Education, University of California, Berkeley, Research and Occasional Paper Series CSHE.1.99 (Spring 1999).

8. See National Academies, *Facilitating,* 16–25. See also Steven Brint, "Creating the Future: 'New Directions' in American Research Universities," *Minerva* 43, no. 1 (2005): 23–50.

9. For federal centers, see National Academies, *Facilitating*, 114–136; and Barry Bozeman and P. Craig Boardman, *Managing the New Multipurpose, Multidiscipline University Research Centers: Institutional Innovation in the Academic Community* (Washington, DC: IBM Endowment for the Business of Government, 2003). For state and private initiatives, see Roger L. Geiger and Creso Sá, "Beyond Technology Transfer: US State Policies to Harness University Research for Economic Development," *Minerva* 43 (2005): 1–21.

10. See Roger Geiger, "Organized Research Units—Their Role in the Development of University Research," *Journal of Higher Education* 61, no. 1 (1990): 1–19; Robert Friedman and Renee C. Friedman, *The Role of University Organized Research Units in Academic Science* (University Park: Pennsylvania State University, Center for the Study of Higher Education, Center for the Study of Science Policy, Institute for Policy Research and Evaluation, 1982); Robert Friedman and Renee Friedman, *Sponsorship, Organization and Program Change at 100 Universities* (University Park: Pennsylvania State University, Institute for Policy Research and Evaluation, Center for the Study of Science Policy, 1986).

11. Treatments on the topic include Michael Gibbons et al., *The New Production of Knowledge* (London: Sage Publications, 1994); Julie Klein, W. Grossenbacher-Mansuy, and R. Häberli, eds., *Transdisciplinarity: Joint Problem Solving among Science, Technology, and Society—An Effective Way for Managing Complexity* (Basel, Switzerland: Birkhäuser, 2000); and Brint, "Creating the Future."

12. William Mallon and Sarah Bunton, "Research Centers and Institutes in U.S. Medical Schools: A Descriptive Analysis," *Academic Medicine* 80, no. 11 (2005): 1005–11. For NIH center programs, see Frederick J. Manning, Michael McGeary, and Ronald Estabrook, eds., *NIH Extramural Center Programs: Criteria for Initiation and Evaluation* (Washington, DC: National Academies Press, 2004).

13. See Walter Cohen, Richard Florida, and W. Goe, *University-Industry Research Centers* (Pittsburgh: Carnegie Mellon University, 1994). For an analysis of the National Science Foundation Engineering Research Centers, see Irwin Feller, Catherine P. Ailes, and J. David Roessner, "Impacts of Research Universities on Technological Innovation in Industry: Evidence from Engineering Research Centers," *Research Policy* 31 (2002): 457–474.

14. Nathan Rosenberg and Richard Nelson, "American Universities and Technical Advance in Industry," *Research Policy* 23 (1994): 323–348, quote p. 323.

15. Rory P. O'Shea et al., "Delineating the Anatomy of an Entrepreneurial University: The Massachusetts Institute of Technology Experience," *R&D Management* 37, no. 1 (2007): 1–16. Former MIT president Charles Vest is among those who argue that greater organizational flexibility and integration of efforts among academic units are needed if universities are to enhance their contributions to innovation. See Charles M. Vest, *Pursuing the Endless Frontier: Essays on MIT and the Role of Research Universities* (Cambridge, MA: MIT Press, 2005), esp. 54.

16. For a review on matrix structures, see W. Richard Scott, *Organizations: Rational, Natural, and Open Systems* (5th ed.) (Upper Saddle River, NJ: Prentice Hall, 2003), 242–244. See also Christopher A. Bartlett and Sumantra Ghoshal,

"Matrix Management: Not a Structure, a Frame of Mind," *Harvard Business Review* (July–August 1990): 138–145.

17. Interview by author (CMS) with a director of a genomics institute at a leading private university, March 2005.

18. Harvard University, "Report from the Task Force on Science and Technology" (May 2004), quote p. 19.

19. Science-based technologies include stem cells, innovative computing, quantum science and technology, systems neuroscience, systems biology, chemical biology, and microbial science. Partial areas are engineering (especially bioengineering), origins of life (especially self-replicating systems), global health (especially applied life sciences), and environment (applied life sciences). The final two areas are clinical medicine and collaborative science. Harvard University, "Task Force on Science and Technology," 2.

20. Harvard University, *Enhancing Science and Engineering at Harvard: The Preliminary Report from the University Planning Committee for Science and Engineering* (July 2006), quotes pp. 4–5, 26.

21. Ibid., 29–37. See also "The Scope and Composition of the Harvard University Science and Engineering Committee," *Harvard Gazette* (January 18, 2007): www.news.harvard.edu/gazette/2007/02.01/99-committee.html.

22. Harvard University, *Enhancing Science and Engineering*, 54.

23. Creso M. Sá, *Interdisciplinary Strategies at Research-Intensive Universities*, PhD diss. (University Park: Pennsylvania State University, 2006), 182.

24. Duke University, *Building on Excellence* (Durham, NC: Duke University, 2001), 165.

25. These were the Center for Biologically Inspired Materials and Materials Systems, Computer-Based Support for Science and Engineering, Fitzpatrick Center for Photonics and Communications Systems, Institute for Genome Sciences and Policy, Nanoscience Initiative, and Program in Neural Analysis. The others involved the social sciences and the humanities.

26. Peter Lange, "Issues in Interdisciplinarity: Building Duke's Interdisciplinary Commitment into Our Organizational Fiber," draft ms. (September 12, 2004), 1.

27. The centers are in genomic medicine, applied genomics and technology, computational biology, evolutionary genomics, population genomics and pharmacogenetics, systems biology, and genome ethics, law, and policy.

28. Duke University, *Making a Difference: The Strategic Plan for Duke University* (Durham, NC: Duke University, 2006), 119; Sá, *Interdisciplinary Strategies*, 188–189.

29. Duke Institute for Genome Sciences and Policy, *Strategic Plan 2007* (Durham, NC: Duke University, 2007). A living and learning community on the "Genome Revolution" was created as part of the Duke Focus program, which admits students into living and learning communities that reside in the same buildings, attend seminars, and benefit from interactions with and mentorship from senior faculty members.

30. Two previously existing initiatives in ethics and public policy, and two that arose after the 2001 plan (social sciences and environment), are also strategic priorities in *Making a Difference*.

31. Duke Institute for Genome Sciences and Policy, *Strategic Plan 2007*, 5.
32. See Duke, *Making a Difference*, 1.
33. John L. Hennessy, "Going Forward: The Challenges Ahead after a Year of Change," annual State of the University address (April 18, 2002), quote pp. 8–9; http://news-service.stanford.edu/news/2002/april24/acadcounciltext.html.
34. For a more detailed examination of these initiatives, see Sá, *Interdisciplinary Strategies*, 159–174.
35. Abbott Vascular, Agilent Technologies, ALZA, Amgen, Boston Scientific, Fuji Film, Genentech, Panasonic Shikoku Electronics, Pfizer, and Philips Medical Systems.
36. See http://thestanfordchallenge.stanford.edu/get/layout/tsc/ TheStanfordChallenge?indexredir=r.
37. "The interdisciplinary synergy resulting from combining these ideas into more comprehensive 'themes' made them both stronger and more comprehensive." University of California at Berkeley, New Ideas Internal Review Committee, Report and Recommendations (June 10, 2003), 2–3, quotes on 6–7.
38. University of California at Berkeley Strategic Planning Committee, "UC Berkeley Strategic Academic Plan" (Office of Planning and Analysis, June 2002), 10–11, 29. For the management of technology program, see http://mot.berkeley.edu/.
39. The academic plans of most leading doctoral and research universities include strategies to focus institutional resources on cross-disciplinary research areas emphasized by federal agencies. Creso Sá, "Planning for Interdisciplinary Research," *Planning for Higher Education* 35, no. 2 (2007): 18–28.
40. Sá, *Interdisciplinary Strategies*, 144. See http://www.biodesign.asu.edu/
41. The centers are in Applied Nanobioscience, Bioelectronics and Biosensors, Bio-optical Nanotechnology, Environmental Biotechnology, Evolutionary Functional Genomics, Infectious Diseases and Vaccinology, Innovations in Medicine, Bioenergetics, Ecogenomics, and Single Molecule Biophysics.
42. Arizona State University, *ASU Vision and University Goals 2002–2012* (Tempe: Arizona State University, 2002), 5, 8–9.
43. For major interdisciplinary facilities in the life sciences, see Sá, "Planning for Interdisciplinary Research," 24–25.
44. Sharon T. Bozovsky, "A Meeting of the Minds," *Rensselaer Research Quarterly* (Winter 2004): 11–13.
45. Mary Sue Coleman, "The Research Mission of Public Universities," in "Riding the Momentum of Research: Leadership Challenges in Public Research Universities," MASC Report no. 108 (Lawrence: University of Kansas, Merrill Advanced Studies Center, 2004), 11–19, quote p. 16. For the number of faculty, see *LSIExplore* 2, no. 2 (2006): 12.
46. For the evolution of Cornell's New Life Sciences Initiative, see Sá, *Interdisciplinary Strategies*, 64. For the quotes, see David Brand, "CU Life Science Building Now Scheduled for Completion in Less than Four Years," *Cornell Chronicle* (June 5, 2003), 3–4. Cornell obtained $25 million from the Gen*NY*sis program to be used toward the construction of the Life Sciences Technology Building.

47. Considering those with assistant, associate, or full professor appointments, as of 2006. The total academic staff rises to 48 including instructors.

48. Elizabeth Redden, "A Raise for the Record Books," *Inside Higher Ed* (June 5, 2007), www.insidehighered.com/news/2007/06/05/albany. For SEMATECH, see Richard A. D'Errico, "Alain Kaloyeros Played Big Role in Sematech Decision," *The Business Review (Albany)* (July 29, 2002); www.bizjournals.com/albany/stories/2002/07/29/story1.html.

49. Based on author's (CMS) interviews with three academic administrators on the Albany campus (May 2006). See http://cnse.albany.edu/about_cnse.html.

50. Richard A. D'Errico, "Partnership Strengthens Albany NanoTech," *The Business Review (Albany)* (October 3, 2005); http://albany.bizjournals.com/albany/stories/2005/10/03/story1.html.

51. Based on interviews with three academic administrators on the Albany campus (May 2006).

52. Candace Stuart, "Gateways to Greatness," *Small Times* 6, no. 3 (2006): 11.

53. Quoted in D'Errico, "Alain Kaloyeros."

54. Chris Przirembel, "Transplanting Industries: The ICAR Project; Embedding the Automotive Industry in South Carolina," presented at the First International Conference on Local Innovation Systems, Boston, MA, December 13, 2005.

55. Lynnley Browning, "Donation Gives BMW Influence at University," *International Herald Tribune* (August 23, 2006), par. 8.

56. Measured by a head count (which includes faculty occupying administrative posts), UW Madison in 1999 had a gap of nearly 150 faculty relative to the level of academic year 1982–1983. The figures for full-time-equivalent faculty show a decrease of 288 between the start and the end of the 1990s. For a case study, see Sá, *Interdisciplinary Strategies,* 123–140.

57. The University of Wisconsin-Madison, *Report of the Ad Hoc Advisory Committee to Evaluate the Cluster Hiring Initiative* (November 2003), 7.

58. Sá, *Interdisciplinary Strategies,* 132.

59. The provost's office invests $200,000 per year in the program, and awards up to $20,000 per year over three years to successful proposals. These grants have supported academic events and graduate students, for example.

60. Sá, *Interdisciplinary Strategies,* 124–141.

61. Thomas K. Wetherell, State of the University Address (September 8, 2006): www.fsu.com/pages/2006/09/08/StateOfUniversity.html.

62. See Florida State University Board of Trustees Meeting, Summary Meeting Minutes (September 19, 2005), and Wetherell, State of the University Address.

63. Jennifer Jacobson, "Managing a Hiring Boom," *Chronicle of Higher Education* (October 17, 2001).

64. RPI president Shirley Ann Jackson stated to the faculty that the endowment needed to be raised to support new faculty, and that the constellations were one way to accelerate that. See "Original Minutes of the General Faculty Meeting, November 15, 2000, Rensselaer Polytechnic Institute Faculty Senate."

65. President Jackson explained, "The search for these constellations is a historic moment for Rensselaer because they represent the means by which we create a national research presence in new areas that are vital to society—and critical to a first-rank research program—but are not now in the Institute's portfolio. We chose these areas carefully, with the assistance of experts who include a Nobel Laureate from Rockefeller University as well as faculty researchers from Harvard, the University of California at San Diego, Georgia Tech, and the New York State Department of Health." Shirley Ann Jackson, "President's View: Time for Transformation," *Rensselaer Magazine* (March 2001): www.rpi.edu/dept/NewsComm/Magazine/mar01/presview.html.

66. "Rensselaer Completes Future Chips Constellation with Two New Faculty Appointments," RPI press release (March 4, 2004): http://news.rpi.edu/update.do?artcenterkey=66.

67. Interview with an RPI senior research administrator, May 2006.

68. Sá, *Interdisciplinary Strategies,* 134–135.

69. RPI Faculty Senate Minutes, November 15, 2000.

70. See Florida State University Board of Trustees, Summary Meeting Minutes (July 26, 2006): http://trustees.fsu.edu/meeting/index.html?2006-07-26M.

71. A. Henig and K. Mangan, "Environmental Institute at USC Makes a 'Cluster Hire,'" *Chronicle of Higher Education* 53, no. 2 (September 1, 2006): A8.

72. Roger L. Geiger, *Research and Relevant Knowledge: American Research Universities since World War II* (New Brunswick, NJ: Transaction, 2004 [1993]), 118–135.

73. As observed over 30 years ago by Stanley Ikenberry and Renee Friedman in *Beyond Academic Departments: The Story of Institutes and Centers* (1st ed.) (San Francisco: Jossey-Bass, 1972), 103; for more recent examples, see William Mallon and Sarah Bunton, *Characteristics of Research Centers and Institutes at U.S. Medical Schools and Universities* (Washington, DC: Association of American Medical Colleges, 2005), 6, 10–13.

74. See Geiger, "Organized Research Units," 6–13.

75. "Proposal for a Graduate Designated Emphasis in Computational and Genomic Biology" (September 11, 2003), 4; http://computationalbiology.berkeley.edu/de_proposal.pdf.

## Chapter 6: Universities and the Promise of Economic Growth

1. Jason Owen-Smith and Walter W. Powell, "Accounting for Emergence and Novelty in Boston and Bay Area Biotechnology," in Pontus Braunerhjelm and Maryann Feldman, eds., *Cluster Genesis: Technology-based Industrial Development* (Oxford: Oxford University Press, 2006), 61–86; Michael R. Darby and Lynne G. Zucker, "Grilichesian Breakthroughs: Inventions of Methods of Inventing and Firm Entry in Nanotechnology," NBER Working Paper 9825 (November 2003); James Flanagan, "Nanotechnology Companies Planning to Sell Shares," *New York Times,* November 20, 2007.

2. J. Scinta, "Industrial Research Institute's R&D Trends Forecast for 2007," *Research Technology Management* (January–February 2007): 17–20.

3. Bruce Kogut, "Conclusion: From Regions and Firms to Multinational Highways; Knowledge and Its Diffusion as a Factor in the Globalization of Industries," in Martin Kenney with Richard Florida, eds., *Locating Global Advantage: Industry Dynamics in the International Economy* (Stanford: Stanford University Press, 2004), 261–282; AnnaLee Saxenian, *The New Argonauts: Regional Advantage in a Global Economy* (Cambridge: Harvard University Press, 2006).

4. Henry Chesbrough, *Open Innovation: The New Imperative for Creating and Profiting from Technology* (Boston: Harvard Business School Press, 2003) and *Open Business Models: How to Thrive in the New Innovation Landscape* (Boston: Harvard Business School Press, 2006).

5. Such is the faith in science that the energy bill passed by Congress in December 2007 mandated the incorporation by 2020 of technologies for biofuels that do not yet exist.

6. I.e., biotechnology, biofuels, biomanufacturing: "North Carolina Lawmakers Fund Major Research, Education, TBED Initiatives," *SSTI Weekly Digest* (August 1, 2007).

7. Holly is vice-provost and executive director of the USC Stevens Institute for Innovation: http://stevens.usc.edu/aword.php.

8. Scinta, "Industrial Research Institute's R&D Trends."

9. Barbara J. Culliton, "Monsanto Renews Ties to Washington University," *Science* (March 2, 1990), 1027; interview of T. Cicero by author (RLG) (December 2000); Christopher T. Hill, "Partnerships in Research: The Evolution of Expectations," in Chemical Sciences Roundtable, *Research Teams and Partnerships: Trends in the Chemical Sciences; Report of a Workshop* (Washington, DC: National Academy Press, 1999), 21–27.

10. Association of University Technology Managers, "AUTM U.S. Licensing Survey: FY 2005."

11. Jeannette A. Colyvas and Walter W. Powell, "From Vulnerable to Venerated: The Institutionalization of Academic Entrepreneurship in the Life Sciences," *Research in the Sociology of Organizations* 25 (2007): 219–259, quote p. 255.

12. Battelle Memorial Institute and SSTI, *Laboratories of Innovation: State Bioscience Initiatives 2004*, prepared for BIO—Biotechnology Industry Organization (June 2004).

13. Harvard University, "Report from the Task Force on Science and Technology" (May 2004), quote p. 19.

14. Harvard University, "Enhancing Science and Engineering at Harvard: The Preliminary Report from the University Planning Committee for Science and Engineering" (July 2006), quotes p. 3.

15. Ross DeVol and Armen Bedroussian, *Mind-to-Market: A Global Analysis of University Biotechnology Transfer and Commercialization* (Santa Monica, CA: Milken Institute, September 2006), 116; National Research Council, *Research-Doctorate Programs in the United States: Continuity and Change* (Washington, DC: National Academy Press, 1995). The composite faculty rankings for the top five were (on

a 5-point scale) MIT, 4.7; UC Berkeley, 4.62; Harvard, 4.6; Caltech, 4.59; and Stanford, 4.55. Other universities mentioned here were among the top 25 with composite ratings of at least 3.7.

16. Goldie Blumenstyk, "Northwestern U. Sells Royalty Rights from Blockbuster Drug for $700 Million," *Chronicle of Higher Education* (December 19, 2007): http://chronicle.com/daily/2007/12/1037n.htm.

17. David L. Kirp, *Shakespeare, Einstein, and the Bottom Line: The Marketing of Higher Education* (Cambridge: Harvard University Press, 2003), 171–174, 217; John L. Pulley, "Raising Arizona: Is Michael Crow's Remaking of a State University a Model, or a Mirage?" *Chronicle of Higher Education* (November 18, 2005).

18. RPI, "The Rensselaer Plan: A Comprehensive Strategic Plan for Rensselaer Polytechnic University," www.rpi.edu/president/plan/goal.html.

19. Judged on their benefits to students, all these models provide opportunities to work with and learn from industry partners, thus providing career preparation.

20. Richard Florida, *The Rise of the Creative Class* (New York: Basic Books, 2002), 291–293.

21. For a review of organizational theories as applied to universities, see Robert Birnbaum, *How Colleges Work: The Cybernetics of Academic Organization and Leadership* (San Francisco: Jossey-Bass, 1988).

22. Creso Sá, "Research Centers and Institutes and the University Matrix," unpub. ms., Center for the Study of Higher Education (May 2004).

23. Cf. Stephen D. Sugarman, "Conflicts of Interest in the Roles of the University Professor," *Theoretical Inquiries in Law* 6, no. 1 (January 2005): 255–275.

24. Daniel S. Greenberg, *Science for Sale: The Perils, Rewards, and Delusions of Campus Capitalism* (Chicago: University of Chicago Press, 2007).

25. Roger L. Geiger, "Expert and Elite: The Incongruous Missions of Public Research Universities," in Geiger et al., eds., *The Future of the American Public Research University* (Rotterdam: Sense Publishers, 2007), 15–34.

# Index

Academic core. *See* Economic relevance of universities
Academic departments, 157–160, 183–184
Academic quality, 124–125, 153–154, 183–185
Advanced Micro Devices, 39
Agricultural R&D, 9
Air Products and Chemicals, 53–54; alliances, 61; evaluation of research, 57–58
Albany College of Nanoscale Science and Engineering, 95–98, 174–176, 192, 197, 201
Albany Nanotech. *See* Albany College of Nanoscale Science and Engineering
American Competitiveness Initiative, 25–26, 125, 189
Amgen, 29, 63
Anticommons in biomedical research, 144–145
Arizona, state policies for TBED, 104–111, 113–115; Biosciences Roadmap, 105–106, 109; Proposition 301, 104–105; Science Foundation Arizona, 107–108
Arizona State University, 200; Biodesign Institute, 106–107, 172–173, 178, 185
Association of University Technology Managers (AUTM), 118, 121, 135, 146, 149, 152, 154, 193
Atkinson, Richard, 88, 90
AT&T, 30

AUTM. *See* Association of University Technology Managers
Axel, Richard, 146–147

Baumol, William, 28–30, 214nn1,4
Bayh-Dole Act (1980), 12, 17, 33, 37–38, 52, 119, 126, 149, 236n81; spirit of, 149–152, 193
Bell Labs, 31, 50
Biotechnology, 33, 36, 40–41, 47–49, 187; and Berkeley-Novartis contract, 65–66; patents, 120–121, 141–142
BMW, 176
Boeing, 61, 191–192
Bok, Derek, 16, 18, 19
Boyer, Herbert, 32–33
Buderi, Robert, 31

California, state policies for TBED, 86–92, 113–114
California Institute for Regenerative Medicine, 82, 86, 91
California Institute of Technology, 137–138, 198, 202
California Institutes for Science and Innovation, 86, 89–90, 114, 197
Carnegie Mellon University, 50, 62
Chevron, 188
Clemson University, 176, 201–202
Clinical trials, 18–19, 48
Clough, G Wayne, 83
Clusters: economic, 41–42, 80–81, 197, 224n34, 228n94; faculty, 180–182

247

248    **Index**

Cohen-Boyer patents, 32, 146
Collaborative research, 59–60; disincentives in universities, 159–160
Columbia University, 146–147, 199
Colyvas, Jeannette, 194
Consortia, 60–61
Consultants, 59
Cornell University, 173–174
Corporate R&D, 20, 23–24, 29–32, 42–45, 67, 69; electronics industry, 49–51; knowledge needs and sources, 45–47; materials industry, 51–54; offshore, 55–56; pharmaceutical industry, 47–49
Crow, Michael, 83, 106, 200

Defense R&D, 10
Deshpande Center for Technological Innovation, 138–139, 234nn60,61
Dow Chemical, 52
Duke University, 19, 166–168
DuPont, 29, 52–53

Economic development, as university mission, 4, 8–15, 186, 209; critics of, 16–18
Economic relevance of universities, 1–7, 15, 68–70, 186–187, 197, 203–210; and the academic core, 156–185; faculty recruitment for, 178–182; and research capacity, 172–177; and science-based technologies, 163–171
Energy Biosciences Institute, UC Berkeley, 90–91, 113, 188, 192
Engineering Research Centers (ERCs), 12–13, 59–60, 219n74
Entrepreneurs, 29, 39, 133, 138
Entrepreneurship at universities, 124, 129

Faculty: clusters, 179–182; culture, 124–126; hiring, 178
Fairchild Semiconductor, 39
Florida, Richard, 202
Florida, state policies for TBED, 115, 230n115

Florida State University, 180
Friedman, Thomas, 21, 26, 186

Genentech, 33, 49
General Electric (GE), 29–31
Georgia, state policies for TBED, 98–104, 113–114
Georgia Institute of Technology, 103, 202; Electronic Design Center, 102, 113, 201; VentureLab started at, 101
Georgia Research Alliance (GRA), 98–102, 197
Globalization, 21–22, 26
Greenberg, Daniel, 18

Harris, William, 108
Harvard University, 15–16, 32, 48, 151, 163–165, 198, 202, 240n19
Hatch Act, 9
Hewlett Packard, 50, 51
Holly, Krisztina, 139–140, 189

IBM. 30–31, 61, 143, 191–192; and service science curriculum, 177–178
Imperial College, London, 61
Indiana University, 132
Industrial recruitment, state policies, 78
Industry-University Cooperative Research Centers, 74
Innovation, 1–2, 21–25, 28–70; corporate imperative, 187–189; corporate track of, 42–54, 68–69, 191, 207; defined, 29; and economic development, 22–23, 28–32; limitations of universities, 206–208; narrative on, 14, 25–27, 208; open innovation, 24; small business track of, 37–42, 68–69, 193, 207; state policies for, 196, 208; at University of Southern California, 139–140
*Innovation America*, 83–84
Intel, 39, 49–50, 177, 217n48; open collaborative research model, 61–63, 220n80
Intellectual property (IP), 34–36; and materials industry, 52–53; and offshore research, 55; and pharmaceutical industry, 48, 142–143

Harvard University Press is a member of Green Press Initiative (greenpressinitiative.org), a nonprofit organization working to help publishers and printers increase their use of recycled paper and decrease their use of fiber derived from endangered forests. This book was printed on 100% recycled paper containing 50% post-consumer waste and processed chlorine free.